THE KINDERGARTEN

Early Childhood Education Series

Kenneth D. Wann, Editor

THE KINDERGARTEN
Evelyn Weber

CHILDREN DISCOVER MUSIC AND DANCE
Emma D. Sheehy

PARENTS AND CHILDREN LEARN TOGETHER
Katharine Whiteside Taylor

SCHOOLS FOR YOUNG DISADVANTAGED CHILDREN
Ruth Hamlin, Rose Mukerji, and Margaret Yonemura

BEFORE FIRST GRADE
Susan W. Gray, Rupert A. Klaus, James O. Miller and
Bettye J. Forrester

NEW DIRECTIONS IN THE KINDERGARTEN
Helen F. Robison and Bernard Spodek

THE KINDERGARTEN

ITS ENCOUNTER WITH EDUCATIONAL THOUGHT IN AMERICA

Evelyn Weber

TEACHERS COLLEGE PRESS
Teachers College, Columbia University
New York, 1969

FOREWORD

Not since the Kindergarten Reform Movement of the early 1900's has the kindergarten come under such far reaching and searching analysis as it now faces in the last third of this century. Fundamental issues concerning the development of kindergarten programs demand careful attention by those concerned with effective education for young children. Divisions between the advocates of play and the proponents of a work-oriented curriculum, between behaviorist-oriented psychologists and those favoring a perceptual psychology, between those who see the function of the kindergarten as socialization and those who view it as a means for developing intellectual powers are only a few of the many issues which must be considered today.

The construction of the kindergarten curriculum was a long and painful process of trial and error involving a break with deeply intrenched concepts of the nature and needs of young children. The impetus came primarily from early childhood educators who had come under the influence of certain newly developed theoretical insights about childhood and the learning process. The battles, and there were bitter ones, were fought largely among the leaders of kindergarten education. Today the impetus for change is coming from numerous groups, many of them outside the field of early childhood education. Educational administrators, psychologists, social reformers, parents, and other laymen as well as early childhood educators have demonstrated fundamental concerns for curricular change in the kindergarten. The proposals for change are numerous, varied, and worthy of careful consideration.

Appropriate curriculum designs for the kindergarten can be developed only after the existing approaches are explored and current theories examined. The many influences which have shaped the kindergarten during this century have validity today in early childhood education. A broad perspective on the development of these influences will be essential if we are to avoid wasteful duplication and the pitfalls of fragmented, opportunistic curricular innovation.

Evelyn Weber has made a valuable contribution to the process of effective curriculum change in the kindergarten. With penetrating insight she has traced the development of significant ideas from the kindergarten's first encounter with the twentieth century up to the present. A study of this account offers a deeper appreciation of the tremendous task which faces educational reformers today and it also clarifies the varied and divergent elements on the current educational scene. Teachers, administrators, laymen— all concerned with the future of the kindergarten will find this book a valuable aid in their work with kindergarten reform.

March, 1969   KENNETH D. WANN

INTRODUCTION

At the turn of the century, members of the International Kindergarten Union heard a clear statement of dissent from accepted practice. With the zeal of a reformer Alice Temple dared to suggest that a child in kindergarten be allowed to make objects for which he could see a direct use. "For example," she explained, "let him weave a little basket of vegetable fiber on a wire frame, or a rug of heavy candlewicking for his playhouse rather than a small, easily torn and comparatively useless paper mat. Let him sew the seams of a doll's dress or a marble bag instead of a conventional design on a perforated card." [1]

This statement, addressed to kindergartners [2] assembled at Brooklyn, New York, in 1900, evoked an ominous and chilling silence.[3] Had they not just heard from such recognized leaders of the kindergarten movement as Susan Blow, Maria Kraus-Boelte, Lucy Wheelock, and Elizabeth Harrison that Friedrich Froebel had designed the ideal play materials for young children? [4] True, these leaders recognized that in the hands of some kindergartners Froebel's

[1] Alice Temple, "Conference on Gifts and Occupations," *Proceedings of the Seventh Annual Convention of the International Kindergarten Union,* (1900), p. 91. [The International Kindergarten Union consistently published proceedings of their annual meetings and had the volumes printed wherever it was convenient. Most volumes, now available only in libraries where they have been preserved, have no publication data.]

[2] "Kindergartner" was a term applied to kindergarten teachers and those training kindergarten teachers in the early literature.

[3] Related to the writer by Mary Leeper and Frances Berry in separate interviews in January, 1963. Both attended the meetings as active members of the International Kindergarten Union. The response was also reported by Patty Smith Hill, "Some Conservative and Progressive Phases of Kindergarten Education," *The Kindergarten and Its Relation to Elementary Education,* Sixth Yearbook of the National Society for the Study of Education, Part II (Bloomington, Ill.: Public School Publishing Co., 1907), p. 64.

[4] Speeches given by these kindergarten leaders in the "Conference on Gifts and Occupations." *Proceedings of the Seventh Annual Convention of the International Kindergarten Union,* pp. 50-58, 69-74.

program had become excessively formal, but the cure for these adverse tendencies was to be found in a greater understanding of the spirit and philosophy behind Froebel's educational principles. Deviation from Froebel's program was not to be countenanced.

The Froebelian program that Susan Blow extolled in her paper (she was too ill on this occasion to deliver her address in person) included the making of small paper mats and working on sewing cards. These activities for young children were the proper "occupations" when used to accompany "gifts." Together, the gifts and occupations were part of the logically organized program followed in a Froebelian kindergarten. The paper mats and sewing cards developed some of the "beauty forms" Miss Blow found essential when she wrote, "Three kinds of exercises, known to kindergartners as the production of forms of life, forms of beauty and forms of knowledge, guide the child in definite directions." [5] These were the forms and objects familiar to most kindergartners at the Brooklyn meeting in 1900. Not only had their training prepared them for the use of Froebelian materials but a cult of Froebelianism prevailed.

The simple proposition by Alice Temple epitomized the growing divergence in points of view concerning the curriculum of the kindergarten. On the surface the difference between having the child weave a paper mat from quarter inch strips of colored paper and having him weave a rug of heavy roving for the doll house may seem simple and insignificant. As we shall see, however, a number of fundamentally opposed premises separated these two practices. They represented different beliefs about the nature of the child and contrasting psychological theories. The views were in conflict on such questions as the use of the "ideal" versus the "real" in the curriculum, directed play versus free play, logical versus psychological continuity, and the meaning of creative self-activity.

The forces impelling change had made themselves felt earlier. Under a restiveness that demanded the consolidation of kindergarten interests and gains, kindergarten teachers had moved their arena of action from the Department of Kindergarten in the National Educa-

[5] *Ibid.*, p. 51.

tion Association to their own autonomous organization.[6] The first few years of the International Kindergarten Union were largely devoted to organizational matters, but at the stirring meeting in 1900 the controversy of the next two decades was clearly outlined.

Alice Temple was not alone in recommending departures from the Froebelian kindergarten curriculum. Patty Smith Hill of the Louisville Training School suggested the child's self-directed activity should replace exercises directed by the teacher. Alice Putnam of the Chicago Froebel Kindergarten Association reported her conviction that the kindergarten should open its doors wide to the "pure interests" of children. Mary Boomer Page, representing the kindergartners from the Armour Institute in Chicago, argued that the great revelations of modern science, which was beginning to recognize the theory of evolution that Darwin had put forward, could not be ignored. At the meeting in 1900, however, their voices were in the minority and the applause was given to those who supported Froebel's kindergarten program.

If within the ranks of kindergarten teachers themselves the conservative element reigned in 1900, proponents of change in the curriculum expressed themselves elsewhere. That same year an issue of the *Pedagogical Seminary* contained an article by Frederick Eby, then a fellow in psychology at Clark University, in which he outlined changes that current study of the child implied for the kindergarten program.[7] John Dewey, also, critically analyzed the Froebelian program and made suggestions for new procedures in *The Elementary School Record*.[8]

The controversy gained momentum, and the meetings of the International Kindergarten Union served as the arena for testing new ideas and for clarifying basic issues. The members of the International Kindergarten Union were largely kindergarten teachers,

[6] The International Kindergarten Union was organized in July, 1892 at Saratoga Springs at the time of the 32nd annual meeting of the National Education Association.

[7] Frederick Eby, "The Reconstruction of the Kindergarten," *Pedagogical Seminary*, VII (July, 1900), pp. 229-286.

[8] John Dewey, "Froebel's Educational Principles," *The Elementary School Record*, I (June, 1900), pp. 143-151.

directors of training schools for kindergarten teachers, or supervisors of kindergarten education in public schools. Involved in the practical aspects of teaching, they discussed the bases for selecting kindergarten activities, the sequential development of experiences, the use of symbolism with children, and similar curriculum problems.[9] They were so concerned about discussing differences in practice that they seldom found time to consider the philosophies undergirding these practices. Feelings ran high among members and the schism between the Conservatives and the Progressives, as the two factions came to be known, gradually widened.

Actually the battle on the kindergarten level reflected in microcosm the vast revolution reshaping intellectual thought in America in the years between the Civil War and World War I. In conflict with an idealistic philosophical outlook, which had embraced the Froebelian kindergarten in its entirety, came new views of man and differing fundamental conceptions of the universe. Investigations in the physical and biological sciences and, above all, the theory of evolution forced a reassessment of inherited beliefs. In the words of Lawrence Cremin, "as new notions of man and society came to the fore, pedagogy too was inevitably caught up in the ferment." [10]

In line with this controversy, as we shall see, the Conservative kindergartners had aligned themselves with an idealism in which truth was viewed as fixed and eternal. Froebel's mystical view of the unity of the universe and the educational principles he derived from it had become law to them. The Progressives, if not direct exponents of scientific and Darwinian thought, did concern themselves with the educational suggestions of those affected by it; the names of John Dewey and G. Stanley Hall figured prominently in their discussions.

For the three decades between 1890 and 1920, the Progressives hammered at the Froebelian kindergarten program. By 1909 it was

[9] See, for example, "Round Table Conference on Programs," *Proceedings of the Eighth Annual Convention of the International Kindergarten Union* (1901), pp. 48-58; "The Value of Constructive Work in the Kindergarten," *Proceedings of the Ninth Annual Convention of the International Kindergarten Union* (1902), pp. 51-58; "Materials and Methods," *Proceedings of the Twelfth Annual Meeting of the International Kindergarten Union* (1905), pp. 72-101.

[10] Lawrence A. Cremin, *The Transformation of the School* (New York: Alfred A. Knopf, 1961), pp. 90-91.

recognized that the major differences between the Progressives and the Conservatives were irreconcilable; by the mid 1920's new programs were presented in written form and the voice of the Conservatives rapidly disappeared. In order to understand the dramatic changes involved, let us turn first to the kindergarten program as Froebel developed it and to the expansion of this program in the United States.

CONTENTS

1

KINDERGARTEN BEGINNINGS

Froebel opened his "kindergarten" in Blankenburg, Germany in 1837, after having spent many years teaching in his own privately run schools or tutoring individual students. By the time of the Blankenburg kindergarten, the flowering of his educational ideas was quite complete. The principles upon which his kindergarten program was based reflected a number of educational and philosophical streams of thought: the absolute idealism of his time, some of the naturalism of Rousseau, aspects of the sense realism of Pestalozzi, Froebel's own tendency toward mysticism, and his understanding of child nature viewed in the context of these other influences. These fundamental aspects of Froebel's kindergarten program will become clear as we look at his educational theory and practice.

THE PHILOSOPHY OF FROEBEL

Idealistic Base

Froebel developed his philosophy in a period when the Idealistic movement pervaded Europe. According to Robert Ulich, "He is the representative of German transcendentalism in the realm of education." [1]

While attending the University of Jena between 1799 and 1801 Froebel concentrated mainly on mathematics and physics and did some work in architecture and surveying. But Jena was one of the

---

[1] Robert Ulich, *History of Educational Thought* (New York: American Book Co., 1945), p. 286.

centers of German philosophical life, and these were the years when the influence of the idealism of Johann Fichte and Friedrich von Schelling were felt at the university. One biographer of Froebel has written "that he absorbed much of this spirit by living in its atmosphere and associating with the students," [2] and suggests that Froebel's later persistent pounding on the inner connection of all things was a reflection of Schelling's writings. Ulich also connected Froebel's concept of unity with Schelling's philosophy of the identity of mind and matter. Froebel himself gave some clues to the outside influences on his thinking. In his autobiography he mentioned that Schelling's *Bruno, oder über die Welt-seele* had moved him profoundly.[3] In general, however, his autobiography is filled with the introspective musings which had been so much a part of his life from early childhood.

He shared the longing of other Germans of this period for a free and united Germany, for a great "Fatherland." This desire and love for his country led him to join the infantry division of Lutzow's corps at Leipzig in 1813 during the Napoleonic wars. The lack of national unity was his greatest concern and deepened his search for unity and harmony on both a national and individual level.

Basic to Froebel's philosophy and the kindergarten program he developed was his conception of the central unity of all things. This notion runs through his entire system of thought. He wrote, "The most pregnant thought which arose in me at this period was this: all is unity, all rests in unity, all springs from unity, strives for and leads up to unity, and returns to unity at last." [4]

Always a searcher for fundamental ideas, he turned to the value and purpose of elementary education as soon as he made his decision to enter the sphere of education. This need for unity became a measuring rod by which Froebel tested the educational program of others; unity, inner connections, an ordered whole became his strictest standards. He complained that his studies at Jena lacked inner connection, that they were merely arranged in an arbitrary series. Lack of unity he found to be the defect of Pestalozzi's school

[2] Denton J. Snider, *The Life of Frederich Froebel* (Chicago: Sigma Publishing Co., 1900), p. 21.

[3] Friedrich Froebel, *Autobiography of Friedrich Froebel*, trans. Emilie Michaelis and H. Keatley Moore (Syracuse: C. W. Bardeen, 1889), p. 40.

[4] *Ibid.*, p. 69.

at Yverdun. Though Froebel was deeply impressed with the warmth and human kindness at the school, he wrote after his second visit,

> The want of unity of effort, both as to means and aims, I soon felt; I recognized it in the inadequacy, the incompleteness, and the unlikeness of the ways in which the various subjects were taught. . . . I could see something higher, and I believed I saw this clearer, though not with greater conviction than Pestalozzi himself.[5]

As Froebel worked out his concept of unity, he saw it stemming from God, and thus encompassing the laws of both physical nature and the human spirit. Thus, Froebel saw no dichotomy *division* between the realm of the spirit and the realm of nature, or between the individual and society. The source of all was the all-pervading unity—God.

Since all things have their origin and existence in God it followed, in Froebel's thinking, that these things revealed an inner connectedness. His much discussed doctrine of *Gliedganzes,* or member-whole, was derived from this recurring theme of inner connection. The whole was seen as working in each of its parts. For example, Froebel conceived of man as both a part and a whole: a whole as a self-determining being, a part as a member of a social group. In a more encompassing sense he expressed the whole-part concept differently: ". . . as the germ bears within itself the plant and the whole plant life, does not the child bear also within himself the whole man and the whole life of humanity?" [6]

Unity, in Froebel's thought, was evidenced by great diversity. One way to comprehend the whole was through the understanding and reconciliation of opposites. As Froebel expressed it, "Every thing and every being, however, comes to be known only as it is connected with the opposite of its kind, and as its unity, its agreement with this opposite, its equation with reference to this is discovered. . . ." [7] The completeness of the sense of unity depended upon a thorough examination of the connecting thoughts or links.

Upon these notions of life-unity, of whole-part relations, of

[5] *Ibid.,* p. 79.

[6] Friedrich Froebel, *Pedagogics of the Kindergarten,* trans. Josephine Jarvis (New York: D. Appleton and Co., 1895), p. 62.

[7] Friedrich Froebel, *The Education of Man,* trans. William N. Hailmann (New York: D. Appleton and Co., 1889), p. 42.

inner connection, and of the law of opposites rests the symbolism of Froebel's educational program. The kindergarten itself was a symbol to this symbolic thinker.

The Nature of the Child

Froebel's idealistic interpretation of the unity of God and man clearly defined the nature of the child as innately good. He took seriously Rousseau's injunction to base education on the development of the child's inner capacities. For this reason Froebel's thought can be placed within the predeterministic theory of child development, in which prominent recognition is given to the child's contribution to his own development, to his developmental needs and status, and to his spontaneously undertaken activities. This is precisely stated in *The Education of Man:* ". . . all the child is ever to be and become, lies—however slightly indicated—in the child, and can be attained only through development from within outward." [8]

The contention that the child was not "a piece of wax or a lump of clay" but a self-generating force was one of the most significant aspects of Froebel's educational conception. It staunchly proclaimed man to be essentially dynamic or productive and not merely receptive. Man was not a sponge to sop up knowledge from without.

The Nature of Learning

Education must be, then, a process of unfoldment. Froebel frequently used an analogy with plant life to emphasize the nature of inner unfolding and as a protest against the idea that learning could be imposed upon the child from without. The educational materials that Froebel devised for the kindergarten were for the purpose of drawing out of the child every potentiality of his nature. By this means Froebel revised the traditional idea of the educational process. And he stated this point with conviction: "The purpose of teaching and instruction is to bring ever more *out* of man rather than to put more and more *into* man." [9] Froebel continually insisted that the curriculum should be built around the inner urges, the native im-

[8] *Ibid.,* p. 68.
[9] *Ibid.,* p. 279.

pulses, the developmental stage of the child—that it should be child-centered.

Sense Perception and Learning

Sense perception played only a partial role in Froebel's educational design. Recurrently expressed in his writings was the need for the child to make "the inner outer and the outer inner." Froebel here was wrestling to unite the dichotomous aspects of reality: inner experience and the outer world, private reality and public truth. Since development proceeded from the connection between the child's inner strivings and his outward expression of them, the senses were involved in both an outward expression of inner ideas and a taking in of outer phenomena.

Eby and Arrowood captured Froebel's ideas about the relationship between sense perception and self-activity when they wrote, "The senses have evolved in order to enable this inner activity to find appropriate expression, and to enable it to interpret the phenomena of outer reality for the sake of further, more discriminating action. For this reason, sense perception and physical activity develop together." [10] This would seem to bring Froebel close to modern behavioristic psychology, but Froebel emphasized this major distinction: the inner activity was primary and there was always something more in the mind which did not get there through the senses.

Creative Self-Activity and Play

Froebel's developmental scheme envisaged the child as vitally fostering the process of unfoldment by "his impulse to creative activity." In the light of the kindergarten program he developed, which was excessively teacher directed, his concept of creative self-activity needs careful assessment.

Here, as in other aspects of his philosophical thinking, Froebel wrote with great ambiguity. The teachers of his day to whom he attempted to explain his system asked for restatements of his ra-

[10] Frederick Eby and C. F. Arrowood, *The Development of Modern Education* (New York: Prentice-Hall, 1952), p. 815.

tionale ". . . in such a manner that it [could] be easily understood." [11]
This request was answered by *Education by Development* which
becomes increasingly, though unintentionally, obscure.

A cursory glance at Froebel's kindergarten program would
lead one to consider it quite devoid of opportunities for the child to
be creatively active. Was this then something that Froebel claimed
in theory but did not apply in practice? Though it could be conceived
that for Froebel the need to awaken the child to "Cosmic Truths"
transcended the child's need to create, this untenable conclusion
would contradict his major premises that so diligently highlighted
the element of unity.

Probably the key idea of the Froebelian doctrine of creativeness is to be found in "rendering the inner outer." By expressing the
incipient ideas and impulses welling up within him, the child may be
led to ". . . produce outside of himself that which he conceives within
himself." [12] Thus the child's natural tendencies to act and to construct are important tokens of his creative impulse; what he tries to
represent and do he begins to understand. Outer reality and his
inner presentiments become unified through constructive activity.
Earlier, in *The Education of Man,* Froebel had been extravagant in
placing value upon perceiving, doing, and constructing when he
wrote,

> We become truly godlike in diligence and industry, in working and
> doing, which are accompanied by the clear perception or even by the
> vaguest feeling that thereby we represent the inner in the outer; that
> we give body to spirit, and form to thought; that we render visible
> the invisible; that we impart an outward, finite, transient being to life
> in the spirit.[13]

The constructed object became important as a means of ob-
jectifying even the vaguest of ideas. In discussing self-activity Froebel declared, "The deepest craving of this inner life, this inner activity, is to behold itself mirrored in some external object." [14] For the

[11] Friedrich Froebel, *Education by Development,* trans. Josephine Jarvis
(New York: D. Appleton and Co., 1899), p. 1.

[12] *Ibid.,* p. 61.

[13] Froebel, *Education of Man,* p. 31.

[14] Froebel, *Pedagogics,* p. 238.

very young child, then, the objects he manipulated and handled could be the "awakener[s] of his inner world." They helped him to image himself objectively, to be self-creative.]

Froebel could thus include imitation and direction within his concept of creative self-activity, for he believed the young child's productive imitation could help to establish the connections between the inner and the outer. Froebel frequently claimed that imitation was an important aspect of creative activity: a "triune phenomenon" of development, "spontaneous activity, habit, and imitation" are referred to in various discussions. Imitative movement and production awakened subconscious thought and nurtured "Universal Truths." For the child's present life this meant that his activities were creative in the sense that he created himself by producing objects that developed his own inner meanings. Thus imitation was a true point of departure for nurture and for subsequent independent production.

This appraisal of "creative self-activity" shows it to be far from the ideas the word "creativity" connotes today. Froebel's notion was not bound tightly to originality or divergent thinking. He did offer, however, a bold, creative view of the educational enterprise for his time. It was daringly new to suggest that a major portion of a child's time in school be used to manipulate and construct objects.

Froebel's perception of the value of the child's self-active qualities led him to recognize the importance of play in the development of the child. Play was to him the perfect medium for encouraging self-development. A few educators, notably John Locke and Johann Basedow, had seen play as a device for motivating the learning of academic subject matter. Others, among them Johann Amos Comenius and Robert Owen, emphasized physical exercise and games for health purposes. It remained for Froebel, however, to perceive play as an educational method suitable for the release of the child's inner powers.

The following excerpt illustrates Froebel's conviction concerning the importance of play: "Play is the purest, most spiritual activity of man at this stage, and, at the same time, typical of human life as a whole—of the inner hidden natural life in man and all things. It gives, therefore, joy, freedom, contentment, inner and outer rest, peace with the world. . . . The plays of childhood are the germinal leaves of all later life; for the whole man is developed and shown in these, in his tenderest dispositions, in his innermost tendencies." [15]

Personal and Social Nature of Education

Froebel's ability to perceive new ways of working with children resulted partly from his continual observation of them. His ideas, though intended for and tested in practice, were nevertheless not products of the scientific laboratory but were essentially intuited. In his frequent invitation, "Come, let us live with our children," Froebel implied a deeper living with them, encompassing a knowledge and appreciation of the child's nature, an ability to enter into his perceptions and interests.

This student of children recognized stages of development, each stage growing out of the preceding one according to what he believed to be a divine-natural law. Each phase in development was itself a whole, but also a part of the continuity of successive stages. The concept of stages also united each individual with the evolution of the world as he unfolded from lower to higher stages of consciousness.

Froebel stressed each unique stage of development when he wrote, "The child, the boy, man, indeed, should know no endeavor but to be at every stage of development wholly what this stage calls for. Then will each stage spring like a new shoot from a healthy bud. . . ." [16] Thus, childhood was not merely preparation for adulthood but a significant stage to be respected and cultivated. This conviction of the importance of each stage was, no doubt, instrumental in leading Froebel to design a curriculum specifically for young children.

As the purpose of life was spiritual union with the Absolute, so the aim of education was the unfoldment of the child's powers in order to achieve this divine unity. Froebel summarized this point when he wrote, "Education consists in leading man, as a thinking, intelligent being, growing into self-consciousness, to a pure and unsullied, conscious and free representation of the inner law of

[15] Froebel, *The Education of Man,* p. 55.
[16] *Ibid.,* p. 30.

Divine Unity, and in teaching him ways and means thereto." [17] Froebel saw the unfoldment of spiritual unity as the ultimate development for the person both as a self-enhancing individual and as a harmonious member of a group. Stripped of the relationship of man to the Absolute, a concept akin to Froebel's unfoldment may be found today in discussions by some psychologists of individual self-actualization.[18]

The spirit of Froebel's writing showed that he envisioned the kindergarten as a happy group of children learning in harmonious relationship. Group activity was essential to development. A recurring expectation of Froebel's was the delight of the child in the activities he proposed. With experiences planned appropriately for each stage of development the child was expected to grow in complete harmony with his environment. Froebel anticipated that the child, given the opportunity to develop according to the laws of his own nature, should gain an evolving sense of unity with his fellow man. Good social relationships were an important outcome of school life and were founded upon a demand for a cooperative rather than a competitive education.

A loving communion of men was expected to help the individual to ascend to the metaphysical unity of the universe. This formed the basis of all moral training. Of later childhood Froebel wrote, "True discipline firmly places the boy, in all his actions, on the recognition and feeling of human worth, and on consequent respect for his own nature." [19]

Summary

At the heart of Froebel's theory of education for young children was his faith in the active nature of learning. Emphasizing the process of unfoldment as central to his learning theory, he denied the validity of an arbitrary or content-centered education; instead he buttressed the building of a curriculum around the nature of the

[17] *Ibid.,* p. 2.
[18] See, for example, Carl Rogers, *On Becoming a Person* (Boston: Houghton Mifflin, 1961); Abraham Maslow (ed.), *New Knowledge in Human Values* (New York: Harper, 1959).
[19] Froebel, *The Education of Man,* p. 250.

child. In his benign view of original nature he attributed to even the young child an intuitive discernment of metaphysical truths.

Froebel's insistence on the unfoldment of the capacities of the child within a loving community added the spirit of harmony to the child's relationships with his teachers and his peers. The individual aim of education was self-realization, which could be best developed in ideal human interaction.

Transcending all these views of the child and of development were Froebel's beliefs about the unity of all creation and about the necessity of man's understanding this unity and the relationship of the parts to each other and to the whole. As man came to acknowledge and master these inner relationships and as he discovered the connecting links, he would be truly educated.[20]

What kind of curriculum for young children grew from these basic beliefs of Froebel? Let us look at the kindergarten curriculum in detail.

FROEBEL'S KINDERGARTEN CURRICULUM

A great deal of impressive originality is to be found in Froebel's kindergarten curriculum. He selected educational experiences for children on an original basis; he developed a precise sequence of activities; and these led him to design completely new materials for children.

Gifts and Occupations

The selection of educational experiences was dictated by two main ideas already discussed: the importance of unfolding in the child's consciousness the inner connection and unity of all things, and the need for enlisting the child's self-active impulses for this purpose. These are exactly what the gifts and occupations in Froebel's program were designed to do. They formed the core of his kindergarten curriculum.

For at least fifteen years Froebel was engaged in planning and inventing the gifts—"gifts" because they were divinely given to

[20] Froebel, *Autobiography,* p. 70.

meet the needs of children. These objects, with their exceedingly formal qualities, reflect his mathematical bent and an earlier interest in crystallography. They were the connecting links in the child's world planned to lead him to discern ultimate truths; they were the opposites that established the completeness of the sense of unity.

Illustratively, the second gift comprised a sphere, a cube, and a cylinder. In play with the sphere the child would learn its sphericity, but Froebel's further expectation was that it would suggest to the child the concept of all-inclusive unity. The cube with its differentiation in form was to induce in the child a concept of diversity. In summarizing their value to the child Froebel wrote, "In *sphere* and *cube* considered in comparison with each other, is presented in outward view to the child the *resemblance between opposites,* which is so important for his whole future life, and which he perceives everywhere around himself, and multifariously within himself." [21] The cylinder was introduced as the reconciliation of the two "opposites"; its possession of some of the characteristics of each linked them together.

The gifts were said to lead the child to active discovery of his world and to fundamental truths. The occupations, which became a part of Froebel's program for young children, were selected to offer an opportunity for controlling and modifying malleable materials. These included such activities as clay modeling, the interlacing of paper strips, and building forms with sticks connected by softened peas. They followed logically from Froebel's valuing of constructive activities.

In the symbolic system of Froebel, the gifts were the objects that the child manipulated in order to objectify his own vague conceptions, and thus they led him to a better understanding of himself and his world. They made use of his urge to creative self-activity. The occupations, a term given to a type of handwork, extended and fixed the impressions made by the gifts.

---

[21] Froebel, *Pedagogics,* p. 105. Froebel himself made no sharp distinction between gifts and occupations. In *Education by Development* he used the term "occupation" to cover activity both with gifts and other materials. The American kindergartners, however, came to view the work with gifts and occupations as two separate, though parallel, series of activities.

The gifts and occupations as enumerated in William Hailmann's translation of *The Education of Man* were: [22]

GIFTS

Solids

First gift: Six colored worsted balls about one inch and a half in diameter

Second gift: Wooden ball, cylinder, cube, one inch and a half in diameter

Third gift: Eight one inch cubes—forming a two-inch cube

Fourth gift: Eight brick shaped blocks, 2 x 1 x ½

Fifth gift: 27 one-inch cubes, three bisected, three quadrisected diagonally forming a three inch cube

Sixth gift: 27 brick-shaped blocks, three bisected longitudinally, six bisected transversely

Surfaces

Seventh gift: Squares—entire and bisected
Equilateral triangles—entire, half, thirds

Lines

Eighth gift: Straight—splints of various lengths
Circular—metal or paper rings

Points

Ninth gift: Beans, lentils, seeds, pebbles

Reconstruction

Tenth gift: Softened peas or wax pellets and sharpened sticks or straw
To reconstruct the surface and solid synthetically from the point

OCCUPATIONS

Solids

Plastic clay, cardboard work, woodcarving

Surfaces

Paper folding, papercutting, parquetry, painting

Lines

Interlacing, intertwining, weaving, embroidery, drawing

Points

Stringing beads, perforating

[22] Froebel, *The Education of Man,* pp. 285-288.

The size of the blocks was significant. If blocks were too small the representations would appear too trivial, if too large, the pupils would fail to grasp the general meaning. Following Froebel's suggestion that "the material for building in the beginning should consist of a number of wooden blocks, whose base is always one square inch," the standard cube found in many of the gifts was exactly one inch square.

The first gift of six soft colored balls Froebel thought was suitable for the mother to introduce to the child at a very early age. Play with these balls would give the child a "new perception of the object as something now clasped, grasped, and handled, and now a freely active, opposite something." [23] A repetition of play with the ball would promote "a feeling and perception deeply grounded in and important to the whole life of man—the feeling and perception of oneness and individuality, and of disjunction and separateness; also of present and past possession." [24]

These first plays Froebel suggested as particularly suitable for a mother with her child, but play with gifts could early become a group procedure. In discussing the fifth gift he wrote: "Children of five years of age . . . can build in common at the same time." [25] An almost unlimited number of possible plays was suggested for these small blocks through division and recombination, implying analysis and synthesis.

For not only did Froebel devise the gifts, but he described with great precision the manner in which children were to play with them. A large portion of *The Pedagogics of the Kindergarten* was devoted to this task. Each gift was to be used alone until all possible meanings were pursued, then they were to be employed in combinations with other gifts for expansion of ideas. The manipulation of each gift and the study of its meaning might require weeks for completion.

An excerpt from the use of the fifth gift will illustrate the thorough directions Froebel provided for the teacher,

Lay four times two whole cubes in an oblong before you; place perpendicularly upon them again four times two whole cubes. Over these two

23 Froebel, *Pedagogics*, p. 36.
24 *Ibid.*, p. 37.
25 *Ibid.*, p. 223.

cubes lay two half cubes, so that they touch in the middle by their sharp edges; with the last two cubes, each of the two half cubes yet required is represented by two quarters. In the long hollow thus made sink four whole cubes. What have you made which now stands before each of you? "A house with an overhanging roof, four cubes high and two cubes broad." [26]

This particular play resulted in what Froebel called a life form—a house. Other plays developed knowledge forms, which were geometric shapes; still other plays resulted in beauty forms, which were designed to appeal to aesthetic appreciation.

By carefully planning and ordering the plays of childhood, Froebel believed he had found "the progressive course of the development and education of the child in a logical sequence." [27] As the gifts proceeded from solid to surface, from line to point, so the occupations paralleled this progress from clay modeling to paper folding, from stick laying to pricking. The movement thus symbolized the unfolding of the universe from absolute unity to the multitudinous diversity of existence. For Froebel, this apparently logical arrangement of materials was also the psychological arrangement since it was "in harmony with the growth of the child." [28] It "mirrored" the processes going on in the child's inner development.

Other Aspects of the Kindergarten Program

Songs, games and movement plays, stories and poetry, and aspects of nature study were all included in Froebel's program for young children. In a letter to a friend Froebel wrote, "The little girl of a neighbor of mine is supplying me with daily demonstrations that song is an essential part of child-life, for she never wearies, all day long, to repeat her few cadences." [29] Song and rhyme to Froebel were natural vehicles for reaching the mind through the senses. Many of the directions accompanying gift work contained rhymes or songs.

A concern for the very earliest nurture of the child led Froebel

[26] *Ibid.*
[27] *Ibid.,* p. 146.
[28] *Ibid.*
[29] Arnold H. Heinemann (ed.), *Froebel's Letters* (Boston: Leland Shepard, 1893), p. 71.

to publish *Mutter- und Kose-Lieder*.[30] This volume contained verses, songs, pictures, mottoes, finger and movement plays, and commentaries in which Froebel instructed the mother on the development of the child. The first verses, songs, and pictures centered on the mother as she played and talked with her child, helping him through imitation to understand his world and strengthen his fingers, arms and legs. Ideal family relationships were presented in plays of "The Family" and "Happy Brothers and Sisters." The child's familiarity with country life was expanded through songs, verses, and pictures of pigeons, weather vanes, fish, or gardening. Included also was the awakening of gratitude for those who serve through their daily labor: the carpenter, the wheelwright, or the charcoal burner, for example. The picture and rhymes abounded with references to animals, birds, workers, and the other country sights so familiar to the German children of the 1830's and 1840's for whom they were written.

Even though the book was considered to have rough, ill-drawn pictures with songs and verses that were distinctly poor, the intent of the book was clear. It was to help the mother guide the developing ideal of the child so that his life might become one of harmony and unity. Froebel admonished the mother of the child to "sacredly guard his simplicity and purity of soul." The medieval knight was used as an ideal of freedom and beauty; the emphasis was always on the romantic and the ideal.

Though the commentaries were written for mothers they came to be regarded as important guides to kindergarten practice. Froebel used them as the foundation of some of his lectures for kindergarten teachers because he felt they illustrated the fundamental ideas of his educational theory. Songs, verses, mottoes, and discussions centering on the pictures found a place in the kindergarten program.

From the earliest years the child's motor activities should be fostered for "Each sure and independent movement, either of his whole body or one of his limbs, gives the child pleasure because of the feeling of power which it arouses in him." [31] The minute descriptions of games and movement plays in *The Pedagogics of the Kin-*

---

[30] Friedrich Froebel, *Mutter- und Kose-Lieder* (Leipzig: A. Pichler's Witwe und Sohn, 1911).
[31] Froebel, *Pedagogics*, p. 241.

dergarten testify to the importance these teacher directed games held in Froebel's kindergarten program. We know that they were often carried on out of doors, as indeed were other parts of the program when tables for gift and occupation work could be placed outside.

Repeatedly Froebel linked movement plays which were forms of rhythmic activity, to the joy the young child experienced as he moved about, gaily hopping up and down or swinging his arms. The inner feelings and vague perceptions attributed to the child as well as his overt activity were considered in planning these plays, for Froebel was convinced that the young child's joy in movement stemmed from more than mere bodily activity. "The true source of their joy," he wrote, "is the dim premonition which stirs in their sensitive hearts (Gemüthe) that in their play there is hidden a deep significance; that it is, in fact, the husk within which is concealed the kernel of living spiritual truth." [32] The games were significant for arousing and strengthening "the ethical feeling of the child." Most of the movement plays were put into circle form to foster the budding sense of unity and harmony. Some were based upon pure motor activities such as walking, running, or swinging; others involved imaginative representations like stars, flowers, or snails. The rhymes and songs that accompanied many movement plays fulfilled a threefold purpose: to move the play forward by supplying careful directions, to awaken a latent sense of rhythm and melody, and to strengthen "the impulse for social cooperation." [33]

Froebel continually emphasized the social advantages expected to accrue from the games, again symbolically conceived. Of the *Snail Game* he wrote, ". . . it unites all the children in one whole of living activity, and finally yields the form of a circle, which is symbolic of wholeness." [34] The different social roles children might play through games were recognized. He suggested that when swinging movement plays were used, "Each member of the circle should have a chance to lead, for it is especially developing to a child to recognize himself on the one hand in his own independent activity, and on the other as the member of a well-ordered totality." [35] Many of the

[32] *Ibid.,* p. 261.
[33] *Ibid.,* p. 268.
[34] *Ibid.,* p. 256.
[35] *Ibid.,* p. 270.

games Froebel copied from traditional plays of children, omitting the rougher features in order to have them conform to his educational ideal.

Nature study and gardening completed the program for young children that Froebel presented in his writings. The ideal garden he outlined had a small plot for each child and a common part with careful divisions for flowers and vegetables. In garden work the child was expected to learn the essentials of the development of plants and also the relationship of the particular to the whole. Gardening was viewed as one of the ways in which the child could watch the working of the "Unseen Power" and also as a way of gaining a first sense of responsibility. Care of pets and walks out into the countryside added informality to the program.

Summary

Froebel's kindergarten program reflected the sense of unity he wished to achieve. The materials he designed to focus the attention of the children in the classroom followed logically from his stated goals and his view of the learning process. His belief in whole-part relations and the inner connectedness of all life was demonstrated in the gifts and occupations. By designing materials with a definite sequence and by supplying explicit directions for their use, Froebel provided an educational system with clear directives for the teacher. The defined sequence also held the program together as a whole. The sense of unity, with which Froebel's kindergarten curriculum was impregnated, fostered its expansion as a totality. This is precisely the manner in which the kindergarten idea spread to the United States.

2
THE ENTRENCHMENT OF
THE FROEBELIAN KINDERGARTEN
IN AMERICA

The kindergarten came to America as the transplantation of Froebel's educational principles and practices. Several circumstances favored the acceptance of the kindergarten program exactly as it developed in Germany; most significantly, its idealistic base was in accord with the philosophy of a number of educational leaders in America. William T. Harris, Elizabeth Peabody, and Susan Blow, avid students of German idealism, were ready exponents of Froebelian principles and this "new education" rapidly gained the support of the National Education Association. Important also were the many German students trained directly in Froebel's educational methods who came to America and were able to explain and demonstrate the precise procedures. As the methods drew interest, the Froebelian materials were made available commercially.

PATTERNS OF EXPANSION

On the basis of what she had learned of Froebel's principles from lectures he gave in Hamburg in 1849, Margaretha Meyer Schurz opened the first American kindergarten in Watertown, Wisconsin, in 1956.[1] Several other members of the Meyer family had also attended the lectures including Margaretha's sister and brother-in-law, Bertha and Johannes Ronge, and a brother, Adolph Meyer. The Meyer family was one of wealth and of liberal social views so

[1] The Library of Congress research department confirmed this as the first kindergarten in America in a report of March 24, 1955. *Watertown Daily Times* (Wisconsin), Centennial Edition, August 24, 1956, p. 4.

their interest in "the new education" was not surprising. Margaretha was only sixteen when she learned about kindergarten procedures, but she developed an intelligent and sincere interest in Froebel's educational plan.

Madame Bertha Ronge helped to spread the kindergarten idea to England by opening kindergartens in Manchester and in London. Her display of kindergarten material at the International Exhibit of Educational Systems in London in 1854 interested a visitor from America—Henry Barnard.[2] For a time Margaretha assisted her sister in the London kindergarten, and it was in the Ronge home that she met Carl Schurz, the young German liberal who took her to America as his wife in 1852.

Carl Schurz had taken part in the abortive German revolution of 1848. Discouraged by the seeming failure of the liberal cause in Europe and not foreseeing the realization of his youthful dream of the unification of Germany under a constitutional government, Schurz turned his attention to the United States. After a brief residence in Philadelphia, the Schurz family located in Watertown, Wisconsin. Desiring the benefits of kindergarten training for her own children, Mrs. Schurz gathered together her two daughters and four of their cousins and put into practice the methods she had learned earlier from Froebel.[3]

At first the kindergarten was held in the parlor of the Schurz home and on the broad front porch. In response to the request that the children of other relatives and friends be allowed to join the group, the kindergarten was moved into a small vacant store in the center of town. Here the mother-teacher used for her curriculum Froebel's gifts and occupations with the addition of the games and songs he prescribed. The children sang and talked in German. The Schurz family's stay in Watertown was brief, so except for being an "historic first" the impact of the kindergarten was not great. Although Mrs. Schurz conducted no other kindergartens, she nevertheless exerted a far-reaching influence upon the expansion of kindergarten in America by arousing the interest of Elizabeth Peabody.

[2] Nina C. Vandewalker, *The Kindergarten in American Education* (New York: Macmillan, 1908), p. 14.

[3] *Watertown Daily Times,* August 24, 1956, pp. 1, 7.

The two women met by chance in Boston, and Miss Peabody became so interested in kindergarten procedures that she opened a school of her own shortly thereafter. Thus, in the beginning, her life-long devotion to the kindergarten was fed by the knowledge that she gained from Mrs. Schurz.

Less romantic but more practical in spreading the kindergarten idea were the efforts of Caroline Luise Frankenburg. A life-long professional teacher and a co-worker of Froebel, she started a kindergarten in Columbus, Ohio in 1858. Miss Frankenburg had established a small infant school in Columbus in 1836, using the educational principles she had learned from Froebel earlier at the Keilhau school. Since this school predated Froebel's innovations at Blankenburg it was never considered to be a "true" kindergarten. Miss Frankenburg returned to Germany in 1840 and taught again under Froebel's direction; with this expanded preparation she later conducted kindergartens in Columbus and Zanesville, Ohio, and Germantown, Pennsylvania. In contrast to the demand for Mrs. Schurz's services, this professional teacher had to scour the neighborhood for enough children to keep her German-speaking kindergarten going.[4]

Other early kindergartens were part of the German-English Academies of the 1860's and 1870's. These academies, most of them bilingual, were established by the Germans who came to the United States as a result of the European Revolution of 1848. The significance of the early kindergarten is thus identified not only with Froebel's own search for unification but also with social liberalism. As early as 1861 the academy in Newark, New Jersey, of which Adolf Douai was principal, added a kindergarten. William N. Hailmann, an ardent worker for the cause, included a kindergarten in the academy he directed in Louisville, Kentucky, in 1865. Hailmann's interest in the kindergarten dated back to his earlier study of schools in Switzerland. Other kindergartens followed this pattern in German-English schools in Detroit (1870) and Milwaukee (1872).[5]

[4] Elizabeth Jenkins, "How the Kindergarten Found Its Way to America," The Wisconsin Magazine of History, XIV (September, 1930), 59.

[5] Caroline D. Aborn, Sarah A. Marble (compilers), History of the Kindergarten Movement in the Mid-Western States and in New York (Washington, D.C.: Association for Childhood Education, 1938), pp. 25, 31.

Dependence Upon Teachers Trained in Germany

As American educators became interested in kindergartens they naturally looked to Germany for explanations of the theoretical background and called for teachers who had been trained in the schools established by Froebel and developed under his direction at Keilhau and Marienthal. Froebel's widow, Frau Luise Froebel, continued to train students in kindergarten procedures in Keilhau, Dresden, and Frankfurt until as late as 1886.[6] The Baroness Bertha von Marenholtz-Bülow, a friend and disciple of Froebel, interpreted Froebel's educational system widely.[7] She had become acquainted with Froebel in 1849 and was thoroughly convinced of the efficacy of his method. She assisted in courses for kindergarten teachers in schools in Berlin and Frankfurt.

When Nathaniel Allen wished to open a kindergarten in his private school in West Newton, Massachusetts, in 1864, he sent to Germany for a properly prepared teacher. Through the influence of the Baroness, Mrs. Luise Pollock, who had learned kindergarten methods in the Berlin training school, came to America to introduce Froebelian procedures in Allen's school.[8] After a few years in West Newton, she moved to Washington, D.C., where a training school for teachers was added to the kindergarten she conducted there.

The largest number of kindergartens directed by teachers trained in Germany was found along the east coast. In New York City, Henrietta Haines, the principal of a "celebrated" ladies school in Gramercy Park, invited Maria Boelte, a pupil of Froebel's widow to open a kindergarten in 1872. The following year Miss Boelte married John Kraus, a personal friend and follower of Froebel. Their mutual interest led them to conduct "The New York Seminary for kindergartners with a model kindergarten conducting class and primary." [9] Together John Kraus and Maria Kraus-Boelte spread

[6] Friedrich Froebel, *Autobiography of Friedrich Froebel,* trans. Emilie Michaelis and H. Keatley Moore (Syracuse: C. W. Bardeen, 1889), p. 143.

[7] See Louis Walter, "Baroness von Marenholtz-Bülow and the Kindergarten," Henry Barnard, (ed.) *Kindergarten and Child Culture Papers,* (Hartford: Office of Barnard's American Journal of Education, 1890), pp. 151-158.

[8] Lucy Wheelock and Caroline D. Aborn (eds.), *The Kindergarten in New England,* (Printing supervised by Charles Edward Newell, President of the Massachusetts School of Art, 1935), p. 10.

[9] *Ibid.,* p. 68.

Froebelian methodology through their training school, speeches, and published literature.[10] Two other students of the Baroness, Mathilde Kriege and her daughter Alma, left Germany to spread the "new educational principles" in America. Madame Kriege established a school for training kindergarten teachers in Boston while her daughter directed the children's class connected with it.

Two pupils even found their way to California and promoted support for the kindergarten idea there. In 1873 Frau Hertha Semler conducted a flourishing German-American kindergarten in San Francisco. Emma Marwedel established the first kindergarten in Los Angeles in 1876 with twenty-five children in the class and "three nice girls" who wanted to learn to be kindergarten teachers.[11]

Trends of Expansion

Two distinct generalizations can be made about these pioneering kindergartens: they were started by people of German origin closely allied to Froebel's original kindergarten ideas; and they followed a pattern of development that helps to explain the way that Froebel's program became formalized in America. At first kindergartens were available only for children whose parents could afford such education; then followed a rapid extension of programs to children in slum areas. The problem of training more kindergarten teachers for the American schools demanded immediate attention. It became a general practice that a recently trained teacher included, along with her work with children, the training of other teachers. This may have contributed to the feeling of some leaders that the materials and detailed practice of Froebel's program became propagated in a manner that lacked the "true spirit" of Froebel's teaching. In her vivid but complex prose, Elizabeth Peabody spoke out against this situation:

Mrs. Kraus-Boelte always cries aloud and spares not in deprecation of recent students and not long experienced kindergartners undertaking

---

[10] Maria Kraus-Boelte and John Kraus, *The Kindergarten Guide* (New York: E. Steiger, 1877).

[11] Barbara Greenwood (compiler), *History of the Kindergarten Movement in the Western States, Hawaii and Alaska* (Washington, D.C.: Association for Childhood Education, 1940), pp. 10-11.

to train others, and has much and most true things to say of the pro-
foundness of insight and depth of experience necessary in order to be
sufficient to undertake the responsibilities of a kindergartner . . .[12]

With a system of education laid out in as complete detail as
Froebel's kindergarten plans, it was easy for the details to be followed even when the reasons behind the minutia were not readily
grasped. Many of the German promoters of early kindergartens must
have shared the significance of Froebel's emphasis upon unity and
social harmony, but a new generation of teachers could easily lose
the principles in the specifics of daily practice.

AMERICAN SUPPORTERS OF FROEBEL

Leadership in promoting the kindergarten in America was not
left to German-Americans alone. Henry Barnard rapidly spread the
news from Europe. William T. Harris, Elizabeth Peabody, and
Susan Blow explained and expanded the guiding philosophy of
Froebel, for in its idealistic base they foresaw boundless possibilities
for the education of the young child. Since the term "idealism"
admits of vast differences in thought and temperament, these three
educators can be included in its scope. Though they interpreted
Froebel differently, placing their personal emphases upon varying
aspects of the theory, all sought to make the basic principles understood by those who would put them into practice.

Henry Barnard

The "new" theory of Froebel was introduced into American
educational literature by Henry Barnard. His enthusiasm for the
exhibit of Froebelian materials and the kindergarten work of
Madame Ronge in London in 1854 was expressed in a report to
the governor of Connecticut, in an article in the *American Journal
of Education,* and in several public addresses. When he first wrote
about kindergarten Henry Barnard was Secretary of the Connecticut
Board of Education and later United States Commissioner of
Education. He edited the *American Journal of Education,* which

[12] Elizabeth Peabody, "Letter from Miss Peabody to the Editor," in
Barnard, *Kindergarten and Child Culture Papers,* p. 12.

was published at Hartford. In his opinion the kindergarten "was by far the most original, attractive, and philosophical form of infant development the world has yet seen." [13]

In order to disseminate Froebelian ideas Barnard assembled the first substantial volume of kindergarten literature in the English language; it included articles by both European and American educators and was published under the title of *Kindergarten and Child Culture Papers*. About half of the collection was devoted to articles about Froebel and his educational work translated by faithful European followers including Wichard Lange [14] and Bertha von Marenholtz-Bülow. The list of American contributors was a veritable roll call of early workers for the Froebelian cause: Maria Kraus-Boelte, Luise Pollock, Elizabeth Peabody, Mary Mann, William Harris, and Susan Blow.

As United States Commissioner of Education, Barnard continued his promulgation of Froebel's program. In the report he submitted to the United States Senate in 1868 he wrote: "as the great formative period of the human being precedes the age at which children now attend the public school, it is necessary that by some formal arrangement, public or private, the age of impression should not be lost for the best purposes. . . . I know of no agency so philosophical and so attractive to these purposes as the kindergarten of Froebel." [15] The influence of Barnard's positions in education, his advice and correspondence, as well as his publications "fathered the kindergarten movement in America, thus helping to add a step on the lower portion of the American educational ladder."[16]

Elizabeth Peabody

If Henry Barnard was the father of the American kindergarten, Elizabeth Peabody was the apostle of Froebel's program. Having

[13] Henry Barnard, "Letter to President of the American Froebel Union," in *Kindergarten and Child Culture Papers*, p. 3.

[14] Wichard Lange was a close associate of Froebel in the winter of 1849-1850. He collected and published much of Froebel's writings—particularly the autobiographical materials.

[15] Barnard, *"Introduction" to Part III, Kindergarten and Child Culture Papers*, p. 370.

[16] Richard Emmons Thursfield, *Henry Barnard's American Journal of Education* (Baltimore: Johns Hopkins Press, 1945), p. 334.

participated in the literary and philosophical activities of the New England Transcendentalists, she was particularly fitted by both nature and experience to enter into the thought of Froebel. She had often discussed philosophical problems with William Ellery Channing and Ralph Waldo Emerson and educational problems with Horace Mann and Bronson Alcott. As a co-worker in Alcott's Temple School in Boston she had become absorbed in his techniques of working with children, had indicated her interest in newer educational methods—and had also suffered from the later discreditation of the school.[17]

Miss Peabody was so rapidly drawn to Froebel's kindergarten that she began to practice his methods with only the barest knowledge of his total educational system. Barnard's article describing the London kindergarten exhibit had aroused her interest; a chance meeting with Mrs. Carl Schurz in 1859 fanned this interest into a flame of enthusiasm. She read the preface to Froebel's *Education of Man* in pamphlet form as it was sent to her by Mrs. Schurz, and with her usual exuberance she hastened to open a kindergarten on Pinckney Street in Boston in 1860. The instant popularity of the school made it necessary to add an assistant director, thus her sister, Mary Mann, became associated with the school, as she had with so many of Elizabeth's educational efforts. That same year they collaborated in writing a *Moral Culture of Infancy and Kindergarten Guide.*

Despite the warm reception of her kindergarten, Miss Peabody began to doubt some of her applications of Froebel's principles: perhaps her attempts at kindergarten education had been premature. Of these early, inadequate efforts she later wrote, "The most noted one was my own in Boston; but I must do myself justice to say that I discovered its radical deficiency, by seeing that the results promised by Froebel, as the fruit of his method, did not accrue . . . ." [18] The financial success of the school and the obvious delight of the children did not satisfy her. So, at the age of fifty-five, Elizabeth Peabody

[17] Louise Hall Tharp, *The Peabody Sisters of Salem* (Boston: Little, Brown, 1951), pp. 91, 111.

[18] Peabody, "Letter," in Barnard, *Kindergarten and Child Culture Papers,* p. 10.

went to Europe to increase her understanding of the Froebelian kindergarten. In Berlin she visited the Kindergarten Seminary run by
Baroness von Marenholtz-Bülow, and her letters show her delight
in the equipment, the music, and the singing games based on folk
tunes.[19] Upon her return to Boston she felt that she must devote her
attention "to the work of abolishing the mischief she had done, and
of spreading the true thing in her native land." [20] Acting on this conviction she spent her last years writing and lecturing about the kindergarten. She revised the *Kindergarten Guide* and later published a
volume of her *Lectures in the Training Schools for Kindergartners*.[21]

Elizabeth Peabody was in great demand as a lecturer at training schools for kindergarten teachers, and while touring the country
she pervaded the atmosphere of their work with her vitality. She
presented her enthusiasm for Froebel forthrightly and movingly;
his theory became the epitome of all she had believed and tried to
formulate. Even though, on her return from Europe, her stated aim
was to inspire "an enthusiasm for educating children strictly on
Froebel's method," [22] her own transcendental thought nevertheless
permeated her lectures. The influence of Channing and Emerson
were ever in evidence. Her concept of the child was more than
benevolent, she revered childhood as the time when communion
with God could most easily be realized. In every child she saw the
possibility of the perfect man; "Every individual child is a momentum of God's creativeness which the human Providence of Education must take as its datum." [23] Goodness was to be found within
the child, but it needed nurture and unfoldment. Thus in her lectures
she stressed the religious and spiritual side of education, telling her
listeners what a lofty and benign influence the kindergarten would
have in setting each young child on the right path in life. "Moral
education," she wrote, "is the Alpha and Omega of the kinder-

[19] Tharp, pp. 322-323.

[20] Elizabeth Peabody, "The Origin and Growth of the Kindergarten,"
Education, II (May, 1882), p. 524.

[21] Elizabeth Peabody and Mary Mann, *Guide to the Kindergarten and
Moral Culture of Infancy* (New York: E. Stieger, 1877); Elizabeth Peabody,
Lectures in the Training Schools for Kindergartners (Boston: D.C. Heath,
1886).

[22] Peabody, *Lectures*, p. 25.

[23] *Ibid.*, p. 161.

garten," [24] thus linking the goal of the kindergarten with that primary goal Horace Mann held for the common school he proposed, moral or character education.

As a means of understanding the nature of the child Miss Peabody heartily endorsed the method of introspection. Her "Psychological Observations" outlined the intuitive awakening of children's thought, which she explained in terms of her own metaphysical reminiscences. This introspection plus Transcendentalism formed the background of thought that paved the way for her ready acceptance of the symbolism of Froebel's program, and led her to recommend the gifts and occupations as eminently suitable material for children. As she crusaded to introduce kindergartens to the American public schools, she also spread her benevolent view of child nature. Unfortunately, however, this belief in the almost unassailable goodness of young children could—and did—readily lapse into mere sentimentality.

Any necessity for modifying Froebel's program to suit American culture was brushed aside. Elizabeth Peabody accepted Froebel's theory not just as a national system but rather as a method of human development applicable to all children. She believed that Froebel's system came to him through revelation, and this clearly made him the authority on the education of young children. She warned against deviations from his suggested procedures. The one cultural concession she made was that it might be harder to govern American children because of their lively energies; this made it all the more important for them to learn order and self-direction.

William T. Harris

The year 1873 marked the first, epoch-making connection of the kindergarten with a public school system. While Elizabeth Peabody was promoting the kindergarten cause in New England, William T. Harris and Susan Blow collaborated to incorporate this "new education" into the public schools of St. Louis. Although eventually the effect of connecting the kindergarten with the public school was to mitigate the insularity of the program and to expose it to the currents of thought playing upon the schools at large, the

[24] *Ibid.*, p. 76.

direct influence of both William Harris and Susan Blow was to reinforce Froebel's kindergarten program.

Neither of these educators, however, shared Elizabeth Peabody's romantic reverence for childhood. Harris, it is true, saw the individual as endowed with a noble and immortal destiny, but for the great masses of children this was to be achieved by adjustment to existing social institutions in which the school played a central disciplinary role. In other words, Harris accepted the kindergarten on grounds other than Froebelian metaphysics. For Miss Blow, also, the disciplinary aspects of development ranked high and her strictures against the naturalism of Rousseau were intense.

The concern of the kindergarten to develop self-active individuals found ready acceptance in the Hegelian philosophy of Harris. Of the process of education he wrote, "Educate the heart? Educate the character? Yes, these are the chief objects, but there is no immediate way of educating these. They must be educated by two disciplines—that of the will in correct habits, and by that of the intellect in a correct view of the world." [25] Froebel's kindergarten principles seemed to Harris so eminently suited to disciplining the will in correct habits that he heartily endorsed them in his official capacities as Superintendent of Schools in St. Louis (1868–1880) and subsequently as United States Commissioner of Education (1889–1906).

Although Harris held that the self-active individual was the end product, he also believed that the school was essential to help man achieve his truest expression. In elucidating the doctrine of self-activity, he stated that through imitation and assimilation the child grew toward a feeling of responsibility and became less mechanical and more spontaneous, finding the rule for the action in his own mind and becoming truly original.[26] Thus Harris contributed to the concept of a disciplined development of creativity, and the full weight of his prestige was used to support the kindergarten gifts

[25] William T. Harris, "Psychological Inquiry," *Addresses and Proceedings of the National Education Association* (Washington, D.C.: The Association, 1885), p. 101. [In subsequent notes these volumes are referred to with only the appropriate year. All volumes were published by the Association.]

[26] William T. Harris, "How Imitation Grows Into Originality and Freedom," *Kindergarten Magazine*, XI (May, 1899), 601.

and occupations as "the best instrumentalities ever devised for the purpose of educating young children through self-activity." [27]

As the manual training movement gained in importance in the 1880's, Harris minimized it as being related too closely to the doctrine of sense training. All knowledge, in his view, was *not* derived from sense perception; elementary education needed to open up more cultural and intellectual aspects of life. Skills of manipulation should be developed at an early age since, he believed, later years must be devoted to the disciplines of reading, writing, and arithmetic. The kindergarten period including children from three to seven years old was the ideal time and Froebelian gifts and occupations were the ideal materials for industrial training. Harris announced to the American Froebel Union in 1879, "I have in this protracted discussion of the significance of Froebel's gifts as a preparation for industrial life, indicated my grounds for believing that the kindergarten is worthy of a place in the common-school system."[28]

Society would benefit by providing rational kindergarten training, Harris argued. Poor children would be kept out of the streets where they developed evil associations; rich children would be kept out of the hands of unskilled servants who ruined them through self-indulgence. "Believing," writes Merle Curti, "that the kindergarten could salvage these pampered children of the rich, a function he considered of at least equal importance with its power to redeem moral weaklings from homes of poverty and squalor, Harris was a pioneer in its behalf." [29]

Harris did not, however, share the belief of some kindergarten enthusiasts that the principles and procedures of the kindergarten should be extended into the primary school. "The genius of Froebel," he wrote, "has provided a system of discipline and instruction which is wonderfully adapted to this stage of the child's growth, when he needs the gentleness of nurture and the rational order of

[27] William T. Harris, "Kindergarten in the Public School System," in Barnard, *Kindergarten and Child Culture Papers*, p. 630.

[28] *Ibid.*, p. 633.

[29] Merle Curti, *The Social Ideas of American Educators* (Paterson, New Jersey: Littlefield, Adams, 1959), p. 324.

the school in due admixture." [30] Kindergarten ideas were excellent
for children when they were in the transitional stage between the
home and school and conventional studies were beyond their grasp;
the methods of the primary school were equally right for children
a little older, when "the method of play gives place to the method
of work; the symbolic yields to the conventional; the kindergarten
methods to the methods of the primary school." [31] In his opinion
it was not the purpose of kindergarten to prolong childhood.

Susan Blow

In 1870 Superintendent Harris had recommended that the
school board of St. Louis adopt the kindergarten as part of the
school system, but it was not until three years later when Susan
Blow volunteered to superintend a kindergarten and to instruct a
teacher that the first step was taken.[32] The school board provided
a room and suitable equipment at Des Peres School. Miss Blow
had just returned from a year in New York City, where she had
studied kindergarten procedures with Maria Kraus-Boelte, and was
eager to test her new educational ideas. Later she looked to the
immediate followers of Froebel for a precise understanding of his
method; the year 1877 found her in Germany studying with Baroness von Marenholtz-Bülow and visiting German kindergartens.
Her writings evidence careful study of Froebel and other German
philosophers of the period.

Like others before her Miss Blow had faith in play as part
of the educative process, the development of creative self-activity
through a disciplined process involving imitation and the use of
Froebel's materials to achieve the prescribed results. She placed
herself squarely in the ranks of those who looked to an introspective
psychology to reveal the most important characteristics of the
child; she found in Froebel's philosophy a "real" psychology. In
the doctrine of *Gliedganzes,* the member-whole concept, Susan

[30] Harris,"Kindergarten in the Public School System," in Barnard,
Kindergarten and Child Culture Papers, pp. 629-630.
[31] William T. Harris, "Kindergarten Methods Contrasted with the
Methods of the Primary School," *Journal of Addresses and Preceedings of
the National Education Association,* 1889, p. 453.
[32] Aborn and Marble, *History . . . Mid-Western States,* pp. 38-39.

Blow found the key to Froebel's practical work and the source of the symbolism, which she believed to be his most original contribution to educational theory. She interpreted the young child's tendency toward animism and his imaginative or "analogous" play as evidences of his ability to think symbolically. Since "The young child not only expresses himself symbolically, but is quick to interpret the symbolism of nature," [33] she felt this could rightly be made the most significant aspect of the educational program.

The child's proneness to impute life to inanimate objects indicated his intuitive understanding of the unity of all things and of all forces as being "derived ultimately from the forces of mind." [34] In concept building she saw the child's tendency to generalize before differentiating as evidence of his ability to recognize the universal from a fragmentary thought. The use of his father's cane as a hobby-horse was an example of the young child's "analogical activity of mind." Susan Blow described these characteristics in detail as evidence to support the wide use of symbolism. Symbolic toys were essential for the child's intellectual development; the too realistic toy chilled the child's imagination, but the true plaything possessed an indefiniteness that permitted many symbolic transformations. The play materials she recommended were, of course, Froebel's gifts, each one capable of varied usage.

Of all of Froebel's contributions to education, Susan Blow found the *Mutter und Kose-Lieder* the loftiest expression of his educational genius. The formal defects of the book, she freely admitted, were halting verse, crude pictures, poor music, and obscure commentaries. Yet she believed that Froebel had taken the typical manifestations of the child and used them to reveal deep and profound meanings. They mirrored the ideal life of childhood and helped each child to understand "ideals of love and gratitude and service." [35] As these images were held up to the child in play, they acted on his character in such a way that he would subsequently strive to attain them. With these values clearly defined,

[33] Susan E. Blow, "The Mother Play and Nursery Songs," in Barnard, *Kindergarten and Child Culture Papers*, p. 590.

[34] Susan E. Blow, *Symbolic Education*, (New York: D. Appleton, 1894), p. 94.

[35] *Ibid.*, p. 182.

Miss Blow suggested that the mother-play sequence should be "the center around which revolve all the concentric circles of kindergarten activity." [36] For the curriculum this meant that each mother-play picture and verse would be the organizing center of activities for several days; the themes being "the symbolic aspects of nature and the ethical ideals embodied in human institutions." [37]

There was more here, of course, than the mere request that the daily themes be selected from material in *Mutter-und Kose-Lieder*. Her suggestion embodied the conviction that to build the ideal person, ideal behavior must be continually presented to the child. The vision of the good to be achieved was the source of the power that led to good behavior, thus avoiding the necessity of adult coercion. "The ideal which he holds up to himself in play," she wrote, "reacts upon his character, and what he represents himself as being he actually strives to become." [38] In fostering the growth of the inwardly self-evolving ideal, adults must ever protect the child from bad models of conduct and supply him with good ones.

"Divine love," Miss Blow believed, was symbolized in the pictures and rhymes depicting the work of the carpenter, the baker, the charcoal burner.[39] As these stirred "in the child's mind some presentment of the beauty of universal service, some sense of his own obligation to serve," [40] the virtues of industry, punctuality, and courtesy were expected to flourish. The knight depicted the ideal of service. It was Susan Blow's opinion that in the "labor plays" Froebel had chosen those occupations in which the dignity of labor was coupled with economic importance. To substitute such services as those of the cabman or the scissors grinder, who ministered to incidental needs, destroyed the ideal of industrial life and minimized the universal characteristics of service.

One further attribute of the *Mutter- und Kose-Lieder* gave it special value for Susan Blow. In the games and songs Froebel had

---

[36] *Ibid.*, p. 164.
[37] *Ibid.*, p. 247.
[38] *Ibid.*, p. 115.
[39] Blow, "The Mother Play," in Barnard, *Kindergarten and Child Culture Papers*, p. 586.
[40] Blow, *Symbolic Education*, p. 185.

captured the elements that have delighted the children of all races and of all ages.[41] The folk-qualities in the songs and games enabled the child to relive the positive aspects of the evolution of the race. For, "It is not necessary for individuals to repeat the abortive experiments of the race. It is not necessary for them to relive what humanity has outlived." [42] In this manner Susan Blow reconciled the use of the ideal with children, while at the same time stressing the parallelism between the development of the individual and that of the race.

The impact of Miss Blow's elevation of "the ideal" was felt even after practices began to change. Her insistence upon the rigid use of Froebelian materials and practices can be understood in the light of her careful analysis of the unity of his writings. Deviations in practice violated the unity that was so essential to the system and destroyed the "universal" meanings underlying specific parts. Susan Blow was the champion of Froebel's program at a time when newer ideas were demanding change. This forced her adamantly to defend the program in its entirety and to try to elucidate the meaning of the program for the development of young children even more clearly. She became the leader of the group of kindergartners who tried to protect Froebel's program from the encroachment of the revolutionary ideas stemming from new scientific ideas.

Support of the National Education Association

Enthusiasm for the Froebelian kindergarten system expanded as it received publicity through the meetings of the National Education Association. As early as 1872, William N. Hailmann presented Froebel's educational principles to a general session. Although Hailmann had faith that Froebel's program aided the continuity of growth, he suggested that "Ever-varying circumstances require frequent modifications of the theoretical direction; for no theory can take into consideration the manifold differences that

[41] Blow, "The Mother Play," in Barnard, *Kindergarten and Child Culture Papers*, p. 576.

[42] Susan E. Blow, *Educational Issues in the Kindergarten* (New York: D. Appleton, 1908), p. 224.

beset practice." [43] He did not propose a blind acceptance of Froebel's ideas but a careful examination of them in light of existing social circumstances in America.

The association responded by appointing a committee to investigate Hailmann's proposal. The committee consisted of Hailmann himself, William T. Harris, Adolph Douai, John Kraus, John W. Dickinson, George Baker, and John Hancock. With the committee largely made up of members widely known for their positive appraisal of Froebel's kindergarten, it is not surprising that the report presented to the general session the following year encouraged the extension of kindergarten education and urged experimentation in connection with public schools.[44] But to at least one member of the committee, John Kraus, the report was disappointing in its failure to suggest any modification of Froebel's program to cultural differences in the United States.[45] The weight of the report was given to the extension of kindergarten in precise Froebelian form. Perhaps the original program was still too new and unknown to be ready for conscious cultural modification.

For the next few years Froebel's kindergarten continued to be explained in speeches to the Elementary Department and occasionally to general sessions. During these early years the prime movers in all discussions were those steeped in the Froebelian procedures — William and Eudora Hailmann, John Kraus and Maria Kraus-Boelte, Luise Pollock, William Harris, and John Dickinson. In 1885, when a Department of Kindergarten Instruction was established, the audience narrowed, but the concerns were largely the same: to explain the application of Froebel's principles, to discuss the training of kindergarten teachers, and to proclaim the value of kindergarten experience for all children. That same year

[43] William N. Hailmann, "The Adaptation of Froebel's System of Education to American Institutions," *Addresses and Journal of Proceedings of the National Education Association,* 1872, p. 141.

[44] Report of the Committee of Seven given by John W. Dickinson, "What Froebel's System of Kindergarten Education Is, and How It Can Be Introduced Into Our Public Schools," *Addresses and Journal of Proceedings of the National Education Association,* 1873, pp. 230-241.

[45] John Kraus, "The Kindergarten (Its Use and Abuse) in America," *Addresses and Journal of Proceedings of the National Education Association,* 1877, p. 204.

a resolution supporting kindergartens and recommending their incorporation into public school systems was again accepted in a general session of the NEA. Thus the influence of the entire organization was placed behind the Froebelian program.

Froebel's Play Materials in the United States

It was not only the ideas and principles of the Froebelian program that were transmitted to America; the outward manifestations of the program, the play materials and translations of the mother-play sequence, became readily available in the United States. As early as 1871 Milton Bradley, a toy manufacturer of Springfield, Massachusetts, began the production of the gift and occupation materials. His published manual of directions contained chapters that Elizabeth Peabody considered "better than those of any other manual I have seen." [46] Publishers such as E. Steiger and Company devoted pages at the end of books about the kindergarten to advertising gift and occupation materials, illustrating their use in great detail.

The mother-play and nursery songs of Froebel were available early in both the original German and translated editions. Later the mother-play verses and mottoes, with commentaries by Susan Blow and Denton Snider, appeared in versions purporting to improve the literary quality of the rhymes and to elucidate the meaning of the plays.[47]

With this exaltation of the Froebelian materials and their ready availability, it is small wonder that in the hands of the first generation of American kindergartners the program became essentially a dry husk of metaphysical symbolism. The explicit directions attached to the gifts and occupations dominated as many teachers lost sight of the original spirit of play. The mother-plays intended for the mother to use with her very young child were marketed for use at school with older children and their original meaning was uselessly attenuated.

[46] Peabody, "Letter," in Barnard, *Kindergarten and Child Culture Papers,* p. 14.

[47] Susan E. Blow, *The Mottoes and Commentaries of Friedrich Froebel's Mother Play* (New York: D. Appleton, 1895); Denton J. Snider, *Froebel's Mother Play Songs* (Chicago: Sigma Publishing Co., 1895).

THE KINDERGARTEN AND SOCIAL REFORM

Regardless of the important factors of intelligent leadership and the availability of Froebelian material on the American scene, these alone do not adequately account for the growth of the kindergarten movement in the three decades prior to 1900. In 1870 there were less than a dozen kindergartens in the United States; in 1880 there were not less than four hundred scattered over thirty states; by 1890 associations working for the expansion of kindergarten education existed in many cities.[48]

A powerful leaven at work in society had helped to make ready for the acceptance of the kindergarten as an educational institution. Early American settlers would hardly have been prepared to adopt the kindergarten, but the attitudes of many people by the latter half of the nineteenth century had been modified by many influences that brought about a general ferment of thought—the animal spirits of a youthful democracy, the disintegration of established religion, the stirrings of a new humanitarianism, and the dissemination of a genuine idealism. The two chief phenomena that help to explain the rapid expansion of the kindergarten in the United States were the idealistic philosophy that generally prevailed in education, which transformed the concept of the nature of the child, and the burgeoning humanitarian interest, which embraced all manner of philanthropic kindergartens. Each aspect of this change in social consciousness supported the kindergarten idea.

Changing Conception of Child Nature

According to philosophical idealism, man was governed by spiritual laws; as the finite expression of the infinite spirit, his spiritual nature transcended his material aspects. The idealist thought of education as the development of the spiritual powers and mental functions that were an innate part of man's endowment. Froebel's educational program was built upon the assumption that the child was endowed with an intuitive ability to discern metaphysical truths; its goal was spiritual union with the Absolute—God. The acceptance of the kindergarten rested upon the romantic, idealistic view of the child.

[48] Vandewalker, pp. 23, 58.

This belief in the child's inherent goodness was a major reversal of the accepted attitude during the colonial period. In Puritan New England the child was viewed as innately depraved, an idea resulting from the belief in original sin. It was believed that the child needed to grow up in an atmosphere of fear and discipline, and the belief was based on a conviction that this was the way to lead him to the possibility of salvation. The child's enthusiasm for play was deplored as an inclination to evil. The key to salvation lay in exact obedience to the Bible; the God of the Puritan child was one who condemned most men to eternal damnation and saved only a few of His elect. From this grew the definition of the duties of the child: to honor, love, and fear God; to be humble, submissive, and obedient to parents and other "superiors"; to retire for secret prayer and a diligent examination of conscience every day.[49] These stern demands upon children delineate the most rigid New England beliefs; the outlooks in other geographical areas reflected a less formidable attitude. Despite the logical consequences of their views of human nature, it is likely that many "Puritan" parents lavished loving care on their children. Indeed, even when Yale was founded, early in the eighteenth century, Cotton Mather complained that Harvard students had been excessively pampered by their parents. In general, however, the impulses of children were viewed as unwholesome.

The relaxation of Puritan belief, together with the growth of a liberal Christianity emphasizing the fatherhood of God, altered these austere requirements. To be sure the change was gradual. Children were taught to live under the eye of God, but, though He punished disobedience, He was seen as a loving, protecting God. The child's duties were altered accordingly: he was to acknowledge God as the author of his being, to love his fellow creatures, to live industriously, and to be mannerly.[50] These changes were exhibited in greater freedom of dress, in a more humane approach to child training, and by a new interest in the personality of the child.

By 1855 the concept of the child had reached the point where discussions were in terms of rights rather than duties. The philosophy

[49] Monica Kiefer, *American Children through Their Books* (Philadelphia: University of Pennsylvania Press, 1948), pp. 41-43.
[50] *Ibid.,* pp. 54-55.

of idealism, the influx of ideas based on Romanticism, and the increasing association of beneficent concepts of the child with American democratic thought, changed the prevailing view of the child's inherent impulses. In the thoughts of many, the innate tendencies of the child came to be viewed as good—as reflections of God's goodness. Play was then accepted as a medium for educational experience, and benevolent nurture came to be viewed as a right of the young child. This sweeping change took place in adult minds, yet it was so significant and far-reaching that "we may yet recognize it as one of the great revolutions of history." [51]

Settlements and Free Kindergartens

The acceptance of a loving, benevolent nurture as a reasonable expectation of childhood coincided with a major social reform movement in the United States. Settlement houses developed in the 1880's and 1890's in answer to the growing concern for the poverty and squalor of urban slums. Drawn to the cities by increasing industrialization, some Americans found only a hard tenement life in answer to their dreams of wealth and better jobs. Many that increased the urban population were immigrants; coming from southern and eastern Europe in the years between 1880 and 1920, they tended to remain in the cities, congregating in the slum areas. The rapid expansion of settlements was one of the most dramatic evidences of an awakening social conscience.[52]

The kindergarten was utilized as a part of settlement work by some philanthropic individuals as a way to alleviate the distress of young children. In addition, however, it was used as a means of acquainting mothers with fundamental principles of child rearing. Above all, in starting children on the correct path in life, the kindergarten provided hope for an improved future generation.

Coming upon the educational scene soon after Horace Mann

[51] James H. S. Bossard and Eleanor Stoker Boll, *The Sociology of Child Development* (New York: Harper, 1960), p. 624.

[52] R. Freeman Butts traces American humanitarianism as stemming from the social humanitarianism of France, the transcendentalism of Germany and the romantic ideals of England. Thus the impetus was very close to that fostering a changed conception of the child. See R. Freeman Butts, *A Cultural History of Western Education* (New York: McGraw-Hill, 1955), p. 439.

had worked so effectively for a common school for all children as a means of alleviating the ills of mankind, the kindergarten became part of the vision of fostering the perfectibility of man and society through education. The stress placed upon the moral goals of the kindergarten led many educators to believe it provided the very foundations of character. Industry, neatness, reverence, self-respect, and cooperation were seen as results of the properly directed Froebelian kindergarten, and these moral benefits were linked to both individual and societal advancement. The early exponents of the kindergarten had done their work convincingly as they attributed to it the power to start each child toward effective social living.

Working under the conviction that the suitable training of children could develop adults who were free from the temptations of the lower appetites, the Women's Christian Temperance Union was instrumental in promoting kindergarten education. The kindergarten department of the WCTU developed a course in Froebelian literature for local unions to use with mothers. WCTU kindergartens were established in at least twenty large cities.[53]

The expansion of kindergartens became tied to the desire to render social services through the organization of kindergarten associations. Kindergartens were a part of many settlements from the very beginning. Nina Vandewalker wrote of the liaison, "So akin are the social settlement and the kindergarten in spirit that several head residents of settlements were originally kindergartners, and several well-known settlements began as mission kindergartens and became settlements by the natural expansion of their work." [54] In the decade between 1880 and 1890, kindergarten associations were formed in cities in all sections of the country. The extension of the kindergarten experience to destitute children and their mothers was the dominant purpose of these organizations. The words "Free Kindergarten Association" appeared in the name of many. Under the aegis of philanthropic women organized into Free Kindergarten Associations, Froebel's program was offered to mill children in Florence, Alabama, and Columbus, Georgia; to children from the stockyards and packing-

---

[53] Vandewalker, pp. 104-105.
[54] *Ibid.*, p. 107. This was true of Neighborhood House in Chicago, East Side Settlement in Detroit, Kingsby House in New Orleans.

house areas of Chicago and Indianapolis.[55] The movement spread rapidly so that in 1897 the United States Commissioner of Education listed over four hundred such associations.

The Cincinnati Free Kindergarten Association serves as an example of the work of many. The organization was formed in December, 1879, by a group of benevolent women to further "the welfare of little children in the poorer districts of the city." Aware that the laws of Ohio prevented the use of public funds for the education of children under six years of age, these women encouraged private contributions. Mrs. Alphonso Taft, the President of the Association, remarked, "If the little ones who wander neglected in our streets are to be reached by this method, private benevolence must come to the rescue." [56] And she appealed to friends of education and humanity to help "without distinction of race, sect, or nationality." [57]

By March, 1880, a free kindergarten was opened on the river front in Cincinnati with a student of Susan Blow as director. Other kindergartens in various parts of the city soon followed. William Harris so impressed the association with the need for training teachers that in the same year they organized a training school offering free courses for students who could not pay. During the first year they financed the training of four young women who agreed to give their time and services for a year in return. Both the kindergartens and the training school were maintained by the Association until 1905 when the kindergartens became a part of the public school system and the training school was affiliated with the University of Cincinnati.

In some places an altruistic individual, convinced of the effectiveness of Froebelian kindergarten methods, maintained a number of kindergartens. A notable example was Mrs. Pauline Agassiz Shaw of Boston. The daughter of Louis Agassiz, a Harvard professor who taught summer courses for teachers of natural history at Nantucket,

[55] Catherine Watkins (ed.), *History of the Kindergarten Movement in the Southeastern States* (Washington, D.C., Association for Childhood Education, 1939), pp. 5, 19; Aborn and Marble, *History . . . Mid-Western States,* pp. 19, 53.

[56] Aborn and Marble, *History . . . in the Mid-Western States,* pp. 13-14. Mrs. Alphonso Taft was the second wife of Alphonso Taft, founder of the Taft dynasty in Cincinnati, and mother of William Howard Taft.

[57] *Ibid.,* p. 14.

she shared the conviction that education could uplift the lot of humanity. After her marriage to Quincy Adams Shaw, she had at her command a large income to use for public beneficence. The two free kindergartens she supported in 1877 were increased to thirty-one by 1883 in Boston, Cambridge, and Brookline. Those within the Boston limits were incorporated into the school system in 1888.[58]

We can see that the kindergarten was carried on a wave of humanitarian interest that was deeply rooted in the belief of the ultimate perfectibility of man and society. In a directly practical vein, the kindergarten program was viewed as especially valuable as preparation for vocational training later given to many of the children attending schools in slum areas. Manipulative work with gifts and occupations was expected to form an excellent beginning for industrial instruction. This aspect of kindergarten education was stressed by Felix Adler in explaining the system of work education at the school maintained by the New York Society for Ethical Culture.

The pattern of kindergarten extension becomes clear through repetition. The first steps were private kindergartens for children whose parents could afford it and mission kindergartens for underprivileged children supported by an association of public-minded men and women. Public school support followed. Frequently, the first step was the provision of a room for the kindergarten, with the addition of equipment and teachers' salaries as the next step in the incorporation of kindergartens into the school system.

Effects Upon the Kindergarten Program

Even when teachers were working within the Froebelian ideology, which was true of the early workers for the kindergarten cause, the program did not remain completely intact. Those who saw Froebel's kindergarten procedures as an expression of unity were reluctant to omit or to replace any of the specific practices he had outlined. Nevertheless, certain aspects of his program received greater emphasis; in particular the use of gifts and occupations was exalted for fostering manual dexterity and for the symbolic meanings derived. Maintaining sequence in using the gifts became a fetish. Frequently an intellectual cramming in the study of gifts predominated, leaving

---

[58] Wheelock and Aborn, *The Kindergarten in New England*, p. 5.

little time for actually playing with them. In a speech chastising kindergarten teachers for allowing their work to become so formal and routinized, William Hailmann called this attenuation of gift-work "a certain one-sided, exclusive, and more or less pharisaical intellectualism that takes pride in wordy phrases and formulas." [59]

The exaltation of the moral value of kindergarten education took several forms. Most teachers relied on symbolism and a continual presentation of ideal behavior for character development. In some kindergartens morning prayers and the learning of moral texts were added; in others more direct methods of character training were employed. In discussing "moral suasion" in the kindergarten at the Ethical Culture School, Felix Adler wrote, "The faults of each child are studied; obstinacy is checked, selfishness is put to the blush, and, by a firm, yet mild treatment, the character is improved." [60] In general in the concept of character training, knowing was equated with doing.

As part of the process of presenting only the ideal and the beautiful to the child, poems, songs, and stories developed that were wrapped in sentimentality. The following poem illustrates this spirit of pretty cleverness:

CLOUDS

In day-time clouds can see to float
In far-off skies of blue,
But when night comes they are afraid
That they will tumble through.

And so the angels tack them up
Between the sky's blue bars,
Then when the golden nails shine bright,
We say, 'Oh see the stars.' [61]

The emphasis upon sentimental personification covered any concern that might have existed about the conceptions the child

[59] William N. Hailmann, "Schoolishness in the Kindergarten," *Journal of Proceedings and Addresses of the National Education Association,* 1890, p. 566.

[60] Felix Adler, "Free Kindergarten and Workingman's School," in Barnard, *Kindergarten and Child Culture Papers,* p. 688.

[61] Marie Ruef Hofer, "Report of Music Committee," *Third Report of the International Kindergarten Union,* 1898, p. 36.

developed from such false images. Nowhere were there more practical challenges to a strict Froebelian program than in the settlement and mission kindergartens. The crowded slums precluded inclusion of gardening and informal nature study as part of the program. Moreover, some of the physical needs of children were so demanding they could not be ignored; cleaning, feeding and clothing the youngsters became necessary preliminary activities. Felix Adler wrote, "The little children often came to us hungry. We found it difficult to give them instruction on an empty stomach." [62] Warm lunches were served daily in the Ethical Culture School, and a "Ladies Committee" distributed clothing and shoes.

The accounts of the Silver Street kindergarten in San Francisco provide clues to the problems encountered and to the varying activities demanded of the teacher. Here in 1878, a young, inexperienced girl, Kate Douglas Smith, started the first free kindergarten west of the Rockies. Young and inexperienced, she nevertheless had a kindergarten diploma in her pocket and a conviction that Froebel's educational system should be extended to all children. The two rooms rented for the kindergarten were in an ugly, crowded, sordid section of San Francisco known as Tar Flats, where "Miss Kate" became known as the teacher of the "Kids Guards"—the tenement interpretation of the unfamiliar word kindergarten.[63] The neighborhood was enthusiastic in offering its offspring, but seats were available for only forty-five out of the hundred children that might have been enrolled. Though the rooms had been planned as an inspiration to cleanliness and courtesy, the ideals were not readily imparted. "Many days were spent in learning the unpronounceable names of my flock," wrote Miss Kate, "and in keeping them from murdering one another until Froebel's justly celebrated 'law of love' could be made a working proposition." [64] The teacher hoped that the new, shiny, colored materials would inspire cleanliness in the children, but she still found direct washing a necessity.

[62] Adler, "Free Kindergarten," in Barnard, *Kindergarten and Child Culture Papers,* p. 688.
[63] Kate Douglas Wiggin, *Children's Rights* (Boston: Houghton, Mifflin Co., 1892), p. 110.
[64] Kate Douglas Wiggin, *My Garden of Memory* (Boston: Houghton, Mifflin, 1923), p. 118.

In *The Story of Patsy,* which Kate Douglas (Smith) Wiggin wrote to raise money for the Silver Street Kindergarten, she pictured the kindergarten teacher as mother, nurse, guardian, provider, and spiritual counselor.[65] The sympathetic understanding of individual problems was evident, yet, underneath was the insistence on making the children conform to her conception of "proper" standards of behavior as rapidly as possible. To Patsy's outpouring of his activities in the vernacular of his home the teacher responded, "please don't talk street words to Miss Kate," illustrating her desire to inhibit whatever did not meet her standards.[66]

Thus in philanthropic kindergartens the insistence upon the ideal became difficult to maintain. The concept of the residual nature of education—the school's undertaking what the home does not accomplish—was difficult to resist. Under the facade of mysticism and sentimentality lay a highly practical impulse to reform society and culture in keeping with the natural needs of the child.

[65] Kate Douglas Wiggin, *The Story of Patsy* (Boston: Houghton, Mifflin, 1889).
[66] *Ibid.,* p. 23.

3
EARLY EFFORTS TO REFORM
THE KINDERGARTEN PROGRAM

Against the general acceptance of Froebelian principles Anna E. Bryan raised a dissenting voice in a speech to the kindergarten department of the National Education Association in 1890. She attacked the slavish following of Froeblian procedures in existing kindergartens, suggesting that a ball might symbolize motion to a young child, but not unity. She criticized the formal, sequential use of gifts: "The child is not creatively active, only mechanically so. He has played with his spinal column, not with his heart. It therefore may be called a barren, uneducative play." [1] Three major problems of Froebelian theory, which would be topics of discussion for years, were exposed in this single protest: the symbolism, the logical sequence, and the lack of self-determined purpose in the child's play.

After graduation from the Chicago Free Kindergarten Association, Anna E. Bryan had returned to her native Louisville, Kentucky. The Chicago school was similar to many other "free" associations that were established in the 1880's to extend kindergarten education to children in the poorer districts and to prepare teachers for the task. There is no evidence that it had distinguishing features or distinguished personnel, and the training Miss Bryan received here was later considered poor even for that time. Nevertheless, in September of 1887, an issue of the *Louisville Courier-Journal* announced, "A Free Kindergarten—Miss Bryan Returns to Her Kentucky Home to Instruct Poor Children; She Will Also Train Young Ladies for

---

[1] Anna E. Bryan, "The Letter Killeth," *Journal of Proceedings and Addresses of the National Education Association,* 1890, p. 575.

Teaching Methods of the Celebrated System." [2] Far from consider-
ing "the Celebrated System" a final and finished product, however,
she encouraged experimentation with method and materials as a
part of her first training class. Patty Smith Hill, a student of great
promise, attended this initial class.

Miss Bryan's initiative in searching for new procedures apparently stemmed from her own native interests and concerns for children rather than from her formal education. From the beginning she
urged students in her training classes to view the kindergarten as a
laboratory for vitalizing teaching practices. She seemed to recognize
independently the significance of purposeful activity, and it was with
her support that Patty Hill began to give the children little problems
that were designed to promote practical solutions; for example, they
were given paper dolls and asked to make a bed to fit them using the
blocks of the fourth gift.[3]

The break from traditional procedure drew attention. The
crude attempts at change won the approval of William Hailmann and
also of Colonel Francis W. Parker of Chicago, who promoted Miss
Bryan's speech to the National Education Association, which drew
further attention to the Louisville kindergartens. As it became known
that something unusual was happening there, educators from all over
the country came to visit. Three thousand visitors were registered in
the guest book of the demonstration school during a single year,[4]
which may indicate a general readiness for change.

Quietly, others who were influential in the training of kindergarten teachers began to make inroads into traditional kindergarten
practices. Eudora Hailmann, who had studied kindergarten procedures in Switzerland and Germany, gradually divorced herself from
the more rigid Froebelian practices. In her work in Detroit, Michi-
gan, and in La Porte, Indiana, she introduced beads designed after
the forms of the second gift, a sand table, a doll-house and some

---

[2] Caroline D. Aborn, Sarah A. Marble, and Lucy Wheelock, (eds.)
*History of the Kindergarten Movement in the Mid-Western States and in
New York* (Washington, D.C.: Association for Childhood Education, 1938),
p. 55.

[3] Ilse Forest, *Preschool Education* (New York: Macmillan, 1927),
p. 173.

[4] Aborn, Marble, and Wheelock, *History . . . Mid-Western States*, p.
57.

enlarged forms of building gifts. The new materials were used to promote a free social interaction among the children, which she believed was increasingly limited in many formalized kindergarten programs.[5]

Alice Putnam had always maintained an independent position on the kindergarten curriculum, though she had studied with both Maria Kraus-Boelte and Susan Blow. As leader of the Chicago Froebel Kindergarten Association she was influenced by the ideas of Colonel Parker and Jane Addams. When Parker was appointed head of the Cook County Normal School, he invited the Froebel Kindergarten Association to make the Normal School its headquarters and asked Mrs. Putnam to give instructions in theory. Later, the training school was transferred to Jane Addams' Hull House so students might study directly the problems of slum children. In these training classes Alice Putnam attempted to open up the use of new areas of science and art with young children. She warned against extreme reliance upon formal materials to carry out a program, telling her students, "I could have a kindergarten in a meadow with a group of children and only the flowers, grasses, earth and my two hands." [6]

THE IMPACT OF SCIENTIFIC THINKING

These individual efforts to revise the kindergarten program gained momentum as they were influenced by the momentous changes in educational thought that were bringing about a ferment in education in general. The two major links between the kindergarten leaders and the increasing influence of scientific thinking in education were G. Stanley Hall and John Dewey; later the psychology of Edward Thorndike influenced the curriculum. Hall and Dewey, however, repeatedly focused attention upon reforms that they felt were needed in the kindergarten, and this immediately drew the attention of the progressive kindergartners.

As the avant-garde kindergartners in search of guidelines for

[5] Barbara Greenwood, "William Nicholas Hailmann," in the Committee of Nineteen, International Kindergarten Union (eds.), *Pioneers of the Kindergarten in America* (New York: The Century Co., 1924), pp. 256-257.

[6] Bertha Payne Newell, "Alice H. Putnam," in *Pioneers of the Kindergarten*, p. 218.

newer practices changed their allegiance, they aligned themselves with an educational philosophy and psychology that were the antithesis of those that undergirded Froebelian principles. Gone was the concept of a fixed and knowable truth. Eminently significant was the reversal in the means for obtaining knowledge from the intuitive discernment of the innermost logic of things to a faith in scientific observation. Perry Miller highlighted the import of the new methodology when he wrote, "Within a few years—or even months—after *The Origin of Species* shattered Victorian complacency, acute minds began to see that the least of its revolutionary meanings was its substantial denial of fixed species, or even its implied discrediting of Christian morality; what struck them was its unprecedented method of investigation." [7]

G. Stanley Hall

The progressive kindergartners were led into the new methodology by Hall, who provided them with techniques of data collection in the form of questionnaires, anecdotal records, and the analysis of products. Through the nationwide surveys that he carried out with some of his students he called attention to previously unstudied characteristics of children in relation to fear, anger, crying, interests, or types of play. The information about children's concepts of nature, numbers, and religion that Hall used in writing *The Contents of Children's Minds* [8] was collected with the assistance of the teachers in the Boston kindergartens supported by Mrs. Pauline Agassiz Shaw. Hall considered this data extremely significant evidence of "the width and depth of the chasm which yawned between the infantile and the adult mind." [9]

After Hall became president of Clark University in 1889, he made it the center for child study, a part of psychology little explored before that date. Anna Bryan, Alice Putnam, Patty Smith Hill, and Jenny B. Merrill attended the summer conferences at Clark in which

[7] Perry Miller (ed.), *American Thought, Civil War to World War 1* (New York: Rinehart and Co., 1954), p. xv.

[8] G. Stanley Hall, *The Contents of Children's Minds* (Boston: Ginn and Co., 1907).

[9] G. Stanley Hall, *Life and Confessions of a Psychologist* (New York: D. Appleton, 1924), p. 381.

child development problems were probed. Their attention was directed to what Hall considered a gross indifference to health problems in the kindergarten; he recommended that more attention be given to the young child's body and less to his soul.[10] Froebel's theory of inner connection and his scheme of analysis from solid to point were fantastic and superficial to Hall; if they had any meaning, he believed, it existed solely for the teacher and not for the child. Moreover, he felt that the devotion to gifts and occupations, which stressed sedentary activities and the use of the late-developed accessory muscles, resulted in fatigue and nervousness on the part of the child. Study of the child showed that development proceeded from fundamental to accessory muscles; the young child needing large, bold movements. Free play with large materials would support this needed development, according to Hall.

Hall's promotion of free play in early childhood was part of his central thesis that ontogeny, or individual development, recapitulates phylogeny, the development of the race. In his concept of developmental stages he accepted an evolutionary development both biologically and behaviorally; each stage needed to be lived through completely for healthy development. The child from four to eight, according to Hall, was in a stage of myth-making and poetic fancy similar to that of a savage. He believed the child needed freedom and rich cultural materials to promote normal growth and to prepare adequately for the next stage. In the young child reason did not abound, and the emotional life was more fundamental than the intellectual. True intellect, Hall argued, was a rather late development for both the individual and the race.

Hall felt that the characteristics of each stage of development as defined by child study were the ideal base for determining the curriculum. He was convinced that any real advance in educational theory and practice would stem from an "ever clearer realization that in the nature of childhood itself and its different stages of development must be found the norm for all the method and matter of teaching." [11]

[10] G. Stanley Hall, "The Ideal School as Based on Child Study," *Journal of Proceedings and Addresses of the National Education Association,* 1901, p. 476.

[11] Hall, *Life and Confessions,* p. 500.

It was only natural that the progressive kindergartners should welcome the child study movement because their own initial attempts to change kindergarten practice had stemmed from empirical observation of the child. Information became available to more teachers as specialists began to appear at other universities and child study associations sprang up in many states.[12] Earl Barnes of Stanford University, William L. Bryan of Indiana University, and M. V. O'Shea of the State Normal School at Mankato, Minnesota, were leaders in the department of child study that was added to the expanding National Education Association, and they supported the progressive kindergartens in their search for new classroom procedures.

It was not surprising that the conservative kindergarten group should regard the new child study movement with suspicion. The study of the child had always been important to them, but the new methodology was anathema; they held adamantly to an introspective psychology. Harris, while recognizing that "physiological psychology" could help in understanding some physical phenomena, insisted upon "the paramount importance of insight into what we shall call pure psychology." [13] Pure psychology, in the opinion of Harris, had to rely on introspection, for mental development could "never be perceived as external phenomena, but only in one's self, and inferred to exist in others." [14] Susan Blow's answer to the new observational techniques was that one man with the eyes of genius could see farther than any multiplication of observers.[15]

This change in methodology was, of course, one of the major issues underlying the controversies between the two factions. In child study the progressives found much to support criticisms of current practice. Although exceedingly helpful in diagnosing the effects of material and methods upon the development of the child, it was less effective in providing clear directives for a changed curriculum. Hall's stipulation that experiences for children should be selected and

[12] For the work of some state associations see Department of Child Study, *Journal of Proceedings and Addresses of the National Education Association*, 1894, pp. 1000-1003; or 1895, pp. 893-906.

[13] William T. Harris, "Psychological Inquiry," *Journal of Proceedings and Addresses of the National Education Association*, 1886, p. 95.

[14] *Ibid.*

[15] Susan Blow, "Discussion," *Proceedings of the Twelfth Annual Meeting of the International Kindergarten Union*, 1905, p. 17.

organized on the basis of their needs and characteristics was easier to state than to put into direct practice.

Eagerly searching for help in planning and carrying out new kindergarten methods, the progressive group turned to John Dewey for aid. Some kindergartners, notably Patty Smith Hill and Alice Temple, developed an affinity for Dewey's social conception of education.

John Dewey

In the laboratory school that Dewey established at the University of Chicago in 1896 to test his educational theories, the four- and five-year-old group was called the sub-primary. Because of his disagreements with Froebelian philosophy, Dewey was unwilling to admit the kindergarten, by name, into his experimental school.

A close working relationship developed, however, between the Dewey sub-primary and the demonstration kindergarten at Armour Institute in Chicago, which was supported by the Chicago Free Kindergarten Association. When Anna Bryan left Louisville and returned to Chicago to direct this kindergarten and the training classes at Armour Institute, some of her students served as assistants in the Dewey sub-primary. In the *Elementary School Record* in 1900, Dewey acknowledged his indebtedness to Anna Bryan for her suggestions for new kindergarten practice.

Dewey agreed with Froebel that education should direct the play experiences of the young child toward effective social living, but Dewey's secular, scientific, pragmatic outlook was at variance with the idealistic, absolutist principles of Froebel. Froebel viewed truth as encompassed in unity and intuitively discernable; for Dewey, on the other hand, truth could only be determined in the light of consequences as ideas were tested.

In Dewey's pragmatic philosophy, ideas were not fixed, but changed with varying circumstances and as new bases for thinking developed. In place of Froebel's logical sequence of ideas symbolically represented from solid to point, Dewey relied upon a psychological continuity of growth. He believed activities for the young child must promote psychological continuity; unless this was true, play resulted "in mere amusement and not in educative growth." Psychological continuity could be judged by the young child's being "carried on to a higher plane of perception and judgment . . . equipped with more efficient habits," and developing increasing "powers of action." [16]

Dewey's functionalism penetrated the formalism of Froebel. The fallacy in gift work, Dewey said, was that it assumed that objects must be known before they could be used. Reversing this method, he held that objects became known as they were used to achieve ends. For these ends to be significant to the child they must be close to some interest and purpose of his own and directly connected with his everyday life. Instead of the symbolic material that would only "teach insincerity, and instill sentimentalism, and foster sensationalism," [17] Dewey recommended material that was as straightforward as opportunity would permit. He would not have children sweep a make-believe room with a make-believe broom, but would involve them in the actual duties of taking care of their classroom. Dewey felt "constructive" work was particularly suited to the young child: it called for acuteness of observation; it demanded clear-cut imagery of the ends to be accomplished; it required ingenuity in planning; it made necessary a personal responsibility in execution; it resulted in a tangible form which enabled the child to judge his own work. Thus did Dewey outline a process whereby the young child could learn to think by managing experience and developing the ability to cope with new situations.

There was no place here for the child's imitation of teacher-initiated activities, which Dewey criticized sharply. He recognized the young child as highly imitative and open to suggestion, but maintained that "Imitation and suggestion come in naturally and inevitably, but only as instruments to help him carry out his own wishes and ideas." [18] The safeguard for this would be to have no activity *originated* by imitation but to have it start with the child. Besides being a defense against mechanical imitation, this elevation of the child's purpose was related to problem-solving. The child's own purpose provided him with the tools for planning and evaluating his work and with the impetus for carrying it out.

[16] John Dewey, "Froebel's Educational Principles," *The Elementary School Record*, I (June, 1900), 149.

[17] *Ibid.*, p. 147.

[18] *Ibid.*, p. 151.

Constructive work, drawing, music, nature study, field excursions, and the school garden all were important in the school curriculum as varying means to one end—"the ascent of intelligence." [19] They provided interest; they provoked intelligent response; they added to the fund of information.

In order to bring activities close to the child's out-of-school life and to afford continuity with his previous experience, Dewey offered "the home" as a subject for study in the sub-primary. As children relived home situations under the conditions of enlarged social interaction that would increase understanding, they were beginning the process of continuous reorganization and reconstruction of experience, which defined learning in Dewey's terms. Dewey expected the central focus upon the home to progress naturally into a series of wider studies including the social occupations upon which the home was dependent.[20]

As a proposed center of interest the home made feasible many activities that would develop a sub-primary group as a miniature community. This would be a major means of providing "the development of social power and insight" basic to Dewey's educational scheme. The child's very first educational experience could be linked to the school's role in social reform:

When the school introduces and trains each child of society into membership within such a little community, saturating him with the spirit of service, and providing him with the instruments of effecive self-direction; we shall have the deepest and best guarantee of a larger society which is worthy, lovely, and harmonious.[21]

The moral goal of education, which for Froebel came through symbolic understanding, Dewey promoted through social interaction. He proposed with great clarity that "the best and deepest moral training is precisely that which one gets through having to enter into proper relations wtih others in a unity of work and thought." [22]

[19] John Dewey, "The Situation as Regards the Course of Study," *Journal of Proceedings and Addresses of the National Education Association,* 1901, p. 347.

[20] Dewey, "Froebel's Principles," *The Elementary School Record,* I, 151.

[21] John Dewey, *The School and Society* (Chicago: University of Chicago Press, 1899), pp. 27-28.

[22] John Dewey, "My Pedagogic Creed," *The School Journal,* LIV (January 16, 1897), 78.

With Hall exhalting the emotional side of development and Dewey putting stress upon social interaction, it is small wonder that kindergartners began to interpret their goals largely in terms of the social and emotional adjustment of the young child.

Edward L. Thorndike

Rather early in the controversy over the kindergarten curriculum, Edward L. Thorndike pointed out the implications of his psychological laws for kindergarten work. Thorndike's thesis was clear: the function of the teacher was to stimulate the formation of acceptable habits and to inhibit inappropriate ones. "The truth is," he told kindergartners, "that a human life is a bundle of habits; that what we mean by knowledge is habits of sequence among ideas; that what we mean by capacity is the possibility of forming a certain set of habits." [23]

In Thorndike's opinion education could advance most rapidly if the teacher would "adopt the custom of working directly for concrete habits and measuring his success by their attainment." [24] The way to establish habits was to build connections between impressions and responses to them. The famous laws of learning were explained by Thorndike in relation to the kindergarten situation. The law of readiness meant that the best time to form a habit was when the tendency was ripening. The kindergarten child was ready to examine and to manipulate concrete objects, to engage in individual imaginative play, and to observe simple social forms. In connection with the law of exercise, Thorndike pointed out that the immature minds of five-year-olds did not hold events in memory for very long, and that this had implications for developing associations. Emphatically he stressed the law of effect pointing out that not all native tendencies of this age should be strengthened by satisfying effects. Although the child's native intellectual curiosity should be fostered, the instincts for display and adornment should be weakened by dissatisfying results.

Thorndike was, of course, relating the laws of stimulus–re-

---

[23] Edward L. Thorndike, "Notes on Psychology for Kindergartners," *Teachers College Record,* IV (November, 1903), 54.
[24] *Ibid.*

sponse learning to the kindergarten program and propounding the behaviorist conception of the human organism as a response mechanism subservient to the control of conditioned stimuli. In defining learning in this manner Thorndike was building up a new theory of the mind which eliminated it as a separate entity but rather interpreted it as "the total response of the organism to its environment." [25]

The response to Thorndike's suggestions for the kindergarten situation was delayed longer than the reaction to the recommendations of Hall or Dewey. The assumptions upon which his psychological theory rested were highly related to laboratory methods and evolutionary doctrine. The laws of learning were tested in the laboratory with animals as subjects; their application to human psychology assumed the continuous evolution of species. No theory could have been more removed from Froebelian principles. Its revolutionary nature impeded its acceptance.

EXPERIMENTAL PROGRAMS

These new, divergent streams of philosophical and psychological thought, exemplified in empirical child study and pragmatic theory, led to a period of confusion and readjustment in curriculum practices. It led also to schism in the ranks of kindergartners and to the prolonged controversy in which problems of classroom practice were more often debated than fundamental issues. However, these issues, as reflected in the curriculum disputes during meetings of the International Kindergarten Union, were the crux of the vigorous pedagogical battle that lasted for more than two decades. A review of some of the programs that took form around the turn of the century as initial responses to revolutionary proposals, involves many curriculum issues that became a matter of concern as the two factions debated possible solutions. In some instances there was a gradual modification of methods and materials; in others the set curriculum was abandoned and a new sense of freedom ensued. Kindergartners took the findings of child study and intended to apply them immediately, but the transition from theory to practice was deterred by

[25] Lawrence A. Cremin, *The Transformation of the School* (New York: Alfred A. Knopf, 1961), pp. 111-112.

practical problems. In the Froebelian program, content had been
built around the symbolic meanings of gifts and occupations, which
acted as organizing centers for the program; if this content were to
be abandoned, some tangible substitute for both content and
organizing centers had to be developed. Teachers lacked appropriate
materials for the child's physiological development as revealed
through child study. At first, despite good intentions, the old Froebelian materials were simply enlarged and used in new ways.

Taking seriously Hall's belief that the young child was living
through a stage of development analogous to a primitive cultural
level, some teachers investigated the culture-epoch theory as a base
for the selection of activities in the kindergarten. The life-styles of
Indians, Eskimos, and cave dwellers were explored, and young children were encouraged to act out the life of Hiawatha or Robinson
Crusoe. Wigwams, canoes, bows and arrows, and igloos were constructed to be used in sand-table models of historic events.[26] It was
soon discovered that children's interest in these activities was superficial and brief; the subject matter was too remote from daily
experiences to be vital.

A Correlated Program

As the search went on for other materials around which to
organize the kindergarten program, the ideas of Johann Herbart were
explored. Vandewalker lists the Herbartian movement as one of the
three major influences of the decade between 1890-1900.[27] It was
not Herbart's five formal steps for organizing a lesson that appealed
to the kindergarten experimenters, but his notion that certain subjects should form the core of the curriculum around which other
aspects could be concentrated. Herbart suggested history or literature as particularly suited to this purpose; the kindergartners chose
literature in order to bring unity to their program — a unity quite

[26] Lucy Wheelock, "The Changing and the Permanent Elements in the
Kindergarten," *Proceedings of the Seventeenth Annual Meeting of the International Kindergarten Union,* 1910, p. 213.

[27] Nina C. Vandewalker, "The History of the Kindergarten Influence
in Elementary Education," *The Kindergarten and Its Relation to Elementary
Education,* Sixth Yearbook of the National Society for the Study of Education, Part II (Bloomington, Illinois: Public School Publishing Co., 1907),
p. 127.

different from that of the Froebelian system. Stories were used to develop centers around which discussion, gift and occupation work, and games were correlated. This interpretation of Herbartian ideas gained no real favor from either wing of the curricular disputes. Both Susan Blow and G. Stanley Hall felt there was little to be gained from what they called the "ultra-analytic treatment of stories" that reduced them to a mere skeleton.[28] When stories did not suffice, some teachers substituted a great man, an event, an animal, or an object as the central focus of the kindergarten program. Susan Blow dubbed this program that subordinated gifts, occupations, and games to the purpose of illustrating a chosen theme, the "concentric program."

This type of correlation is illustrated by an excerpt from a four-day sequence built around the life of Abraham Lincoln. It was planned by a kindergarten teacher in celebration of Lincoln's birthday and received a prize of fifty dollars given by the Patria Club of New York for the best kindergarten program designed to train children in patriotism.

THIRD DAY

Morning Talk—Lincoln as captain, storekeeper, postmaster, surveyor. Walked one hundred miles in his homespun clothes to help make the laws in the Legislature. Kindness and honesty as a lawyer. Lincoln and the pig. Lincoln's belief concerning slavery.

Gift—Sticks; measuring and counting lesson. Connect with Lincoln's surveying experiences, giving names of different forms and making as graphic as possible.

Occupation—Fold beauty forms in red, white, and blue paper, by dictation, to make a frame for Lincoln's picture.[29]

It can be readily seen that little had been done but to replace the Froebelian sense of unity with a concept of Herbartian correlation. Hall responded that while kindergartners evidenced originality in devising such programs, much of the work was ill-adapted to children.

---

[28] G. Stanley Hall, *Educational Problems,* I (New York: D. Appleton, 1911) 27; Susan Blow, *Educational Issues in the Kindergarten* (New York: D. Appleton, 1908), pp. 81-85.

[29] Blow, *Educational Issues,* pp. 3-4.

The idea of correlation evidently so fascinated some teachers that they carried it out in minute detail. In showing the extremes to which the notion had been carried, Geraldine O'Grady described a kindergarten in a large city school where she counted nineteen exercises on chickens in a week. "Can we suppose that those children had no thoughts but of chickens and needed no room for others?" she queried.[30]

The Free Play Program

Hall's recommendation that kindergarten children should have freedom of movement stimulated more radical departures in the program. At Santa Barbara, California, a free play period became a significant part of the three-hour kindergarten day. Under the leadership of Superintendent of Schools Frederic Burk, supervisors and kindergarten teachers spent the school year of 1898-1899 probing the implications of child study for the kindergarten curriculum. Since Burk had spent some time at Clark University as a student of Hall, he could help his teachers become familiar with child-study literature as the first part of the study. The second step included experimentation with materials and procedures, during which they tested children's spontaneous reactions to Froebelian materials and found many of them—sticks, rings, slats, lentils—practically "a dead-weight."

The kindergarten was opened up to new "incentives" to free play—seesaws, swings, dolls, toy dishes, beanbags, sandpiles, garden tools. The use of materials was carefully recorded and children's play was found to be characterized by: (1) activity—persistent and varied, (2) spontaneous representation of familiar objects, (3) individual activity rather than social, and (4) close concentration on activities of interest to them.[31]

The Santa Barbara experimenters believed the children's favorable responses to the free play situation justified its inclusion in their program. By January they were ready to adopt the following schedule:

[30] Geraldine O'Grady, "Guidance of Attention: The Child's Part and the Teacher's," *Proceedings of the Eighteenth Annual Meeting of the International Kindergarten Union*, 1911, p. 61.

[31] Frederic Burk and Caroline Frear Burk, *A Study of the Kindergarten Problem* (San Francisco: The Whitaker and Roy Co., 1889), p. 95.

I. Prayer, Singing, Movement Songs, Stories, Aesop's Fables, Anderson or Grimm.
II. Blackboard Illustration of Story. Children tell story.
III. Recess. Free Play. Balls, Incentive for Individual Plays— dolls, reins, toys, bubbles, the sandpile, etc.
IV. Number—Counting or groups with objects. Beads or other suitable kindergarten material.
V. Use of objects, pictures and picture books as language incentives.
VI. Recess—Free play with incentives.
VII. Free use of clay, sand table, paper cutting or other kindergarten material without dictation.[32]

For the teachers under Burk's supervision free play became the rational solution to Froebel's plea for self-activity, but it was such a radical departure from current kindergarten programs that the periods were labeled "recess." Directed work gave way to free choice and manipulation; traditional games were replaced by dramatic play and free physical action.

Susan Blow was right when she stated that the "concentric program" conceived of the child as "preponderantly a learning being"; the basis for selecting and organizing experiences was the content to be learned. Perhaps she was right too, when she claimed that the free play program conceived of the child as "a sentient being who reacts upon stimuli from his environment," [33] for the greatest innovations were new incentives to stimulate play. The new basis for selecting materials was an attempt to use a broader concept of the child and his needs.

The Industrial Program

Still one other type of program was initiated around the turn of the century that looked to society and social development for determining curriculum experiences. The central theme of the so-called industrial program was a belief in the dignity of work and service. The emphasis might be on a neighborhood worker—the baker, carpenter, fireman, or street-cleaner. When the organizing center was the street-cleaner, gift blocks were used to make pavements and

[32] *Ibid.*, p. 20.
[33] Blow, *Educational Issues in the Kindergarten*, p. 158.

houses; cardboard, spools and buttons were used to make wagons, shovels, and brooms. Reporting on these experiences in which an understanding of social service predominated, Lucy Wheelock wrote, "This program is an outgrowth of the idea of social education which is leavening the school curriculum, but it seems to follow only one line of social contact namely,—with the industrial world." [34] Other kindergarten programs, categorized as "industrial," centered around home "industries,"—preparing potatoes, making starch, washing and ironing doll clothes.

Dewey's "Industrial Program"

Of the urge to "curricularize cooking, washing, ironing" Hall wrote, "John Dewey carries the industrial experience still further." [35] Indeed, the sub-primary program in the Dewey school did focus on the domestic occupations and the necessary supporting services. Here, there was no mere superficial change, such as using gifts and occupations for different purposes, but a radically reorganized program based upon Dewey's social theory of education. The term occupation no longer stood for constructive handwork but for the realistic tasks of the home and community. In the sub-primary as well as in the rest of the school, efforts were made to build a miniature community in which children would prepare for social life by engaging in social life. The aim was not merely to instruct the child about occupational activities nor even to adjust the individual to social institutions, but to deepen and broaden the range of social contact and experience so the child would be prepared to make future social relations worthy and fruitful.

Morning lunch was served daily. The simple menu might consist of one tablespoon of prepared cereal with cream and sugar, a cracker and a glass of milk. The children were entirely in charge of serving, arranging the tables, washing and putting away dishes. Number and language development were naturally involved in the daily activities. Children planned together, counted spoons, measured food.

The five-year-old children equipped a playhouse with furniture

---

[34] Wheelock, "Changing and Permanent Elements," *Seventeenth Annual Meeting of the IKU*, p. 213.
[35] Hall, *Educational Problems*, I, p. 30.

made of wood and rugs woven of candle wicking on large frames, which they made themselves. Their teacher reported that, "the children were thrown largely upon their own resources for planning and making the objects they needed and wanted." [36] In the handwork period the children used a wide variety of materials—wood, leather. yarn, clay, sand—to carry out their self-initiated ideas.

The teacher functioned as guide and helper who supported each child's endeavor through making suggestions instead of dictating or providing a model to be copied. A compromise between dictation and abdication to the child's whims was deemed possible and was expressed in the report of the Dewey School that nothing seemed "more absurd than to suppose that there was no middle term between leaving a child to his own unguided fancies . . . and controlling his activities by a formal succession of dictated directions." [37]

Constructive work with blocks and raw materials was featured in the program whenever it seemed best fitted to secure "initiation in the child's own impulse and termination on a higher plane." [38] It was also considered suitable for fostering the child's own conceptual images, however crude these might be. As the child set about making something to fulfill his own purpose, he could judge its utility by its compliance with his own specifications. A copy or model was excusable only as it could assist the child in imaging more definitely what he really wanted to produce. Dewey's belief in the importance of play was bound to his idea of producing conceptual images in concrete form. "Play is not to be identified with anything the child externally does. . . . It is the free play, the interplay, of all the child's powers, thoughts, and physical movements, in embodying, in a satisfying form, his own images and interests." [39]

It took courage for the teachers to discard the old materials and to trust to the child's own selective and productive powers. Besides the support of Dewey in devising new learning possibilities the

[36] Alice Temple, "The Kindergarten in America—Modern Period," *Childhood Education,* XIII (April, 1937), 359.

[37] Katherine Camp Mayhew and Anna Camp Edwards, *The Dewey School* (New York: D. Appleton Century, 1936), p. 62.

[38] Dewey, "Froebel's Principles," *The Elementary School Record,* I, 149.

[39] *Ibid.,* p. 144.

teachers had the assistance of Anna Bryan as she continued to direct
the Chicago Free Kindergarten Association at Armour Institute.

By 1900 the daily program in the sub-primary had developed
as follows:

9:00 – 9:30	Handwork
9:30 – 10:00	Songs and Stories
10:00 – 10:30	Handwork
10:30 – 10:40	Games, such as Follow-the-Leader, while room is being aired and personal wants cared for
10:40 – 11:15	Luncheon
11:15 – 11:45	Games and Rhythms [40]

The schedule was viewed as a flexible framework of the daily activities. Outdoor play, excursions, and gardening were commonly a part of the sub-primary day. During the large blocks of time there was ample opportunity for children to develop and carry out their own purposes, to plan and organize experiences cooperatively, and to have a variety of social contacts. A visitor to the school gives us a picture of children working independently, spontaneously, and with considerable individuality.[41]

All of these early experimental programs departed from Froebelian traditions. Some involved changes at superficial levels, others were reflections of completely divergent educational theories. The curriculum as it was developed at the Dewey School was the most completely developed, with obvious relations between theory and practice. The free play programs and the Dewey sub-primary were to have the greatest impact upon succeeding programs.

THE FROEBELIAN KINDERGARTEN AND THE
DEWEY SUB-PRIMARY CONTRASTED AND COMPARED

The contrasts between the Froebelian kindergarten and the Deweyan sub-primary curriculum highlight the underlying ideological differences and their implications for practice. The one had an

[40] Georgia P. Scates, "The Sub-Primary (Kindergarten) Department," *The Elementary School Record,* I (June, 1900), 141.

[41] Geneva Mary Clippinger, "A Visit to the Sub-Primary Class of Dr. Dewey's School," *Kindergarten Review,* XI (March, 1901), 424-426.

idealistic, introspective base; the other was pragmatic and scientific in its point of view. In Froebel's idealistic opinion the young child held within him the "seeds" of understanding, and it was the task of education to unfold symbolic premonitions and spiritual ideals. In Dewey's pragmatic view, the young child had only the potential for growth, which was shaped by interaction with environmental forces. It was the task of education to channel the resultant action along a socially acceptable course.

For both the ultimate aim of education was character building, but the educational process through which this was accomplished led to dissimilar learning activities and quite opposite roles for the teacher. In the Froebelian kindergarten character was expected to be achieved through play with symbolic materials that led to an understanding of universal, fixed truths. The teacher was the precise director of these learning experiences in a program outlined in such detail that the teacher's initiative was not great. In Dewey's sub-primary individual development was promoted through play that was closely related to daily experiences and elicted problem-solving on the part of the child. The teacher's role was that of a guide who promoted social skills through providing the opportunity to practice them. As guide, the teacher could discard authoritarianism and embrace a democratic procedure in working with children. Growth was facilitated as children had a part in planning, organizing, and evaluating their own experiences. The demand for teacher initiative and responsibility was extremely great.

The Froebelian program relied upon a sequence of logically designed symbolic materials. The psychological continuity of growth became the watchword in the Deweyan sense of individual development. Experiences were sought that had their roots in children's current concerns, but would also lead them to higher planes of thought and action.

Both educational leaders started with the young child's interest in activity and play. Froebel expected to promote creative self-activity through a process of imitative production; through early, disciplined experiences the creative power within the child would be released. Dewey's concept of productive activity embraced the child's immediate creative expression of his own ideas.

With both idealism and pragmatism, in the forms of the rigid Froebelian kindergarten program and the Dewey sub-primary curriculum coexisting on the educational scene, it is no wonder the meetings of the International Kindergarten Union were the occasions for emotionally tinged debates.

4
CONFLICTING THEORIES: FROEBELIAN PRINCIPLES, SCIENTIFIC PROGRAMS, AND THE MONTESSORI METHOD

The Kindergarten world was shaken by disputes stemming from the conflicting theories. As the progressives became increasingly convinced that curriculum changes were necessary and inevitable, the conservatives argued more adamantly that Froebel's program must remain intact. The experimental programs inaugurated at the turn of the century were regarded by the conservatives as a genuine danger to the values inherent in "pure" Froebelian methods. Bitter controversy dominated the conferences of the International Kindergarten Union. In their own autonomous organization, kindergarten leaders could, and did, test ideas and interpret practice during this period of great debate.

THE INTERNATIONAL KINDERGARTEN UNION

The idea of a separate organization for kindergartners had not started with the formation of the International Kindergarten Union. As early as 1878 an American Froebel Union was established by Elizabeth Peabody. When it was reorganized in 1882 into the Froebel Institute of North America, Miss Peabody retained the honorary presidency, but William Hailmann became the active leader of the group.

Of this reorganization, which took place in Detroit, Hailmann wrote, "The transfer of the interests of the American Froebel Union had become desirable because the Middle West had practically become the center of the kindergarten movement at this time." [1] The first task the new Froebel Institute undertook was to nationalize the kindergarten movement by organizing a Kindergarten Department of the National Education Association. The Kindergarten Department of the NEA was formed during the second meeting of the Froebel Institute in Madison, Wisconsin, in 1884. The National Education Association was holding its annual convention there at the same time. Before the sessions ended, members of the Froebel Institute established the new Kindergarten Department with Dr. Hailmann chosen as the first president. In 1885 when the National Education Association met at Saratoga Springs, the Froebel Institute was formally merged with the new Kindergarten Deparment.[2] Only a few years lapsed, however, before another independent kindergarten organization was instigated. Again this took place during the meeting of the National Education Association and again at Saratoga Springs. In 1892 Sarah Stewart of Philadelphia proposed the formation of a new union to bring into "active cooperation all kindergarten interests." [3] The crowded agenda of the NEA meetings seemed to give kindergartners too brief a time to gather and disseminate knowledge of kindergarten growth and change.

To their long-range goal of elevating the kindergarten to a prominent place in the educative process, the members of the new Union added an immediate purpose, to present a kindergarten exhibit at the Columbian Exposition in Chicago in 1893. The large expositions that were held in different sections of the country from the 1880's through the early 1900's were used regularly to acquaint the general public with the merits of kindergarten education. Impressive rooms for model kindergartens were provided in the Children's Palace at the Chicago World's Fair where observers could watch a kindergarten in operation. The kindergartners were also given the

---

[1] Caroline T. Haven, "International Kindergarten Union: Its Origin— Why It Was Organized," *Proceedings of the Fifteenth Annual Meeting of the International Kindergarten Union*, 1908, p. 116. Letter from Dr. Hailmann quoted by Miss Haven.

[2] *Ibid.*, p. 117. For a record of this first meeting see the *Journal of Proceedings and Addresses of the National Education Association*, 1885, pp. 349-368.

[3] Sarah Stewart, "Aims," *First Report of the International Kindergarten Union*, 1892, pp. 6-7.

responsibility of decorating the interior of the building, while a kindergarten literature committee distributed information calling attention to their work for young children.

Nothing very dramatic happened within the new Union until after 1895, when the meetings of the regular kindergarten department of the National Education Association were so "full and interesting" that the International Kindergarten Union "was in danger of losing its existence." In the meeting of 1896 strong organizational leadership emerged, and the 1897 convention in St. Louis became "the first really large meeting of the Union." [4] Programs began to include problems of everyday practice, which drew the interest of large numbers of kindergartners.

When the curricular problems that were at issue became the core of conference meetings, the membership mushroomed. From the small organizational meeting in 1892 at Saratoga Springs, it increased to an association of sixty-five branches and 6,225 members by 1900. When the silver anniversary of the organization was celebrated in 1918, it was considered the third largest educational body in the world with 132 branches and 18,000 members.

The free kindergarten associations already active joined as branches of the IKU; nine became affiliated in 1892.[5] This branch structure was highly suited to the dissemination of ideas, for two arenas for debate were thus supplied: national meetings of the IKU and local branch meetings.

The national meetings drew individual and branch members from all sections of the country as the concern for the kindergarten curriculum accelerated. In 1900 the largest share of participants were from the east and the mid-west though there were some from the far west and Canada. Ten years later even a partial list of delegates revealed wide representation from all parts of the country. Travel was facilitated by a fare adjustment made by leading railroads. In the usual arrangement the IKU member could make the return trip for one-third the regular fare providing the return was over the same

[4] Annie E. Laws, "Its Past—What It Has Accomplished" (IKU), *Proceedings of the Fifteenth Annual Meeting of the International Kindergarten Union,* 1908, p. 120.

[5] Statistics from early reports of the International Kindergarten Union.

railroad and the ticket had been validated at the annual conference.[6]
These special railroad certificates were available for members attending the conference in 1900. Well into the 1920's this arrangement
helped to bring together members who were widely separted geo-
graphically.

Clarifying Positions

There were perennial debates in the national meetings about the
use of symbolism, free play, teacher direction, and creative activity.
Remarkable persistence was exhibited year after year as members
listened to each other and tried to resolve their differences. At the
height of the curriculum controversy "round table" discussions were
held in which chosen leaders in kindergarten education presented
their views on a controversial topic; these opinions were then
supported or challenged in open discussion following the initial presentations. In the flowing rhetoric of the period Mary McCulloch,
Supervisor of the St. Louis Public School Kindergartens, opened one
round table discussion by remarking, "In the days of the past the
poets sang of the Knights of the Round Table. The poets of the future
will sing of the kindergartners' Round Table, and their song will tell
of gatherings of workers who came together with one theme to discuss, each contributing to it her thought, her point of view, and listening eagerly to hear the words of others." [7]

Despite warnings to be "discriminating but tolerant," the divergence between the members' points of view could not be minimized. Differences increased with each succeeding year. Only one of
the selected speakers for the "Round Table on Gifts and Occupations" in 1900 presented the progressive point of view—she was
Mary Boomer Page from the demonstration kindergarten in Armour
Institute, Chicago.[8] The use of gifts and occupations in careful sequential order was supported by Josephine Jarvis, Lucy Wheelock,

[6] Preliminary Programs of the International Kindergarten Union from
1900 to 1927, Wheelock College Collection.

[7] Mary McCulloch, "Round Table Conference on 'Stories,'" *Proceedings of the Eighth Annual Convention of the International Kindergarten
Union*, 1901, p. 74.

[8] Mary Boomer Page, "Conference on Gifts and Occupations," *Proceedings of the Seventh Annual Convention of the International Kindergarten Union*, 1900, pp. 41-47.

Susan Blow, Maria Kraus-Boelte, Caroline G. Hart, and Elizabeth Harrison.[9] In the short talks that followed the major addresses, however, the progressives spoke out. Alice Temple of Chicago presented Dewey's demand for purposeful activity on the part of the child. Patty Hill of Louisville claimed that much gift work required children to express adult ideas rather than self-active play. Alice Putnam and Bertha Hofer-Hegner continued the exposition of the progressive side. A similar cleavage may be found in the round table presentations on free play, with the conservative faction finding only danger in abandoning the process of imitation and the progressives finding important possibilities of growth in freedom of activity. Two defined groups opposed each other in the round tables on programs (1901) and home discipline (1902).

The Committee of Nineteen

To stem the tide of dissension, a Committee of Fifteen was established in 1903 charged with the task of formulating a clear statement about contemporary kindergarten thought.[10] Susan Blow was chairman of a committee of three to appoint the remainder of the group. Soon after its organizational discussions four more members were added to enlarge this group to a Committee of Nineteen. Such outspoken progressives as Alice Temple or Bertha Hofer-Hegner were not selected for the committee.

In 1907 the committee presented their divergent views to the International Kindergarten Union. To introduce the report, Lucy Wheelock, who had succeeded the original chairman, hopefully stated, "the kindergartners are approaching a larger spirit of unity through a process of reconciliation of differences. We are illustrating the Froebelian law of mediation in our recognition of the harmony possible even where widest differences of opinion exist or are toler-

---

[9] Speeches—"Conference on Gifts and Occupations," pp. 36-74. Josephine Jarvis, a translator of Froebel's books, was from Cobden, Ill. Caroline C. Hart, a student of Susan Blow, was from Baltimore. Elizabeth Harrison was from the Chicago Kindergarten College. Lucy Wheelock was from the Wheelock School in Boston.

[10] "Report of Special Committees," *Proceedings of the Tenth Annual Convention of the International Kindergarten Union,* 1903, p. 38.

ated." [11] This optimistic introduction failed to mask the basic differences in thought; a realistic look at the practices under discussion revealed beliefs too much at variance to permit reconciliation. The "law of mediation" was so inadequate for this task that by 1909 separate reports were formulated. By this time it was clearly recognized that the liberal position stemmed from concepts of biology and psychology that had an evolutionary base. The authors of the liberal report wrote, "The theory of evolution too, became an accepted hypothesis, and an effective method of research along lines bearing upon human development. As a result the new psychology came into existence, with its significance for education. When the psychologist brought to the school the contribution of scientific research along the line of human development, a new era began for American education." [12] There was no longer any doubt that the liberal faction was aligned with the scientific movement and was reaching out into the new era. Liberal members were embarking on a period of curriculum reconstruction that eventually placed kindergarten theorists on the forefront of the progressive education movement.

In presenting the 1909 reports to the International Kindergarten Union, Annie Laws, the current chairman of the Committee of Nineteen, described the tribulations of devising a report: "three reports were finally authorized, one to represent the conservative or Froebelian point of view; another to show the liberal view; and a third to represent those who, with Aristotle, find virtue in 'a mean state.' " [13] The conservative report was clearly Froebelian and was signed by ten members of the committee. The allegiance of the other committee members vacillated. Convinced that some Froebelian principles could no longer be supported, they still found it difficult to release certain cherished beliefs, and it was an even more perplexing problem to state new principles that could be heartily endorsed.

The liberal report made two salient claims: that education must

---

[11] Lucy Wheelock, "Report of the Committee of Nineteen," *Proceedings of the Fourteenth Annual Meeting of the International Kindergarten Union*, 1907, p. 41.

[12] "Views of the Liberal Kindergartners of the Committee of Nineteen," *Proceedings of the Sixteenth Annual Meeting of the International Kindergarten Union*, 1909, p. 125.

[13] Annie Laws, "Report of the Committee of Nineteen," *ibid.*, p. 115.

base its methods upon scientific knowledge of human development and that the aim of education must be socially determined. Though the liberal report was signed by six members, five of them also affixed their signatures to the liberal-conservative report, which tried to blend the heritage of the past with ideas gleaned from the scientific movement. Of the nineteen committee members, Nina Vandewalker of the State Normal School in Milwaukee alone endorsed unreservedly the liberal point of view.

The culmination of the work of the Committee of Nineteen was the publication of three rewritten reports in book form.[14] In order to divest themselves of any stigma attached to the terms conservative and progressive, the committee members merely numbered their reports. Susan Blow, in her 230-page report, in contrast to the 63-page report of the progressives, ranged widely into past and present philosophic thought to find support for Froebel's principles. The second report, written by Patty Smith Hill, highlighted the dual problem of selecting among children's interests those that were favored by the children as well as useful in leading to significant educational experiences. She drew heavily on Dewey's conception of constructive work that would secure two factors: "initiation in the child's own impulse and termination upon a higher plane." [15] There was an initial attempt to list children's instincts and social needs in a generalized way. The report was signed unqualifiedly by five other members of the committee. Two members of the committee who felt pulled into the maelstrom of scientific thought but who nevertheless clung to much that was Froebelian, presented a five-page compromise report; it was written by Elizabeth Harrison and signed by Lucy Wheelock.

The publication of their lengthy report in *The Kindergarten* constituted the last valiant effort of the conservatives to rally the entire group to the acceptance of their philosophy. It testified dramatically to the tenacity of inherited beliefs. The imbalance of committee members with more in favor of the Froebelian view could not have been representative of the thinking of kindergartners who were exerting leadership in the International Kindergarten Union at that time, for the voice of the conservatives rapidly disappeared from

[14] Committee of Nineteen, *The Kindergarten* (Boston: Houghton Mifflin, 1913).
[15] *Ibid.*, p. 247.

discussion. In the years immediately following the publication of the reports, discussions no longer considered which philosophical system should be implemented in classroom practice; the focus of attention became the practical problems of aligning the kindergarten program with scientific thinking.

In these few years idealism lost the field to scientific knowledge. Those who had seemed very much alone in the enterprise of curriculum change in 1900 were joined by many like-minded progressives by 1920. And hidden in one of the reports was a hint of the new focus soon to demand the attention of the Kindergarten Union—the concept of habit formation in the kindergarten. The 1909 liberal report stated that "emphasis upon the child's physical development and upon the formation of correct habits of acting, feeling and thinking is the best method of furthering the development of the mental and moral powers." [16] Habit formation as Thorndike described it was beginning to affect thinking about the curriculum. By the time William Heard Kilpatrick's examination of the kindergarten principles of Froebel appeared in 1916, the issues had already been clearly defined.[17] His critical estimate of the psychological deficiencies of Froebel's system unmistakably strengthened the cause of the progressive faction. Among the essentials in early learning Kilpatrick listed "the psychology of habit formation by which the child grows to the use or disuse of a particular response."

THE MONTESSORI METHOD

Just at the time the Committee of Nineteen was ready to publish their report, a system of education which they considered to be a rival—the Montessori method—gained national attention. There was a wave of brief, intense investigation on the part of American kindergartners, and some of them traveled to Italy to observe the Montessori school first hand.

There was a general consensus that the Montessori system was

[16] "Views of the Liberal Kindergartners of the Committee of Nineteen," *Proceedings of the Sixteenth Annual Meeting of the International Kindergarten Union*, 1909, p. 129.

[17] William Heard Kilpatrick, *Froebel's Kindergarten Principles Critically Examined* (New York: Macmillan Co., 1916).

not an educational panacea and was much more limited in its general outlook than the American kindergarten. Elizabeth Harrison, who was sent to Rome by the National Kindergarten Association of New York, returned with a skepticism of the system that she felt left so little room for self-expression on the part of children.[18] At the request of Dr. P. P. Claxton, United States Commissioner of Education, the Harrison report was published in 1914. Patty Smith Hill, as well, had little to recommend to American teachers as a result of her observations. In her opinion the Montessori method overlooked some of the most vital aspects of kindergarten learning and vaunted those with less significance. Anne E. Logan, in an address to the IKU, also expressed grave doubts about the ultimate merits of the system. But it was Kilpatrick who wrote the thorough critical appraisal of the Montessori method after his trip to Italy.[19] With clear insight into the philosophical issues and the psychological basis on which the educational experiences rested, Kilpatrick unveiled the limitations of the system. Though Kilpatrick's analysis of Froebel's educational principles had appeared belatedly, his examination of Montessori's educational concepts was timed with precision. Undoubtedly his critical insight aided the rapid decline of interest in the method.

Kilpatrick delivered the keynote address before the International Kindergarten Union in 1913, when "the magic word of Montessori assembled the largest gathering of any daytime session during the meeting." Others analyzed and compared the Froebelian and Montessori systems, and though there was general approval of the less directive role of the teacher in the Montessori school, a greater breadth of understanding of the educative process was accorded Froebel. Since this meeting came in the midst of the period of transition for the kindergarten curriculum, it made a big difference whether the comparisons were made with the rigid American Froebelian kindergarten or the more progressive programs. Kilpatrick, quite conversant with the experimental procedures being carried out in the

[18] Elizabeth Harrison, "The Montessori Method and the Kindergarten," *United States Bureau of Education Bulletin,* No. 28 (Washington, D.C.: Government Printing Office, 1914).
[19] William Heard Kilpatrick, *The Montessori System Examined* (New York: Houghton Mifflin Co., 1914).

kindergarten at Teachers College, was well aware of promising new practices.

The 1912 and 1913 meetings of the Kindergarten Department of the NEA also focused on the educational procedures carried out in the "children's houses" in Italy. These meetings, plus a flurry of articles in the *Kindergarten Review,* exhausted the interest of the kindergartners in Montessori practices. By 1916 there was no further mention of Montessori in these meetings, and attention was centered again upon the controversy within their own ranks.

Robert Beck has traced a similar pattern in the interest of certain lay leaders in Montessori. Supporters of the Montessori method included S. S. McClure, editor of *McClure's Magazine,* who ran a regular column on the method; Mrs. Alexander Graham Bell, who served as president of a Montessori Society in the United States; and Margaret Wilson, the daughter of the president, who helped arrange a gala reception for Maria Montessori on her visit to the United States in 1913.[20] The ebb and flow of general interest is illustrated by Beck's count of fifty-eight articles addressed to the Montessori method listed in the *Reader's Guide to Periodical Literature* between 1910 and 1914, whereas only eight appeared between 1915 and 1918.

Origin of the Montessori Method

What was this educational method that had attracted such widespread interest? It had started quietly enough when Maria Montessori was asked to plan an educational program for children of working mothers in a large tenement improvement project in Rome. The first *Casa dei Bambini* was opened in the San Lorenzo area of Rome on January 6, 1907. Here, in one of the regions most infected by poverty and vice, new housing had developed as a private philanthropy to replace over-crowded, dingy living quarters by housing where light and sanitation prevailed. The "children's houses" were to provide light and healthful conditions for the children beginning with youngsters of three years of age. Because the mothers of these children were

---

[20] Robert W. Beck, "Kilpatrick's Critique of Montessori's Method and Theory," *Studies in Philosophy and Education,* I (November, 1961), 155.

employed, the school assumed care of them from six to eight hours a day.

Dr. Montessori's background for such an undertaking was work with mentally deficient children. After study in medicine, psychology and anthropology, the last two in their initial empirical phases, she had assisted in a psychiatric clinic in Rome. This aroused her interest in mentally handicapped children, and she investigated the work initiated earlier by Edward Séguin in France, which he developed to lead the mentally retarded child to the acquisition of knowledge and skill. On the basis of Séguin's work, Madame Montessori built an elaborate system of "didactic materials" designed to give practice in activities that might otherwise come only fortuitously. Graded exercises were prepared to help the child clarify his own images of form, color, texture, or quantity. These eventually became the "auto-educative" materials used in the children's houses.

Classroom Organization

Maria Montessori broke completely with surrounding school tradition by organizing activities for the individual rather than for the group. Formal class teaching was dispensed with, along with desks, benches, and stationary chairs. These were replaced by moveable chairs, shelves and cupboards the children could reach, and, more significantly, an organization of learning that promoted individual instruction. Learning was to develop from the auto-educative materials, and the child was given freedom to use material of his own choosing either individually or with a small group of similarly interested peers.

This doctrine of liberty, a much-discussed aspect of the Montessori method, was contrasted to the teacher directedness of the American Froebelian program. Whereas the American kindergarten children were pictured as little birds in a nest waiting to be fed by the mother, the Montessori children were portrayed with an individual animus for learning. Indeed this did expose the kindergarten teacher who demanded intricate results obtainable only with teacher help. Teacher direction and intervention were contrasted to the child's voluntary work on self-selected tasks, for long periods of time were

set aside in a Montessori school for the use of materials and apparatus among which the children could choose.

This emancipation of the child from the imposition of authori-
tarian teaching was the source of true discipline according to Dr.
Montessori. Explaining her view she wrote, "A room in which all
the children move about usefully, intelligently, and voluntarily, without committing any rough or rude act, would seem to me a classroom
very well disciplined indeed." [21] Many visitors found this to be true
in the Montessori classrooms; they were impressed with the orderliness and diligence of the children. Indeed, the thoroughly humane
atmosphere and utter respect for individuality aroused the admiration of many observers. Not only was a freedom from restraint or
repression in evidence, but also a sensitivity to the importance of
self-confidence and success in future learnings. If a child did not
understand the use of a material, the teacher was not to correct him,
but to suspend the learnings associated with it until a more propi-
tious time. Nor was the child to be given any feeling of failure. Dr.
Montessori proposed that the words, "no, you have made a mistake,"
were a form of reproof that the child would vividly remember and
that would act as a deterrent to future learning.[22]

Exercises in Practical Life

The daily schedule extended from eight or nine in the morning
to four or five in the afternoon, depending on the season. It included
large blocks of time for "practical life exercises," sense training, gym-
nastics, games, manual work, and, of course, luncheon. The exercises for sense training and those for practical life formed the core
of the program.

The tenement house origin of the *Casa dei Bambini* impelled the
immediate introduction of many practical features. Children were
taught to dress and bathe themselves, brush their hair, and otherwise
care for their personal needs. Frames for lacing, buttoning, and tieing
were developed to promote these skills. Care of the room was also
added to the daily ritual. Children busied themselves sweeping floors,

[21] Maria Montessori, *The Montessori Method,* trans. Anne E. George
(New York: Frederick A. Stokes, 1912), p. 93.
[22] *Ibid.,* p. 226.

dusting furniture, replacing objects in cupboards in perfect order, or caring for plants. Their obvious delight in these activities plus a growing sense of independence impressed over-solicitous mothers.[23] Such activity was not too surprising, however, to kindergartners acquainted with the Deweyan sub-primary, where children also served lunch and washed the dishes.

Sense Training

Though the atmosphere and interaction in the Montessori classroom commanded admiration, the Americans were doubtful of the theory undergirding the total program. Kilpatrick's exposé clarified the vague dissatisfactions: he found the educational practice to be predicated upon the thesis that sense perception formed the sole basis for mental development. The "didactic apparatus" devised to make possible the proper training of the senses and to make the method auto-educative pointed in this direction. Most of the materials were expected to serve two distinct purposes: promoting sense discrimination and developing the skills of reading and writing. Cylinders, geometric forms, and color spools helped to train in sense discrimination and muscular coordination. Sandpaper letters, cylinders, and blocks led directly to an early mastery of the elements of writing, reading, and arithmetic—for work in the Montessori school was expected to culminate in the three R's.

One of the first sense exercises for very young children consisted of solid geometric cylinders of graded size to be fitted into a wooden frame. Since the exercise could be completed only if the child put each cylinder into the opening that corresponded in size, the apparatus was called self-corrective. Materials became increasingly complex: wooden tablets were carefully weighted to cultivate a baric sense; metal bowls were filled with water to promote thermal sensitivity; a multitude of color hues were used to promote a chromatic sense capable of fine discrimination.

Maria Montessori stated her aim in these sense exercises to be the differential perception of stimuli with increasing precision. In her own words, "It is exactly in the repetition of exercises that the educa-

[23] See Dorothy Canfield Fisher, *A Montessori Mother* (New York: Henry Holt and Co., 1912), pp. 141-164.

tion of the senses consists; their aim is not that the child shall know colours, forms and the different qualities of objects, but that he refine his senses through an exercise of attention, of comparison, of judgment." [24] Kilpatrick recognized this goal as tied to an outmoded theory of formal discipline, which depended for its support upon the concept of general transfer. To Kilpatrick, well acquainted with Thorndike's theories of learning, methods and materials based on training innate faculties for an assumed transfer could not form an adequate educational system. This led him to reject each aspect of the process:

We conclude, accordingly, that Madame Montessori's doctrine of sense-training is based on an outworn and cast-off psychological theory; that the didactic apparatus devised to carry this theory into effect is in so far worthless; that what little value remains to the apparatus could be better got from the sense-experiences incidental to properly directed play with wisely chosen, but less expensive and more childlike playthings.[25]

Freedom of Choice vs. Intellectual Freedom

Further analysis revealed that the absolutely determined nature of the materials denied the widespread assertion of freedom for the child. The much-vaunted "libertarian education" did not include intellectual freedom. In the first place, the exercises were formal and exact, and in the second, the child was expected to use the apparatus in the prescribed manner. If a child was found playing train with the blocks of "the long stair" instead of arranging them in graded order, the blocks were removed.[26] As insightful as Dr. Montessori was in some aspects of the learning process, she failed to recognize the rigid control that was placed on learning by limiting the materials and by forbidding any transformation in their use. The young child in need of adult approbation was readily molded into the pattern the program demanded by the quiet reinforcement of certain responses and the non-reinforcement of others.

---

[24] Montessori, p. 360.

[25] Kilpatrick, *Montessori . . . Examined*, p. 52.

[26] Anna E. Logan, "Montessori and Froebel" (Address to the International Kindergarten Union), *Kindergarten Review*, XXIII (April, 1913), 553-561.

To those educators philosophically allied with Dewey, a grave deficiency of the method was its failure to utilize the child's initiative or motivation to solve problems. The problems in Montessori schools were always those provided by the directress, not those created by the child. Further, the situations presented in order to develop the senses were so isolated from the out-of-school experiences of the children that information and skills were acquired merely as ends in themselves. The true auto-education, in the Deweyan sense, arose from situations in which the child could judge the effectiveness of materials by bending them to suit his own desired outcomes. The solution was tested by the exigencies of the life problem. "This is life's auto-education," wrote Kilpatrick, "and a right good pedagogic scheme it is." [27]

To many of the kindergartners just beginning to free themselves from the curricular domination of one set of materials, a new set had little appeal. Especially was this true since the equipment lacked the possibility of creativeness on the part of the child. William Hailmann's response was to disclaim any method with so little stimulation for the child's imagination or his constructive and creative instincts. For many kindergartners, freedom apart from self-expression was a contradiction in terms.

Imaginative activities were purposely omitted from Maria Montessori's program for children. Stories had no place. The explanation for this rested in her conviction that all activities of the mind were derived through sense impressions and thus all learning should be kept within the realm of personal experiencing.[28] Dr. Montessori's background with mental defectives was apparent in this viewpoint. She believed that imagination led to illusions that produced false reasoning and the "concomitants of delirium." [29]

"Explosion into Reading and Writing"

The sense training was extended to the development of skills in reading and writing for four- and five-year-olds. This promise of

---

[27] Kilpatrick, *Montessori . . . Examined,* p. 35.
[28] Harrison, p. 32.
[29] Maria Montessori, "Education in Relation to the Imagination of the Little Child," *Journal of Addresses and Proceedings of the National Education Association,* 1915, pp. 663-664.

early literacy was the source of the great attraction the method held for many lay enthusiasts. The "explosion into writing" was no mystery, however, to one acquainted with the method and with Thorndike's laws of learning. The children followed routinized procedures set up in several stages, each providing for mastery of an isolated component of the writing act. Continual tracing around geometric forms developed the ability to manipulate the writing instrument; endless tracing of sandpaper letters formed a mental image of each letter. When children found they could put these elements together and write words, they expressed a "frenzied joy at writing." [30] The understanding that learning theory now gives of the difficulty involved in learning meaningless material makes the reader of *The Montessori Method* wonder about the endless effort children must have devoted to the development of skill in writing through this approach.

To the image of the graphic sign the letter sound was attached. The purely phonetic nature of the Italian language, in which words are pronounced with full value given to each letter, facilitated the linking of sounds to formulate words. To the child who is methodically but uncomprehendingly repeating the accumulation of sounds, the teacher commands "faster, faster" until "finally the word bursts upon his consciousness." [31]

With all this development of "psycho-motor channels," so divorced from the content of reading, it is little wonder that Dr. Montessori wrote, "The real difficulty is in the *interpretation* of *the graphic signs.*" [32] It was discovered that though children could parrot words, no meaning was attached to them. Of this difficulty Earl Barnes wrote, "She has shown us how they can pass over into a knowledge of letters and words, but she has not shown us how they can pass over into thoughts, feelings and imaginings that need letters and words for their expression." [33]

Madame Montessori protested that no child was forced to read and write; she explained, "almost all of the normal children treated

[30] Montessori, *Method,* p. 289.
[31] *Ibid.,* p. 298.
[32] *Ibid.,* p. 318.
[33] Earl Barnes, "Comparison of Froebelian and Montessori Methods and Principles," *Kindergarten Review,* XXIII (April, 1913), p. 490.

with our method begin to write at four years, and at five know how to read and write." [34] An environment that otherwise furnished only easily mastered sense exercises and that gave such approval to the three R's was compulsion enough. The kindergartners, like Kilpatrick, questioned not the ability of young children to learn to write and read but the advisability of concentration upon these skills at this age level. Anna Logan questioned the desirability of exchanging for a mere tool, the rich content of experience related to concrete situations that would arouse problems in the child's mind and develop initiative. Children, she felt, needed to explore alternative plans for solving problems. To Kilpatrick, the idea of a school without books for the young was Froebel's greatest glory.[35] The real danger was pinpointed as that of robbing the curriculum of vital learning situations arising through a never-ending interaction with an environment that gave purpose and meaning to the learning process. An over-concern for the early learning of skills was believed to divert attention from other vital parts of education and to monopolize the major share of time in the curriculum.

Summary

In Kilpatrick's estimation auto-education was achieved at too great a cost to the child; the learnings were too limited in scope, the opportunities for self-expression too meager. Without the stimulus of creative activities and of individual initiative and purpose there was a deadened curriculum precisely at a period of the child's life when spontaneity should reign. In the progressive kindergarten sense training was only incidental to constructive and imaginative activity in which children were pursuing larger ends than the mere arrangement of form or color.

The results of the investigation of the "rival" system upon the American kindergarten was to make some leaders more aware of a non-directive role for the teacher. Many felt that the didactic materials could find a place among other available equipment. The importance of letting little children participate in the practical work of the schoolroom was also impressive to some kindergartners. The

---

[34] Montessori, *Method*, p. 303.
[35] Kilpatrick, *Montessori . . . Examined*, p. 60.

examination of the reading and writing activities in the Montessori plan only confirmed the American kindergarten tradition of excluding the three R's from the preschool: both factions of the kindergarten group felt that the goals for this age-level were much broader.

Kilpatrick's analysis undoubtedly aided the kindergartners in clarifying their position. Elizabeth Ross Shaw, a member of the Child Study Department, Public Schools, Evanston, Illinois, summed up the Montessori system in this manner, "Montessori's strong point is that she trains the cerebellum and spinal cord—she deliberately tries to make the child an efficient automatum." [36] The Americans felt that kindergarten had to be more than a formal and mechanical system of sense training. With the Montessori system assessed to their satisfaction, the kindergartners returned to the problems they had been discussing before the "rival" method deflected their attention.

[36] Elizabeth Ross Shaw, "The Effects of the Scientific Spirit in Education upon the Kindergarten: Its Relation to the Distinctive Characteristics of the Montessori Method," *Journal of Addresses and Proceedings of the National Education Association,* 1913, p. 442.

5
APPLYING NEW INSIGHTS
TO THE CURRICULUM (1900-1925)

During the first quarter of the twentieth century the kindergarten came into the mainstream of American education. Kindergartners turned away from the theories of European educators and placed their reliance upon the proposals of educators on the American scene. Kilpatrick's critique helped them analyze the Montessori system. Selected arguments from Hall's child study and Dewey's pragmatic beliefs led to the repudiation of the idealistic philosophy of Froebel. When the progressive kindergartners openly recognized that the theory of evolution was an accepted hypothesis on which to base research in human development, the language of empirical science began to appear in the literature about kindergartens.

The insights of educational psychologists and philosophers implied radical changes in classroom practice. Although a number of experimental programs had been tried in the early 1900's, the full, practical implications of the new thought were yet to be explored and implemented. New curricula that was consistently based on theoretical innovations did not appear until the middle of the twenties, but the curricular discussions of the first two decades are not insignificant. They illustrate the slow, tedious process of curriculum change in which each aspect of the program was carefully scrutinized to bring it in line with prevailing beliefs.

The period between 1900 and 1925 was one of curricular confusion, experimentation, and redirection. The results of child study were used to examine the appropriateness of each part of the curriculum for young children. The concern for character building and creative expression did not diminish, but new means to attain these goals had to evolve. There was still no consensus concerning the content areas that would replace the "cosmic truths" of the Froebelian program, therefore the subject of the selection of experiences was continually debated.

CHILD STUDY AND THE CURRICULUM

Not until the major task of clarifying differences between the conservative and progressive factions had been accomplished was the International Kindergarten Union free to pursue child study interests. There had been an early flurry of activity. A questionnaire prepared by Hall in 1896 to ascertain prevailing opinion on disputed points in kindergarten practice had instigated the formation of a child study committee. The first work assigned to the committee, appointed after the annual meeting of the IKU in 1896, was assisting in securing returns to the questionnaire. The question, "What differences, if any, has the Modern Child Study Movement made in your method of using the Gifts?" provoked a great variety of responses. The reaction to these had led to the round table on gifts and occupations in 1900 and the subsequent work of the Committee of Nineteen.

Reports of a duly appointed Child Study Committee were not resumed until 1914, when study was focused upon children's interests as revealed through their drawings and undirected play. In the intervening years concepts based upon child study permeated the discussions of practice. The ideas can be summarized into three major points: the use of symbolism as a basis for selecting experiences, the fineness of materials, which caused over-exercise of the accessory muscles and produced fatigue, and the unhygienic conditions that existed in some kindergartens.

Hall had called the lack of room space, the fatigue-inducing activities, and the shared towels and drinking cups a "heinous offense against health." [1] In the expansion of the kindergarten, many children were put into any available space; frequently a church basement sufficed. Cynthia Dozier of New York City exclaimed, "It is

---

[1] G. Stanley Hall, "The Pedagogy of the Kindergarten," *Educational Problems,* I (New York: D. Appleton, 1911), 20.

a shock to go into some of those kindergartens, and see the chairs, the dirt, the bad light, the bad sanitary conditions. There is everything against, and nothing for, an ideal system of education." [2] The child study movement turned attention to the need for large, light, clean, well-ventilated rooms with additional open-air spaces for gardens and playgrounds. Spurred on by the general concern for hygiene, health training for the child became a part of the curriculum.

Probably no doctrine from child study had a greater impact than Hall's insistence on the order of development from fundamental to accessory muscles: [3] in other words, large muscle movements preceded manipulative detail. Some teachers, at least, willingly discarded the "wonderful contrivances attempted with peas and sticks which to the great grief of the little workers, failed to hold together until completion," and the perforating "done with needles so small that in order to handle them with any degree of facility it was imperative that they be secured in a piece of cork." [4] The intricate products often meant that the teacher spent many hours after the children's departure straightening out what small hands had attempted. Careful observation revealed that fatigue and nervousness resulted from work with such delicate materials. Some kindergartners turned to free play as the ideal way of developing the fundamental muscles as it allowed the child to follow a natural pattern of development.

As the size and symbolism of the Froebelian gifts became unacceptable, experimentation with new materials began. In 1900, during the Conference on Gifts and Occupations, Alice Temple had recommended larger and heavier building blocks, a supply of dolls, a playhouse with utensils and toy animals. The emphasis on constructive activities made a workbench and tools a necessity. Since these materials required the exercise of large, fundamental muscles, they were approved by child study specialists.

[2] Cynthia Dozier, "Round Table Conference on Supervision," *Proceedings of the Eighth Annual Convention of the International Kindergarten Union*, 1901, p. 43.

[3] G. Stanley Hall, "From Fundamental to Accessory in Education," *The Kindergarten Magazine*, XI (May, 1899), 559-560.

[4] Jane Hoxie, "The Development of Occupations," *Proceedings of the Seventeenth Annual Meeting of the International Kindergarten Union*, 1910, pp. 189-190.

In investigating new media mistakes were made. Children were found to work with courage and determination on projects that interested them in spite of hard wood and nails that bent. At Teachers College experimentation in the designing of large blocks went on for twelve or thirteen years. These blocks, named for Patty Hill, were suitable for building large structures and utilized the child's fundamental muscles in their manipulation.

Influence of Child Study on the Selection of Literature

While the philosophy of idealism prevailed, kindergartners had selected a story for its contribution to "character building" by inciting the child to right action. "The first use of stories," was "to help the children form ideals." [5] Emilie Poulsson, a writer of children's stories herself, believed that "the supremely valuable kindergarten story presents some beautiful ideal to the child's imagination in such a way as to win his allegiance." [6]

To those convinced of the character-building importance of stories, Hall's suggestions, developed from the recapitulation theory, were shocking indeed. Hall described children from four to eight as being in the "stage of myth-making and poetic fancy of the *savage*" and exalted myths and fairy tales as suitable literature for this age level. Far from being detrimental to the child, these stories, Hall believed, facilitated development by providing activity for the imagination and by giving vent to the animistic quality of the young child's mind. "If you do not give them gracious lies of poetry and imagination, they make them. That is play—the play of the mind," he said.[7] Fairy tales expressed the play of the mind, and myths helped the child live in the world of fancy. Hall recommended Grimm, Aesop, Old Testament tales—even Homer. In his opinion, stories of blood and thunder fit the needs of the child at this age.

But the kindergartners found it hard to accept the slaughter and the daring of some of the tales. The Committee on Myths and

[5] Mary F. Hall, "The Story in Early Education," *Child Study Monthly*, III (June-July, 1897), 66-74.

[6] Emilie Poulsson, "The Story," *Proceedings of the Fifteenth Annual Meeting of the International Kindergarten Union*, 1908, p. 144.

[7] G. Stanley Hall, "Address to the National Educational Association," *Kindergarten Review*, XII (September, 1901), 45.

Fairy Tales in 1897 stated general approval "of myths and fairy stories properly introduced and *modified*," though some members argued that they belonged to a later period of the child's life. Others questioned the effectiveness of stories based continually on moral themes, though their protest was not as dramatic as Hall's. "That the story may be applied like a plaster or medicine for moral weaknesses is a great fallacy," a noted story-teller, Gudrun Thorne-Thomsen, told the IKU convention in 1903.[8]

The standards for the selection of stories were gradually revised until it was made clear that "all stories of subtle symbolism and worldly wise conversation should be avoided." [9] In 1921 the criteria for suitable stories reflected the advice of child study specialists to relate the literature to the young child's interests; they included dramatic incidents, much dialogue, little descriptive detail, appeal to curiosity, and culmination in satisfying endings. Probably the greatest impetus for new literary products came a little later through the recognition of the child's dominant interest in the present. The identification of this natural characteristic of early childhood stimulated the search for realistic stories closely related to the child's every day experiences.

The change in the basis for the selection of literature for young children was gradual but dramatic. It exemplified the response to Hall's demand to use the data provided by child study as the criteria for selecting the content of educational experiences. Thus child study assisted in the adaptation of distinct parts of the program to the expanding knowledge of the characteristics of young children. However, it never presented a complete rationale that was useful for the reconstruction of all kindergarten practice. The added insight supplied by a new psychology of learning was required before a truly new program emerged.

CHARACTER BUILDING AND THE CREATIVE PROCESS

Character building was retained as an essential goal of kindergarten, but as faith in idealism declined, new means for shaping the

[8] Gudrun Thorne-Thomsen, "The Place of Literature in Child Life," *Kindergarten Review*, XIII (June, 1903), 589.

[9] Report of the Literature Committee, *Proceedings of the Twenty-Fifth Annual Meeting of the International Kindergarten Union*, 1918, p. 54.

child's character were considered and had to be related to specific curricular undertakings. By 1915 two conceptions of the process of character building had been carefully presented and illustrated in practice. The first was the idealistic conception of building an inwardly evolving ideal through the continual presentation of "perfect" models of behavior; and the second was Dewey's view of moral training through social interaction and the thoughtful reconstruction of experience. These were followed by belief in a new means of character training that gradually developed until it dominated the discussions of the twenties—the formation of habits that would enable the child to perform according to the standards set as desirable.

The merging of one process of moral training into another is illustrated by the debates of kindergartners in their national meetings. The idealists had maintained that, as the kindergarten child acted out the ideal, only those ideal thoughts would "enter as germs into the child's mind" and there unfold "freely into the image of the ideal." [10] To the idealist, the ideal mother, not the savage mother, should be exemplified in the child's dramatic play. In practice, however, teachers working in the slum areas discovered that it was difficult to insist only on ideal thoughts. Geraldine O'Grady told of children in a mission kindergarten in New York City who commonly played "the policeman taking men to jail, and especially drunken men to jail." [11] To the conservative group, this play needed to be replaced by the ideal of the soldier or the knight as a means of leading ideals to a higher plane; "the putting of the life of a policeman before them, something so everyday and common, would tend to lower their ideals." [12] But Alice Temple maintained that "the ideal of the policeman is quite within the good environment of the city child. . . . We cannot be safe unless we keep pretty close within his experience." [13] Thus the Deweyan view of moral training as social learning gained through immediate social interaction was restated on

[10] Susan Blow, "Round Table on Home Discipline," *Proceedings of the Ninth Annual Convention of the International Kindergarten Union,* 1902, p. 43.

[11] Geraldine O'Grady, "Round Table Conference on Programs," *Proceedings of the Eighth Annual Convention of the International Kindergarten Union,* 1901, p. 50.

[12] Annie M. Perry, *ibid.,* p. 53.

[13] Alice Temple, *ibid.,* p. 51.

the kindergarten level. Patty Hill also supported the use of daily experiences when a program was planned to secure for children "more intelligent and valuable adaptation to their environment."

The deeper meaning of Dewey's proposal, however, involved social learnings that derived from the children's participation in the little school community, where they pursued personally significant activities and where there was a continual reconstruction of their daily experience. If children were to learn from situations of actual social interaction, freedom of movement and activity were essential. This was such a reversal of the teacher-directed and dominated program of the American Froebelians that the innovators felt called upon to expound the social and moral merits of free play.

Patty Hill explained the essence of the moral act as free choice. Free play exercised and trained the will as the child was allowed to select, choose, and decide in relation to his own self-selected enterprises. The resulting self-reliance prevented any tendency toward over-dependence on others. Not completely convinced with her own arguments, she later proposed that free play be balanced with imitative and guided activities. Others, however, with more singleness of purpose, advanced the need for free play as a strengthener of individuality and as a promoter of imagination, spontaneity, self-assertion, and self-revelation.

What was being outlined was a process of training in self-discipline. Some feared that the result would be an anarchic willfulness; the crux of the problem was how to free a child and, at the same time, to shape him. According to Alice Temple, the requisite freedom was limited and controlled by conditions that the child himself recognized as significant. The objective of free play was the enlarging and clarifying of ideas and the development of individual powers to the fullest. "To this end," she explained, "he should have freedom in the use of his play materials—not freedom in the sense of being always left to follow every fancy and caprice, but freedom in the sense that his activity is stimulated by his own motive and directed by his own imagery." [14]

When Alice Temple spoke of the child's working from his own

[14] Alice Temple, "Material and Methods," *Proceedings of the Twelfth Annual Meeting of the International Kindergarten Union,* 1905, p. 98.

imagery, she was expressing not only a process of training for self-discipline, but also a concept of creativity that eclipsed the "creative self-activity" of Froebel. Giving expression to an image or idea by means of some medium—drawing, speaking, or building—meant fostering individuality. This was the concept of creative self-expression included in the liberal report of the Committee of Nineteen in 1909. It was reinforced by observation of the young child's spontaneous products and was generally applied to the creative arts on the kindergarten level. Art and rhythmic expression illustrate particular modifications that developed in daily practice.

Art as the Expression of Mental Images

One effect of the earlier use of the occupations had been to place a high value on preciseness of production. As we have seen, the products were achieved by the dictation of the teacher, and the child rarely saw at the beginning of the lesson what the termination of his effort would be. Under this regime the child had no better alternative than to follow the teacher's directions, nor any opportunity for initiative. Intricately detailed paper designs demanding delicate manipulations were frequent products, which caused Hall to protest: "I do not like to see the kindergarten made into a factory for paper work, or any other kind of work, even at Christmas time." [15] Sometimes the occupations were merely replaced by other types of hand work. Though children were often involved in the planning of a street parade or a farmyard scene, teacher-made patterns tended to replace precise directions. But there were early protests against a mechanical use of patterns. "A crude, free hand drawing, all finger marks perhaps, but indicating an effort to express some *idea* which the child had in mind, would have far more meaning and educational value than any number of these daintily executed designs, which are mere lifeless copies of teacher's patterns," wrote Charlotte Martindell in 1899.[16]

Empirical studies of children revealed that drawing began with a scribble and proceeded through stages, similar to the development of speech; the first vague meanings grew only gradually into definite

---

[15] Hall, "Address to the NEA," *Kindergarten Review*, p. 47.
[16] Charlotte Sherwood Martindell, "New Developments in Kindergarten Work," *Kindergarten Review*, IX (February, 1899), 359.

representations. Walter Sargent, a member of the art department at the University of Chicago, explained that little children drew from memory and imagination and needed freedom to set forth their own ideas and observations.[17] Drawing, painting, and clay modeling began to be freed from teacher dictation though it was hard for teachers to give up the pretty, showy products that were formerly achieved. Thus we find an increasing belief in activity that was considered creative only when it was the expression of the child's own mental image, no matter how far removed from adult representation. Nina Vandewalker summarized this development: "The child's mental image became a recognized means of education, and the free expression of his images a necessary part of the educational process, not alone in art work but also in music, language, and other forms of school effort." [18]

In essence, the kindergartners were evolving a new kind of symbolism in the education of the young child, which was based upon their enlarged understanding of his developmental process. In their view, symbolic representation in art closely paralleled the child's ability to conceptualize and give form to his vague ideas. It was suggested that as the scribble grew into the expression of ideas, the child's mental images gained strength and clarity through the process of giving them form. Artistic expression, then, must be an outgrowth of what the child experienced.

A similar freedom was proposed for rhythmic movement and illustrated a great reversal of earlier formalism. Early games had formalized the child's love of movement and had linked this movement to Froebelian symbolism. After scrutinizing the games to determine their appropriateness for children, efforts were made to relate movement to the on-going experiences of the child.

[17] Walter Sargent, "The Beginnings of Arts in the Kindergarten," *Proceedings of the Seventeenth Annual Meeting of the International Kindergarten Union*, 1910, pp. 218-219. See also Mrs. A. E. deLeeuw, "Conference on Training Teachers," *Proceedings of the Eighth Annual Convention of the International Kindergarten Union*, 1901, pp. 101-105.

[18] Nina C. Vandewalker, "The History of the Kindergarten Influence in Elementary Education," *The Kindergarten and Its Relation to Elementary Education*, Sixth Yearbook of the National Society for the Study of Education, Part II (Bloomington, Illinois: Public School Publishing Co., 1907), 126.

Observation of little children also revealed that they did not voluntarily play organized games to any great extent, but normally played individually or only in small groups.[19] Awareness of these characteristics led to efforts to drop highly organized movement plays.

Children were allowed more freedom of expression in movement—they imitated the gallop of horses, the flight of birds, or the whirl of a merry-go-round to the accompaniment of the piano. Rhythmic response was valued as providing both wholesome exercise for the body and a consciousness of the relation of motion and rhythm. A "wave of rhythm work" swept the kindergarten as marches, skips, and gallops became part of the typical kindergarten day. Instead of the customary procedure of the child responding to the teacher's suggestion and the musical accompaniment the proposal was made that a greater spontaneity would result if children were allowed to suggest their own ideas and subjects for rhythmic representation. Rhythms were thus related to the child's awakening understanding of life around him. It was further suggested that children be given a larger part in helping to organize and develop the games that remained in the program.[20]

The practical implementation of creativity was simpler by far than the promotion of Dewey's view of character training. To permit freedom of expression with materials and to provide situations that induced individual response were demands that the teacher could fulfill with reasonable ease; but character development through full social interaction was a most evasive plan to put into action. The teacher's judgment must be depended on to recognize and to utilize social situations that would promote individual growth. The lack of concrete directives for the teacher made it difficult for her to insure the learning of initiative, independence, judgment, or social coopera-

[19] Patty Smith Hill, "Some Conservative and Progressive Phases of Kindergarten Education," *The Kindergarten and Its Relation to Elementary Education,* Sixth Yearbook of the National Society for the Study of Education, Part II (Bloomington, Illinois: Public School Publishing Co., 1907), 81.

[20] Katherine Martin, "Plays and Games," *Proceedings of the Twentieth Annual Meeting of the International Kindergarten Union,* 1913, pp. 115-116. See also: Grace A. Harrington, "Questions of Interest Regarding Kindergarten Games," *Kindergarten Review,* XXIV (April, 1914), 495-500.

tion. Furthermore, some objective measure of individual growth seemed necessary in order to give convincing evidence of the results of the process. The answer to the dual problem of facilitating the task of the teacher and of assessing the child's adjustment was to appear later as character training through habit formation, the third conception of the process of character training that dominated the 1920's.

CONTENT AREAS IN THE KINDERGARTEN PROGRAM

Throughout the period of curriculum change and experimentation, the problem of selecting experiences for kindergarten children continued to demand attention. Recommendations were placed in two distinct contexts: one group tended to relate experiences to organized bodies of subject matter; another group talked consistently in terms of children's needs and interests. In an effort to add depth to Dewey's problem-solving approach to curriculum planning, some kindergarten leaders turned to subject matter for assistance. The consideration of children's needs and interests in decisions about the curriculum obviously stemmed from child study.

Classifications of Subject Matter

In a speech to the kindergarten department of the NEA, Alice Temple categorized the subject matter of the kindergarten into three major classes: (1) natural objects and phenomena—*nature study,* (2) human beings and human activities—*home and community life,* and (3) the products of human intelligence, *literature, music, and art.*[21] When a committee from the IKU prepared a bulletin for the Bureau of Education in 1919, they utilized the three categories of subject matter to outline the kindergarten curriculum. Home and community life were advocated, but not because of the knowledge they could supply; their merit lay in the possibilities they offered children to extend and organize experience and to solve problems. For children who were leaving the family environment for the first time, the home was a tangible link for study. Through play about

[21] Alice Temple, "Subject Matter in the Curriculum," *Journal of Proceedings and Addresses of the National Education Association,* 1919, pp. 175-178.

family life, the kindergarten could provide opportunities for the child to relive his life experimentally and for social ends. The method included the recall of family activities and their extension through new objects and excursions and was developed from Dewey's principle of the reconstruction of experience.

Examples of home and community life activities show kindergarten pupils actively engaged in reconstructive experiences. The children in the experimental kindergarten at Teachers College constructed houses and made clothes and furniture for their doll families.[22] At the University of Chicago laboratory school they prepared a meal for the group, which involved a trip to the market, for the home neighborhood was deemed the second source of study material. Because holiday celebrations and seasonal activities were a meaningful part of home experiences, these also became a major part of the kindergarten curriculum.[23]

Excursions to woods and rivers and the care of real gardens where children could take full responsibility were considered an aid to deepening the child's sense of kinship with nature. Gardens were maintained by many kindergartners around the turn of the century in spite of almost insuperable difficulties. Articles appeared regularly in the issues of the *Kindergarten Magazine* and *Kindergarten Review* relating experiences with gardening in crowded city areas. Some writers told of removing debris from adjacent vacant lots; others explained the detailed procedure for developing flourishing gardens. In the opinion of the writers, the children's growing understanding of living things far outweighed the effort put into overcoming of practical obstacles.[24] In 1898 Jenny Merrill reported twenty out-of-door gardens in connection with kindergartens in Philadelphia as well as several in Chicago kindergartens.[25]

[22] Bertha Hofer-Hegner, "The Kindergarten Program in Relation to Home Environment and Activities," *Proceedings of the Twenty-Second Annual Meeting of the International Kindergarten Union,* 1915, p. 156.

[23] See, for example, *The Kindergarten Curriculum,* Bureau of Education Bulletin, No. 16, 13-14; Alice Temple, "Subject Matter in the Curriculum," *Journal of Proceedings and Addresses of the National Education Association,* 1919, p. 177.

[24] Ruth W. Norton, "An Experiment with Children's Gardens," *Kindergarten Review,* XVII (April, 1907), 483-489; Clarence M. Weed, "Crops for Children's Gardens," *Kindergarten Review,* XVII (April, 1907), 489-492.

[25] Jenny B. Merrill, "Children's Gardens," *Kindergarten Review,* IX (September, 1898), 46-50.

Nature study also included examination of many natural phenomena that could be brought into the classroom, such as butterflies, chicks, snails, shells, goldfish, and geraniums. Coinciding as it did with a general nature study movement in the schools, this interest in natural phenomena in the kindergarten had the added support of Anna Comstalk and Liberty Hyde Bailey, writers for kindergarten journals. The chief advantages of nature study for young children, according to Miss Comstalk, were the development of accuracy of eye and truthfulness of expression.[26] Short, snappy, spicy observation of the natural environment was Bailey's recommendation for the development of an inquiring and sympathetic spirit.[27] This close observation had to be done in the spirit of scientific fact-finding, which meant the complete elimination of sentimental stories that falsely represented nature's laws.

The playful, imaginative work of some kindergartners, a residue of the sentimentalism that developed under idealism, is illustrated by the story of a primary teacher who gave each child three leaves to observe. Children who had attended kindergarten responded: "I have some little boats," or, "I have three fans," or, "I have a mamma and a papa and a baby." But Pat, who had never been to kindergarten stated, "I ain't got nothin' but three, old leaves." [28] Sentimental playfulness had no place in a study with the emphasis upon "seeing the things one looks at" and drawing "proper conclusions from what one sees." [29]

Only when parents, ever anxious to have their children become literate at an early age, put pressure upon the kindergarten, was the question of reading discussed. It was readily recognized that children could learn to read at an early age; the crucial point was whether it should be given high priority in the development of kindergarten children. Alice Putnam answered that children needed to concentrate on gathering first-hand material to stimulate their own thoughts

[26] Anna Botsford Comstalk, "Nature Study in the Kindergarten," *Kindergarten Review*, XXV (September, 1914), 28-35.

[27] L. H. Bailey, "What is Nature Study," *Kindergarten Review*, VIII (October, 1897), 85-86.

[28] Susan P. Speed, "How Far Should Imaginative Terminology Be Used in Nature Study?" *Kindergarten Review*, XVII (October, 1906), 91.

[29] Bailey, p. 85.

rather than being inducted too soon into the thoughts of others.[30] Greater rapprochement between the kindergarten and the primary school during the first quarter of the century failed to increase discussion about reading. In one of the infrequent references to reading, Barbara Greenwood of the State Normal School in Los Angeles proposed that flexible grouping might make it possible for a few kindergarten children to receive instruction in the first grade for one period of the day.[31] By 1925 the term reading readiness was not yet in common use.

Efforts to explain the curriculum in terms of subject matter apparently stemmed from the desire to add depth to the problems children were encountering in school. Though teachers tried to plan valuable experiences using nature study, community life, literature, or music as subject matter, it is clearly evident that these bits of knowledge were not the principle objective. The merit of each subject was determined by its ability to assist children in confirming and extending their daily life.

"Needs and Interests" in the Curriculum

While some kindergartners probed subject matter areas, others talked frankly about children's needs and interests as a basis for curriculum development. Amy E. Tanner, a member of the faculty of Clark University, identified the child as the center and source of kindergarten activities and placed her emphasis upon the child's need for a wealth of sensory experiences. The vital needs arising from the child's daily living conditions were held to be the starting point for organizing a curriculum with meaning, according to Luella Palmer, an assistant director of kindergartens in New York City. As explained by Nina C. Vandewalker, the program was a working scheme based on the needs of a particular group of children. Since these needs were not static and could be known only through obser-

[30] Alice Putnam, "Shall Reading and Writing be Taught in the Kindergarten?" *Journal of Proceedings and Addresses of the National Educational Association,* 1894, pp. 327-328.

[31] Barbara Greenwood, "The Kindergarten Curriculum," *Proceedings of the Twenty-Second Annual Meeting of the International Kindergarten Union,* 1915, p. 144.

vation, the kindergarten teacher must be her own curriculum maker.[32] Edna Dean Baker proposed that a balanced kindergarten program would supply activities that fulfilled the child's needs for motor activity, sensory investigation, and communicative opportunities.[33]

It was fine to propose, as so many did, that the problems and materials that formed the organizing centers of the curriculum must be based upon the interests, the impulses, and the native capacities of a specific group of children, but little help was given to teachers in selecting among these for educative purposes. Little wonder that one answer to the dilemma was characterized by the absence of program; free organization and free use of materials prevailed. The recommendations to make the curriculum child-centered were fraught with practical difficulties that went unresolved until the behaviorist credo of habit formation provided new answers to the selection of experiences.

[32] Nina C. Vandewalker, "The Kindergarten Curriculum as Modified by Modern Educational Thought," *Proceedings and Addresses of the National Education Association*, 1919, p. 172.

[33] Edna Dean Baker, "The Balanced Program," *Proceedings of the Thirtieth Annual Meeting of the International Kindergarten Union*, 1923, pp. 132-133.

6
THE DEEPENING THRUST OF SCIENCE

As kindergartners leaned more and more heavily on leaders in American education to give new direction to school practice, they responded to efforts to make education more efficiently scientific. Such movements were systematically affecting all of education by the 1920's. One aspect of the scientific thrust was the development of new psychological theories with special emphasis on the learning process. Modern psychologies based upon objective observation of overt behavior developed in various directions with different terminologies; the kindergarten was particularly affected by the connectionist psychology of Edward L. Thorndike and behaviorism as promoted by John B. Watson.

Another phase of the effort to develop a science of education was the formation of a vast scheme of quantitative investigation including intelligence and achievement tests. Aided effectively by Charles Hubbard Judd at the University of Chicago and by Thorndike at Teachers College, the work to quantify human behavior permeated elementary education in the twenties. Educational measurement brought with it the promise of efficiency in education. Efficiency and scientific analysis were also applied to the problems of curriculum construction. Specialists in the area of curriculum making began to analyze the components of curriculum development. Among those who had some effect upon the kindergarten leaders were Franklin Bobbitt and Werrett Wallace Charters. In the pursuit of efficiency there was even a Committee on Minimum Essentials in Kindergarten and Primary Grades, which coordinated its efforts with an NEA Committee on Economy of Time.

NEW PSYCHOLOGIES

Edward L. Thorndike—Connectionism

While Hall had aroused interest in observational techniques, he was not diligent in compiling data; he became, instead, the interpreter of child study, continually pointing out its implications for teaching. Thorndike wrote in 1925 that Hall's interest in psychology did not include "detailed experimentation, intricate quantitative treatment of results, or rigor and subtlety of analysis." [1] In this statement Thorndike was listing the skills at which he himself excelled.

William James once stated that more than any of his other pupils Thorndike had the quality most essential to a scientific man, the ability to see things objectively, apart from acquired perspective and personal reference.[2] It was while Thorndike was a student at Harvard and registered in a course with James that he began his first work with animal learning, a line of experimentation so novel that he was not permitted to carry it out in the university laboratories. His investigation of animal learning was based upon the assumption that a demonstration of the conditions of animal behavior under laboratory conditions could help solve the general problems of psychology. The assumption, of course, represents a synthesis of scientific method and evolutionary doctrine, since in the absence of the latter animal learning would hardly have been considered a suitable topic for a psychologist.[3]

As kindergartners came to accept the assumptions upon which Thorndike's work was based, they began to consider his work important in reconstructing their own curriculum plans.

The process by which animal responses became increasingly more efficient and economical, Thorndike called learning. As a result of his experimentation he formulated laws of learning that had a great influence on education in America. As a professor of psy-

---

[1] Edward Lee Thorndike, "Biographical Memoir of Granville Stanley Hall: 1846-1924," *Biographical Memoirs*, XII (Washington, D.C.: National Academy of Science, 1925), 139-140.

[2] J. McKeen Cattell, "Thorndike as Colleague and Friend," *Teachers College Record*, XXVII (February, 1926), 461.

[3] Lawrence A. Cremin, *The Transformation of the School* (New York: Alfred A. Knopf, 1961), p. 111.

chology at Teachers College, Columbia University, Thorndike taught many hundreds of students over a span of forty years and instilled in many of them an esteem for the scientific spirit. Among them was Patty Smith Hill, who was pioneering in the reconstruction of the kindergarten curriculum at Teachers College at the time that Thorndike's scientific theory of learning was being formulated.

Learning, according to Thorndike, consisted of specific bonds of connection between a situation (S) and a response (R). As Thorndike stated it in one of his early books called *The Principles of Teaching:* "Using psychological terms, the art of teaching may be defined as the art of giving or withholding stimuli with the result of producing or preventing certain responses." [4] Stimuli included the "teacher's words, gestures, and appearance, the condition and appliances of the schoolroom, the books to be used, and objects to be seen"; responses included an "infinite variety of thoughts and feelings and bodily movements." This broad explanation included motor expression, moral training, and reasoning. In each area the premium was put upon the development of skills and habits by an application of the dictum: "Put together what you wish to put together. Reward good impulses. Conversely; keep apart what you wish to have separate. Let undesirable impulses bring discomfort." [5]

Thorndike enunciated three laws of learning useful for modifying behavior: the laws of readiness, exercise, and effect. The law of readiness held that since learning was a selective response conditioned by the learner's attitudes and mental set, in order to learn successfully a student must be enthusiastic and motivated at the outset. Learning should make use of those "conduction units" that were in readiness to conduct. The law of exercise stated that the more frequently a bond was exercised the more readily available it was for subsequent use. The third law, that of effect, asserted that satisfaction on the part of the learner increased the strength of the S→R bond.[6]

[4] Edward L. Thorndike, *The Principles of Teaching* (New York: A. G. Seiler, 1906), p. 7.
[5] *Ibid.,* p. 110.
[6] Edward L. Thorndike, *The Psychology of Learning,* II (New York: Columbia University Press, 1913), 1-5.

Thus in Thorndike's psychology of learning, which proclaimed the need to exercise and reward desirable connections and to prevent or punish undesirable ones, it was the teacher who specified the bonds or connections to be established. It became the responsibility of the teacher to set the stage for the process of fixing the S→R bonds; the teacher functioned as the master designer. It was precisely this conception of the teacher as one who would provide appropriate stimulus to build desired responses that greatly influenced the development of new kindergarten programs.

Behaviorism—John B. Watson

While Thorndike was formulating laws of learning in the field of educational psychology and making the S→R a well-known symbol, John Broadus Watson was experimenting with infants and young children at Johns Hopkins University and laying the groundwork for a new school of psychology called behaviorism. Openly proclaiming that a science of human behavior could be built around the study of overt behavioral manifestations, Watson discarded introspection as a method of study and refused to place any reliance on such an illusive concept as "consciousness." [7] In dismissing introspection as the major method of psychological investigation and turning to the study of objectively observable behavior, Watson made infants and small children legitimate subjects for psychological experimentation.

At the center of the behaviorists' explanation of learning was the technique of conditioning. The first experimentation that led to a belief in a conditioned reflex was the work of the celebrated Russian, Ivan Pavlov. Pavlov had established that when a dog was making a definite response to a particular stimulus, any frequently accompanying stimulus was likely to be responded to the same way: in other words, a dog presented at the same time with food—to which he responded by a flow of saliva—and the sound of a bell, would eventually respond by salivating to the sound of the bell alone. No introspection was either possible or necessary; the dog learned to respond to a presented stimulus. The behaviorists postulated this

[7] John B. Watson, *Behavior* (New York: Henry Holt, 1914), p. 27.

process of conditioning through associated stimuli as the fundamental process of all learning and all behavior.[8]

Watson applied the conditioning technique to newborn infants. He was interested in emotional development and used conditioning to demonstrate how emotional responses were acquired. All unlearned, unconditioned reflexes he reduced to three unadulterated emotions: fear, love, and rage. He attributed all other human responses to nurture rather than nature, and he argued that they were learned by the process of conditioning whereby thousands of new and more complicated stimuli were associated with the earlier and simpler reflexes. Thus the use of conditioning was extended beyond the realm of emotions to include all learning.

Since, in Watson's view, the conditioning process began with the newborn infant, the kindergarten teacher was confronted with a group of very complex organisms, each conditioned by parental slants and twists. Part of the teacher's work was to undo some of the wrong responses established by parents. The conditioning of "systemized and definite habits" such as responsibility, neatness, and perseverance, Watson considered to be the primary work of the kindergarten teacher.[9]

By his painstaking methodology and his complete discreditation of introspection as a procedure, Watson put new life into the child development movement, thus serving to catalyze child psychology as a whole. His direct effect upon the kindergarten was to reinforce the importance of stimulus situations and to emphasize the significance of the child's early training.

Application to the Curriculum

The view of character training as habit formation, reinforced by the work of Thorndike and Watson, appeared to be the solution both to facilitating the task of the teacher and to assessing the child's adjustment. The proposal to mold specific habits through structuring

[8] For accounts of the conditioning technique see R. Freeman Butts and Lawrence A. Cremin, *A History of Education in American Culture* (New York: Henry Holt, 1953), p. 501.

[9] John B. Watson, "Pre-Kindergarten Age—A Laboratory Stage," *Proceedings of the Twenty-Sixth Annual Meeting of the International Kindergarten Union,* 1919, p. 205.

appropriate stimulus situations seemed also to solve the dilemma of freeing the child from teacher dictation while at the same time shaping him toward socially acceptable goals. The major efforts at application of this moral training to the curriculum originated at Teachers College, Columbia University, and Thorndike's connectionism was undoubtedly the impelling force.

The implementation of this view demanded the restatement of the teacher's task in terms of the habits, skills, attitudes, and ideas that could or should be inculcated. Teachers College took the lead in devising such a habit inventory in the kindergarten department headed by Patty Smith Hill. The result of the study was a curriculum formulated to provide children with the experiences that would call forth desired responses and exercise them until they became thoroughly ingrained. *A Conduct Curriculum* [10] was the expression of this view of character building as the desiderata of kindergarten. Moral training could thus be defined as "the sum total of these manifold mental qualities and dispositions directed toward certain ends," ends that were slowly shaped in the individual.[11] This new thinking cast aside the older notions of character education that equated knowing with doing in favor of an essentially behaviorist outlook. Not virtue in general but goodness in particular became the goal as habits expected were stated in terms of washing hands before eating, using judgment in selecting materials, or cooperating with other children.

THE MEASUREMENT MOVEMENT

The scientists' precise measuring devices and statistical principles were also transferred to education. As early as 1906 Thorndike wrote,

Just as the scientist, though he has made his facts as accurate and his argument as logical as he can, still remains unsatisfied until he verifies his conclusion by testing it with new facts, so a teacher, after planning

[10] Agnes Burke, *et al.*, *A Conduct Curriculum for the Kindergarten and First Grade* (New York: Charles Scribner's Sons, 1923).

[11] Agnes L. Rogers, "The Relation of an Inventory of Habits to Character Development," *Proceedings of the Twenty-Ninth Annual Meeting of the International Kindergarten Union,* 1921, p. 138.

and executing a piece of work as well as he can, must "verify" his teaching by direct tests of its results and must consider uncertain any result which he cannot thus verify.[12]

Though tests had been used for some time by psychologists, the real breakthrough for education came in the form of an intelligence scale developed by Alfred Binet and Theodore Simon in France. The scale idea was soon applied to achievement as well and taken up by American educators as they devised a vast scheme of quantitative investigation that touched every phase of the school curriculum.[13]

Thorndike at Columbia University and Charles Hubbard Judd at the University of Chicago were effective promoters of the measurement movement, which promised to bring efficiency to education. Both men helped to lay the groundwork for the measurement of educational achievement and enunciated the principles that were unfolded in the work of their students. In 1918 Thorndike announced the basic tenet of the quantitative investigators: "Education is concerned with changes in human beings; a change is a difference between two conditions." [14] He believed the success of educational procedures could be determined only by measuring the products of changed behavior—things made, words spoken, and acts performed.

Charles Judd shared Thorndike's dream of building a genuine science of pedagogy. "The recognition of the science of education as a separate discipline," he wrote, "can be urged on the ground that the scientific methods which were applied to the problems of mental development have opened up every aspect of school organization to

[12] Thorndike, *Principles,* p. 258.

[13] For accounts of the measurement movement and the influence of Judd and Thorndike see Lawrence A. Cremin, *The Transformation of the School* (New York: Alfred A. Knopf, 1961), pp. 185-192; R. Freeman Butts and Lawrence A. Cremin, *A History of Education in American Culture* (New York: Henry Holt, 1953), pp. 438-439; Adolph E. Meyer, *An Educational History of the American People* (New York: McGraw-Hill, 1957), pp. 291-297.

[14] Edward L. Thorndike, "The Nature, Purposes, and General Methods of Measurements of Educational Products," *The Measurement of Educational Products,* Seventeenth Yearbook of the National Society for the Study of Education, Part II (Bloomington, Illinois: Public School Publishing Co., 1918), 16.

scientific study." [15] Judd urged the scientific view as a means of opening up "all the results of school work to full inspection and evaluation." [16]

Judd had been a companion of Thorndike as an undergraduate at Wesleyan University in the 1890's. Judd went on to specialize in psychology, obtaining his doctorate from Wilhelm Wundt at Leipzig. Inspired as he was with the methods of science, he spent most of his career as director of the school of education at the University of Chicago, making it a center for the scientific study of education. "Be exact," was Judd's advice to his students, for precise knowledge formed the most defensible basis for solving educational problems. In promoting the measurement of educational products he wrote, "standardization is nothing but a systematic effort to deal with educational problems explicitly and in the light of exact information." [17]

Measurement in the Kindergarten

This feverish activity in test making had its effect upon the kindergarten. Though the tests constructed to measure academic achievement in specific subject areas had no immediate use in the kindergarten, the idea of measuring the results of the teacher's efforts caught on.

From 1915 to 1921 the reports of the various child study committees of the International Kindergarten Union were devoted to knowing more about child nature, and this led them right into the measurement movement. If a psychological continuity of growth was to be relied on, instead of a precise sequence of activities, some means of measuring this growth had to be devised. The Committee of 1915 recognized two measurement problems: the need for measures of progress in various activities during the kindergarten year and the determination of minimum standards of accomplishment. The quest for measurement devices led the committee, in 1917, to approach leading educators about "a few simple tests" with the result that "all the Professors . . . unanimously testified that no

[15] Charles Hubbard Judd, *Introduction to the Scientific Study of Education* (Boston: Ginn and Co., 1918), p. 303.

[16] *Ibid.*, p. 12.

[17] *Ibid.*, p. 228.

such tests existed" that were applicable to kindergarten children.[18] Within the next five years the Detroit Kindergarten Test, the Pintner-Cunningham Mental Test, and others had been reported.[19]

Could young children be measured? Should they be measured? Could the elusive kindergarten goals be stated in a manner that made objective measurement possible? With the availability of tests and the stress on quantitative studies in general, the answer had to be positive. The Bureau of Education Committee of the IKU selected a series of kindergarten activities, devised tests for initial and final measurement, and invited a number of kindergartens to try them. A session of the annual meeting in 1923 was devoted to the problems of record keeping in the kindergarten. The concept of evaluation as a component of the curriculum was growing.

Indeed, extravagant claims were made for tests as a tool for the teacher. "The development of physical science meant the control of the material world and mental tests will ultimately mean the control of human behavior," Dr. Agnes Low Rogers dramatically stated.[20] In an elaborate analysis of six parallel and interrelated ages —chronological, physiological, mental, educational, social, and moral—Bird T. Baldwin, Director of the Iowa Child Welfare Research Station, proposed the possibility of defining a "normal standard child." [21] The search for standards revealed the vast range of individual performance and achievement. The kindergarten could not remain immune to the discussions of individual differences. Frank N. Freeman, a guest speaker at the IKU in 1922, outlined and op-

[18] Elizabeth Ross Shaw, "Report of the Child Study Committee," *Proceedings of the Twenty-Fourth Annual Meeting of the International Kindergarten Union*, 1917, p. 82.

[19] Henry J. Baker, "The Detroit Kindergarten Test," *Proceedings of the Twenty-Eighth Annual Meeting of the International Kindergarten Union*, 1921, pp. 188-195; Bess V. Cunningham, "A New Series of Group Tests for Use in the Kindergarten and Primary Grades," *Proceedings of the Twenty-Ninth Annual Meeting of the International Kindergarten Union*, 1922, pp. 164-188.

[20] Agnes Low Rogers, "The Scope and Significance of Measurement in Early Elementary Education," *Proceedings of The Twenty-Sixth Annual Meeting of the International Kindergarten Union*, 1919, p. 183.

[21] Bird T. Baldwin, "Measuring Childhood," *Proceedings of the Thirtieth Annual Meeting of the International Kindergarten Union*, 1923, pp. 161-166.

posed the belief that the inherited determinants of intellectual capacity made the function of education extremely limited. In his recognition that individual differences were large and significant, Freeman based his own position on the Watsonian concept of the plasticity of human nature. In conclusion he stated:

The function of education is important, both because the limits of individual differences are less definite and precise than have often been supposed, and our means of measuring them are less reliable than is sometimes implied, and also because, regardless of these individual differences, all persons alike are what they are very largely because of the training which they have received.[22]

To provide the richest and most challenging training to which a child could respond meant that more than personal opinion was involved in measuring growth. This implied objective measures. "The purpose of measurement," stated one lecturer, "is not to make all alike. It is rather to discover differences and the reason for their existence. Most of all it is to give some adequate means of determining progress or change." [23] Thus, though the initial impetus for measuring devices was the assessment of individual growth, continued testing led kindergartners to a concern for standardization and greater efficiency.

Standards *vs.* individual differences, observational records *vs.* objective measures, habit inventories *vs.* freedom in development: each dichotomy received attention as evaluation was increasingly considered an integral part of curriculum structure.

CURRICULUR EFFICIENCY

The notion that the study of education should be conducted with the detached and sober outlook of science was applied in other ways to curriculum building. The efforts of curricular revision involved committees as well as individuals. In 1911 the Department of

[22] Frank N. Freeman, "The Limitations Upon Education Set by Individual Abilities," *Proceedings of the Twenty-Ninth Annual Meeting of the International Kindergarten Union,* 1922, p. 163.

[23] Bessie M. Park, "The Application of Method in Kindergarten Education," *Proceedings of the Twenty-Fifth Annual Meeting of the International Kindergarten Union,* 1918, p. 150.

Superintendence of the National Education Association appointed a Committee on Economy of Time in Education, requesting it to formulate definite proposals to prevent wasting time during the school program and to substitute economical and efficient methods of teaching. Surveys and measurement devices were prime tools for assessing the amount of pupil learning so that norms of performance could be established for each subject area.

At the suggestion of some of the members of the Department of Superintendence Committee in 1915, the International Kindergarten Union appointed a cooperating group to determine minimum essentials for kindergarten education. The IKU committee became involved in its own surveys; they devised tests of fundamental arithmetic concepts and developed questionnaires pertaining to the selection of literature. But this initial rigor in establishing minimum essentials rapidly declined. By 1919 the committee turned from precise recommendations to state rather generally; "The main effort of the kindergarten and the primary grades should be to provide for the youngest children an environment that will promote activity and growth along right lines and that will at the same time protect the child from retarding or harmful influences." [24] By 1920 the committee no longer functioned, but the earlier efforts of the kindergartners demonstrated their concern to keep pace with major educational movements. If any of them recognized the divergence between planning a curriculum around child-centered notions and basing it upon minimum essentials for all children, this recognition was never stated.

Franklin Bobbitt

The efforts at curricular analysis were reinforced by professors of education who began to apply the analytical process of science to the components of curriculum structure. Franklin Bobbitt, a coworker of Judd, looked for efficient curriculum construction in his major work called *How to Make a Curriculum*. Comparing the curriculum maker to an educational engineer, he set the task of dis-

[24] H. Grace Parsons (Chairman), "Report of the Committee on Minimum Essentials of Kindergarten and Primary Education," *Proceedings of the Twenty-Sixth Annual Meeting of the International Kindergarten Union,* 1919, p. 74.

covering the goals in a general way and then planning the outlines of the routes to be traveled to their attainment. "The pupil's activities and experiences," he wrote, "are the steps which make up his journey toward these goals. The activities and experiences *are* the curriculum." [25] In the opinion of Bobbitt, education was primarily preparation for adult life; goals could be determined through an analysis of the broad range of human experience. As objectives were derived from "the actual activities of mankind," Bobbitt expected the school to break loose from the concern over subject matter and to radically reconstruct the curriculum. Extreme departures from traditional procedures demanded the conscious formulation of the principles of curriculum making. Though searching for broad principles of curriculum construction, Bobbitt actually made his goals so specific that they delineated a precise curriculum geared to the existing social structure.

Werrett Wallace Charters

W. W. Charters, a member of the faculty of the Carnegie Institute of Technology, was another leader in the analysis of the curriculum who believed that the increasing emphasis on changing conduct necessitated fundamental changes in the organization of school work.[26] He also insisted that the first step of curriculum construction was to determine objectives by studying the life of man in his social setting. The criterion of social utilitarianism was given high priority as Charters defended the technique of job analysis as a means of determining appropriate school activities. Further steps in curriculum planning, outlined by Charters, included some rational means of selection among objectives and the organization of instruction according to the psychological nature of the child.

Though Charters believed that desirable traits developed from many specific experiences that brought about the habituation of right behavior, he left room in his curriculum planning for a release of intellectual powers through problem solving. Norman Woelfel has written of Charters' curriculum proposals, "To the scientific refine-

---

[25] Franklin Bobbitt, *How To Make a Curriculum* (Boston: Houghton Mifflin, 1924). p. 44.

[26] W. W. Charters, *Curriculum Construction* (New York: Macmillan, 1923).

ment of the existing school machinery he would make significant additions of genuine problem and project work. This is true compromise with no apologies for retaining the old or none for incorporating the new." [27]

One of the effects of the work of Charters and his colleague Franklin Bobbitt was the promotion of the idea that curriculum development involves more than simply the outlining of courses of study in various subjects; they prepared for the later development of a curriculum geared to the persistent problems of social living.[28] The more immediate effect of their work, however, was to reinforce current attempts to identify precise objectives and to stipulate means for their attainment. Conduct, behavior, and activity were the watchwords here, also. In writing to the kindergartners Bobbitt proclaimed, "Not only is behavior the end of life it is also the process of life, and equally the end and process of education, for life and education are one process and never should they diverge." [29] And he endorsed the work of kindergartners as they began to plan a curriculum around the behavior identified as desirable.

THE PROJECT METHOD

Not all leading educators of the period relied on the efforts of science to improve the educative process. Kilpatrick warned against the possible restrictions placed on the curriculum through an overemphasis on objective tests. "Great care is necessary," he wrote in stating his position, "that testing should not, as too often it has done, so act as to shift the teacher's endeavors into narrow and wrong lines.

---

[27] Norman Woelfel, *Molders of the American Mind* (New York: Columbia University Press, 1933), p. 114. Woelfel categorizes Charters and Bobbitt with Judd, Thorndike, and Ernest Horn as educators stressing the ultimacy of science.

[28] Curriculum theorists generally recognize the origin of the persistent problem-of-living approach to curriculum making in the work of Bobbitt and Charters. See, for example, Hilda Taba, *Curriculum Development: Theory and Practice* (New York: Harcourt, Brace and World, 1962), p. 447; Virgil E. Herrick, *et al., The Elementary School* (Englewood Cliffs, New Jersey: Prentice-Hall, 1956), p. 140.

[29] Franklin Bobbitt, "Education as Growth Through Experience," *Childhood Education,* I (October, 1924), 52.

This danger is the greater because, so far, we can measure better the more mechanical types of outcomes." [30]

As an interpreter of Dewey's ideas, William H. Kilpatrick influenced a whole generation of teachers. A part-time teaching assignment at Teachers College in 1909 marked the beginning of Kilpatrick's lifelong association with the school where, as lecturer and teacher during the years when the institution was training large numbers of professional educators, he exerted an enormous influence. To the kindergartners, who had leaned upon Dewey to help them redirect their curriculum, Kilpatrick became another recognized leader to help them put progressive views into practice. What attracted the kindergartners to Kilpatrick's writings was an essay called "The Project Method," [31] which presented his idea for organizing the curriculum around the child's "wholehearted purposeful activity proceeding in a social environment." Making individual purpose the key to curriculum organization solved a number of knotty educational dilemmas, in Kilpatrick's opinion. Significantly, to base education upon purposeful acts meant, "to identify the process of education with worthy living itself." As life was a succession of purposeful acts, so education could not only best prepare the child for later life, but could also approximate the entire process of living by focusing upon the purposes of learners.

Kilpatrick developed the relationship between the project method and Dewey's emphasis on social reconstruction, writing that the school regimen of purposeful activity presented the best possibility for building moral character. Moral character was derived from "shared social relationships," or "the disposition to determine one's conduct and attitudes with reference to the welfare of the group." [32] By living in a social milieu that promoted, under competent supervision, shared coping with a variety of situations, Kilpatrick expected to develop skill in judging experiences, as well as to strengthen ap-

[30] William Heard Kilpatrick, "Statement of Position," *The Foundations of Curriculum Making,* Twenty-Sixth Yearbook of the National Society for the Study of Education, Part II (Bloomington, Illinois: Public School Publishing Co., 1930), 140.

[31] William Heard Kilpatrick, "The Project Method," *Teachers College Record,* XIX (September, 1918), 320.

[32] *Ibid.,* p. 329.

propriate response bonds. More than just outward conformity would, thus, result from the pursuit of a rich variety of purposes, some individual, others "conjointly" conceived. Furthermore, Kilpatrick viewed the project method as capable of reconciling Dewey's conception of education with Thorndike's laws of learning. "The whole-hearted purposeful act," on which the project method relied, brought into operation the laws of readiness and effect. Individual purpose or "set" brought into action bonds ready to act, thus maximizing the motivation necessary to learn successfully. Purpose, further, insured satisfaction when success was attained, and satisfaction strengthened those bonds modified in the facilitating action. Not only the primary learning of knowledge and skills, but the concomitant learning of attitudes, ideals, and standards were, according to Kilpatrick, satisfied and thus reinforced in the project method. The third law of learning, the law of exercise, was necessarily a concomitant of purposeful projects.

Kilpatrick made the project method appealing and usable to kindergartners through the inclusion of a variety of projects. Good projects involved manual and motor activities as well as intellectual and esthetic experiences. In outlining four types of projects Kilpatrick named: (1) construction or the embodiment of a plan in some external form (for example, building a boat, or presenting a play), (2) appreciation or the enhancement of esthetic enjoyment (listening to a story or appreciating a picture), (3) problem solving or the straightening out of some intellectual difficulty (such as finding out whether or not dew falls), and (4) obtaining some item of knowledge or degree of skill (for instance, learning to write grade fourteen on the Thorndike scale).[33] Stated in these terms, projects for kindergarten children could be readily identified.

Projects in the Kindergarten

When the project method appeared on the educational scene it was quickly utilized by kindergartners as a means of selecting and organizing curriculum experiences. Kilpatrick's essay was published in 1918; in the 1921 sessions of the International Kindergarten Union there were not only discussions of the method but also reports of projects that had been carried out in kindergartens. Whether

---

[33] *Ibid.,* pp. 322-333.

or not they recognized the project "as a pedagogical principle capable of reconciling Thorndike's connectionism with the Deweyan view of education," [34] they welcomed it as a means of promoting behavioristic goals in a social situation. Edna Dean Baker saw it as "a greater chance for development of initiative, purposefulness, persistence and cooperation on the part of children than any other," and recognized Kilpatrick's definition of a project as an activity that the child attacked with understanding and purpose in a social setting.[35] Adapting the project method to the kindergarten, Patty Smith Hill warned, meant teachers must remember that projects might need to be transitory and done in frequently-changing groups. But her endorsement was given to the method, "Try the project method, but take it in homeopathic doses. It means more than any method I have seen for character development, morality and social training." [36]

Kilpatrick's own emphasis on the moral values of projects appealed to kindergartners ever concerned with character development, but one suspects that the reason for the rapid acceptance of the project method was that it provided an effective means for organizing kindergarten experiences. Projects involved children in art, science, and language growth. Some teachers became so engrossed in encompassing all the possible *kinds* of project that the point of purposeful activity was missed. Teacher-selected projects satisfied those who were anxious to enrich the child's experiences by giving him problems to solve. According to Edna Dean Baker's assessment, the largest proportion of projects were "constructive" in nature.

These new theoretical positions, out on the cutting edge of educational thought in the 1920's, constituted major additions to the educational background on which kindergarten leaders drew to formulate subsequent programs. In an era demanding scientific management of schools, the kindergarten could not ignore some of the aspects promoting scientific determination of educational programs. As we shall see, connectionism, measurement devices, and curricular analysis all played a part in the new curricula.

[34] Cremin, p. 217.
[35] Edna Dean Baker, "The Balanced Program," *Proceedings of the Thirtieth Annual Meeting of the International Kindergarten Union,* 1923, p. 135.
[36] Patty Smith Hill, "The Project, An Adaptation of a Life Method of Thought and Action," *Proceedings of the Twenty-Eighth Annual Meeting of the International Kindergarten Union,* 1921, p. 155.

7
THE EVOLUTION OF THE KINDERGARTEN-PRIMARY UNIT

The links between the kindergarten and other influential movements in elementary education were not forged by theoretical discussions alone but also by some very practical considerations. During the first quarter of the twentieth century kindergarten enrollments almost tripled, and kindergartens increasingly became a part of public school systems. The healthy expansion of kindergartens and the absorption of private kindergartens into public systems accounted for the increase of publicly supported kindergartens.[1] Of course, part of this growth was due to swelling population in urban centers, which increased school attendance in general. As kindergartens became a part of public school systems, teachers could no longer maintain the self-worshipping aloofness so characteristic of earlier days; they were forced to promote continuity between the child's kindergarten experience and the first grade programs. During this period the kindergarten-primary gradually evolved as an educational unit.

PROVIDING CONTINUOUS EDUCATIONAL EXPERIENCE

The extension of the principles and philosophy of the kindergarten into the elementary school years had long been advocated

---

[1] Frank M. Phillips, *Statistics of Kindergartens—1923-1924,* United States Bureau of Education Bulletin, 1925, No. 20 (Washington, D.C.: Government Printing Office, 1925), 1; see also Mary Dabney Davis, *Nursery-Kindergarten-Primary Education in 1924-1926,* United States Bureau of Education Bulletin, 1927, No. 28 (Washington, D.C.: Government Printing Office, 1927), 15.

by ardent leaders of kindergarten education. They viewed kindergarten as a unique adventure in education that could bring about radical improvements in home and school life. Nina C. Vandewalker expressed it this way: "The kindergarten embodied a new ideal of education; it implied a different attitude toward childhood; it utilized for the child's development means other than traditional ones; it employed different methods of procedure." [2] Early leaders felt they were telling the world something new and, therefore, with flaming missionary zeal they hurled their ideals at ancient institutions. They expected motherhood to take on a new and higher significance; above all they expected the primary school to be transformed as the result of kindergarten influence.

Colonel Francis W. Parker shared the conviction that kindergarten principles should revolutionize education at all levels. He phrased his opinion in the idealistic rhetoric of the early period:

In the kindergarten is the seedcorn and germination of the New Education and the New Life. The seed has been planted, the buds and flowers are turned toward the sun: let not the chilling frost of traditional teaching blight and wither them. One and all of the true principles of education are applied in the kindergarten; these principles should be applied (simply changing the application to adapt it to different stages of growth) through all education, up to the gates of heaven. [3]

The theme that the primary school should continue to utilize the "universal" principles of growth employed in the kindergarten was a reiterated one.

Kindergarten Influence on the Primary School

The earliest comparisons, of course, were a protest against the rigidly formal 3 R's curriculum, which characterized the primary school. It must be recognized that, "Kindergartens were introduced into this country while the schools were steeped in the formalism

---

[2] Nina C. Vandewalker, "The History of the Kindergarten Influence in Elementary Education," *The Kindergarten and Its Relation to Elementary Education,* Sixth Yearbook of the National Society for the Study of Education, Vol. II (Bloomington, Illinois: Public School Publishing Co., 1907), 116.

[3] Francis W. Parker, *Talks on Teaching* (New York: E. L. Kellogg and Co., 1896), p. 157.

of academic education, and for years they [kindergartens] stood for an ideal which was opposed in spirit and practice to every tradition of the educational scheme." [4] Because of this lack of agreement in philosophy and practice, the experiences of children in kindergarten and first grade were decidedly discontinuous in nature. The spirit of cooperation and comradeship of the kindergarten contrasted sharply with the strictly individual recitations of the primary school. The kindergarten child's freedom to learn through play activities and his joy in constructive work accentuated the contrastingly rigid atmosphere of the primary school where drill and mastery of skills prevailed.

There is evidence that some of the hopes of early kindergartners for the transformation of the primary curriculum eventually were realized. The wide gap between the kindergarten and first grade narrowed as the progressive education movement changed the curriculum of both. The primary school of the 1920's was the complex product of many influences, and chief among the forces transforming the primary curriculum was the kindergarten. William Thomas Root, a professor of educational psychology at the University of Pittsburgh, expressed his delight in the change when he wrote, "I have been pleased and often amused to see one after another of the informal play methods of the kindergarten find their way into primary teaching." [5]

The leavening influence of kindergarten was credited with producing a "naturalized discipline" and a "deference to individual needs," in some first grade classrooms. Children were allowed greater freedom of movement as physical activity was accepted as a part of learning in early childhood. Some of the handwork and games of the kindergarten found their way into the first grade curriculum. New

[4] Margaret Giddings, "The Relative Advantages and Disadvantages of Having One Supervisor of Kindergarten and Primary Work in the City School System," *The Coordination of the Kindergarten and the Elementary School,* Seventh Yearbook of the National Society for the Study of Education, Part II (Bloomington, Illinois: Public School Publishing Co., 1908), 50.

[5] William Thomas Root, "Pre-First Grade Training," *U. S. Bureau of Education Kindergarten Circular,* No. 13 (Washington, D.C.: Government Printing Office, 1923), 7; see also the article previously cited by Vandewalker; and Samuel Chester Parker and Alice Temple, *Unified Kindergarten and First Grade Teaching* (Boston: Ginn and Co., 1925), p. 14.

materials that promoted freedom of expression became common in primary rooms. R. Freeman Butts has summarized the kindergarten's influence and placed it in historical perspective: "The kindergarten's emphasis upon development of the individual child's capacities through play activities, greater freedom of movement, and social attitudes of cooperation gradually helped to relieve the rigid discipline and formal atmosphere of the elementary school." [6]

Unification of Kindergarten–Primary Education

Not all educators felt that the curricular adjustment should be one way alone. Administrators began to inquire into the ways the kindergarten prepared the child for his primary school experience. Efficiency demanded a closer unification between these two levels; school administrators protested what they considered to be illogical breaks in children's education. [7]

There were some attempts to explain kindergarten work in terms of subsequent school organization. Dr. Jenny B. Merrill, Superintendent of Kindergartens in New York City, classified kindergarten experiences under the same headings as the course of study used for first grade: nature study, handwork, drawing, language, form and number, music, physical training, and moral training. Her reason for doing this was to facilitate explanations of kindergarten experience and coordination of kindergarten education with that of the primary school. [8] Later, Mary G. Waite, a specialist in kindergarten education at the U. S. Bureau of Education, traced the fundamental

---

[6] R. Freeman Butts, *A Cultural History of Western Education* (New York: McGraw-Hill Book Co., 1955), p. 492.

[7] Benjamin C. Gregory, "The Necessity of Continuity Between the Kindergarten and the Elementary School," *The Coordination of the Kindergarten and the Elementary School,* Seventh Yearbook of the National Society for the Study of Education, Part II (Bloomington, Illinois: Public School Publishing Co., 1908), 22-34.

[8] Jenny B. Merrill, "Plans of Work," *Proceedings of the Twelfth Annual Meeting of the International Kindergarten Union,* 1905, pp. 123-125. For a more detailed analysis of this approach by the same author see "Ways and Means of Securing Organic Continuity Between the Kindergarten and the Primary School in the Development of the Child," *The Coordination of the Kindergarten and the Elementary School,* Seventh Yearbook of the National Society for the Study of Education, Part II (Bloomington, Illinois: Public School Publishing Co., 1908), 7-21.

roots of primary subjects to typical kindergarten activities.[9] She explained how the kindergarten program promoted the ability to interpret symbols and stressed sequences of ideas and vocabulary growth, thus furnishing valuable preparation for learning to read. Actual counting of objects and measuring of materials formed the basis for more formalized arithmetic. In general, Mary Waite maintained that, "through furnishing vital experiences and helping the children to organize them and to relate them to their fundamental interests and previously established ideas, the kindergarten provides much of the preliminary material necessary for the teaching of the primary school arts." [10]

These explanations of the relationship between kindergarten and primary school learnings were not precise enough for certain administrators. Requests were made for the standardization of kindergarten practice in order to produce a more efficient continuity of learning. "A widespread desire to determine standards for kindergarten procedures," was noted among "superintendents, and their assistants, supervisors and teachers." [11] The demands that the kindergarten period be used efficiently to prepare children for first grade were insistent enough to yield protests. To view the kindergarten merely as a time of preparation for the more formal schooling to follow was to overlook the "serious danger that organization works to the advantage of system, but at the sacrifice of the boy and the girl," according to Professor J. L. Meriam of the University of Missouri.[12] William Root found value in kindergarten regardless of whether or not it helped in first grade work: "I would justify kindergarten for the brimming cup of simon-pure joy it brings to hundreds of thousands of children, and for the enrichment of concepts it brings

[9] Mary G. Waite, "How the Kindergarten Prepares Children for Primary Work," *U. S. Bureau of Education Kindergarten Circular*, No. 15 (Washington, D. C.: Government Printing Office, 1924).

[10] *Ibid.*, p. 6.

[11] Julia Wade Abbott, "Kindergarten Education 1918-1920," *U. S. Bureau of Education Bulletin 1921*, No. 19 (Washington, D. C.: Government Printing Office, 1921), 10.

[12] J. L. Meriam, "Practical Means of Unifying the Work of the Kindergarten and the Primary Grades," *Addresses and Journal of Proceedings of the National Educational Association*, 1916, p. 430.

to the vital job of living childhood exhuberantly and in all its fullness." [13]

Regardless of individual stands upon the merits of kindergarten as preparation for succeeding school years, there was a growing conviction that the period in a child's life between the ages of four and eight was psychologically one; therefore, no discontinuities in his educational experiences could be condoned. The "gap" that existed in practice stemmed not from children, whose interests were logical and connected, but from "teacher's conceptions of concepts and methods." [14] Therefore, to build an organically functioning bond between the kindergarten and public school systems, teachers of kindergarten and of primary grades needed a common background for work with children.

The assault upon the lack of continuity eventually took two forms: uniting the training of the kindergarten and the primary teacher, and designing curricula encompassing both the kindergarten and the first grade. Patty Hill believed that the kindergarten and primary teachers should know each other's problems and methods. "Until there exists this mutual insight and understanding," she stated, "we can neither expect intelligent cooperation between kindergarten and primary teachers, nor a bridging of the gulf between the kindergarten and the primary school." [15] That the place to work for unbroken continuity was in teacher training institutions was more than a theoretical proposition by the 1920's: it became a practical reality. It was from the most stimulating of these new centers, where educa-

[13] Root, p. 3.

[14] Stella Louise Wood, "The Unity of Aims and Principles of the Kindergarten and Early Grades," *Addresses and Journal of Proceedings of the National Education Association,* 1921, p. 464.

[15] Patty Smith Hill, "Some Conservative and Progressive Phases of Kindergarten Education," *The Kindergarten and Its Relation to Elementary Education,* Sixth Yearbook of the National Society for the Study of Education (Bloomington, Illinois: Public School Publishing Co., 1907), p. 84. For examples of other statements of this position see Bertha Payne, "How Can the Training of Kindergartners and Primary Teachers Contribute to Economy in Education of Children?" *The Coordination of the Kindergarten and the Elementary School,* Seventh Yearbook of the National Society for the Study of Education (Bloomington, Illinois: Public School Publishing Co., 1908), pp. 45-49.

tional programs included the instruction of teachers for work in both kindergarten and primary grades, that new curricula encompassing both educational levels emanated.

TRAINING KINDERGARTEN TEACHERS

Throughout the years of kindergarten expansion the demand for teachers exceeded the number available. Early kindergartens frequently enrolled large numbers of children, which the teacher managed by having an assistant whom she trained "on the spot." With the teacher herself assuming the responsibility for training assistants almost as soon as she began her own teaching, a mechanical transfer of methods and materials resulted, but at least a supply of workers was provided for the cause. In urban centers, special training schools were established by 1880 to spread ideas gleaned from Froebel's writings. Even here the task of mastering techniques in "kindergarten instrumentalities" was central; the prospective kindergartner learned the mother plays, manipulated gifts, prepared beauty forms, and followed innumerable sequences of folding, cutting, and sewing.

With the revision of the kindergarten curriculum, changes in teacher education were indicated. "Nice girls," trained in a few precise techniques, would no longer do. It was argued that teachers working with young children needed an extensive understanding of human development. Indeed, Hall maintained that the need for psychological knowledge "increased inversely with the age of the students." [16] Watson agreed, for he believed the kindergarten instructor had "the most difficult, and at the same time, the most responsible place in the scheme of education today." [17] The changing role of the teacher also demanded a broader professional and intellectual competence. Of the Froebelian program Patty Hill wrote, "No primary or elementary course of study in existence leaves so little to the initiative or judgment of the teacher." [18] But the newer programs made a

[16] G. Stanley Hall, "The Pedagogy of the Kindergarten," *Educational Problems,* I (New York: D. Appleton, 1911), 1.

[17] John B. Watson, "The Pre-Kindergarten Age—A Laboratory Study," *Proceedings of the Twenty-Sixth Annual Meeting of the International Kindergarten Union,* 1919, p. 41.

[18] Hill, "Conservative and Progressive Phases," in the Sixth Yearbook of the NSSE, p. 69.

curriculum maker of the teacher herself. A curriculum that was planned in advance only in very general terms called for a teacher with judgment, skill, and knowledge.

As kindergartens were added to the public school system the teacher's preparation came under the scrutiny of administrators. They found some kindergarten teachers unable to justify the experiences they provided for children. One young superintendent asked, "Why cannot kindergartners give a better reason for doing given things than that it is the kindergarten way?" [19] Obviously, the training of the kindergarten teacher needed to include an understanding of the basic principles upon which the program rested. Administrators began to insist that kindergarten teachers should meet the same certification standards required of all other teachers. The requirements of higher scholarship and a broader educational perspective made the course of study in the training school a vital topic in kindergarten circles. Granted that the preparation of kindergarten teachers would have to change, the direction of change needed to be determined. It was not just a matter of what should be included in training courses but where this training should take place. There were two alternatives: to broaden the scope of the program in private training schools, or to have kindergarten training become a part of normal schools and colleges. To strengthen their program special kindergarten training schools tried borrowing instructors from nearby universities.

In 1906 there were 137 private kindergarten training schools as opposed to 54 kindergarten departments in normal schools or colleges. That same year the "Conference of Training Teachers and Supervisors" held during the annual meeting of the International Kindergarten Union calculated practically all the advantages to be with the larger institution over the isolated training school. Courses in psychology and history of education, laboratory experiences in botany and zoology, an expanded library, the stimulus of other teachers—all these were listed as advantages the larger institution could provide. In 1920, when the available training schools were listed,

---

[19] Nina C. Vandewalker, "The Curriculum and Methods of the Kindergarten Training School," *Proceedings of the Tenth Annual Convention of the International Kindergarten Union,* 1903, p. 64.

the balance had changed; only 31 private kindergarten training schools remained while 109 were part of established normal schools or universities.[20]

The professionalization of education between the years 1890 and 1930 made it inevitable that the private training schools be swallowed up by normal schools, teachers colleges, and universities. During this period, normal schools were rapidly changed into teachers colleges, and there was an increasing growth of departments and schools of education at the university level. It was also a time of lengthening and differentiating educational curricula and of elevating them to the graduate level. Kindergarten training was drawn into this expansion of teacher education, and as kindergarten enrollments more than tripled between 1900-1930, the preparation of teachers for kindergarten and primary teaching became a major activity of colleges and universities.[21] The small private kindergarten training school could hardly compete economically or culturally with this spreading professionalism.

As kindergarten training was transferred to normal schools and colleges it was joined with the preparation of the primary teacher. Statistics accumulated by the U. S. Bureau of Education demonstrate the intensity of the drive for unification. Of the 39 state teacher training institutions that offered kindergarten courses in 1913, only one was listed as a kindergarten–primary course. Less than a decade later (1922), 60 of the 83 state colleges that gave some measure of kindergarten training designated the courses as combining kindergarten–primary instruction.[22] In a few more years 80 per cent of the teacher training institutions were reported as combining the prepara-

[20] These statistics are from addresses in the *Proceedings* of the International Kindergarten Union—the Thirteenth Annual Meeting, 1906, and the Twenty-Seventh Annual Meeting, 1920.

[21] Benjamin W. Frazier, "History of the Professional Education of Teachers in the United States," *U.S. Office of Education Bulletin, 1933*, No. 10, V (Washington, D.C.: Government Printing Office, 1933), p. 43. (The figures given here are 225,394 kindergarten pupils in 1900 and 717,899 in 1930.)

[22] Nina C. Vandewalker, "An Evaluation of Kindergarten-Primary Courses of Study in Teacher Training Institutions," *U. S. Bureau of Education Bulletin, 1924*, No. 3 (Washington, D. C.: Government Printing Office, 1924), 3.

tion of teachers at the two levels.[23] Thus, by 1930, the first major step in the unification of kindergarten–primary education had been at least nominally carried out; teachers were trained to understand and work with both kindergarten and primary grade children. The second major step toward unification, that of the development of new curricula designed for both educational levels, was essentially an outgrowth of the work in these newly established departments of kindergarten and primary education.

THE DEVELOPMENT OF CENTERS FOR CURRICULUM CHANGE

Two kindergarten departments at leading universities became the recognized centers for advanced study in kindergarten–primary education: one at Columbia University under the directorship of Patty Smith Hill, the other at the University of Chicago with Alice Temple as chairman. Both kindergarten specialists had their early kindergarten training under a teacher who was breaking with the Froebelian tradition; both found inspiration from the leaders of the educational scene and were conversant with the new theoretical ideas that appeared; each served at the head of newly established kindergarten–primary departments.

Patty Smith Hill

Shortly after James Earl Russell was made Dean of Teachers College in 1897, he drew to the institution a number of pedagogical pioneers who rapidly raised the youthful college to a place of leadership in education. Between 1899 and 1909 such notables as Thorndike, Dewey, Kilpatrick, and Frank McMurray joined the faculty, and their efforts helped to build a tradition "destined in two decades to make the college one of the primary forces in American educational thought and practice." [24] Alert to leadership at all educational levels, Dean Russell invited Patty Smith Hill first as a visiting lecturer in 1905 and then as a regular faculty member of Teachers College a year later.

[23] Davis, p. 2.
[24] Lawrence A. Cremin, David A. Shannon, Mary Evelyn Townsend, *A History of Teachers College, Columbia University* (New York: Columbia University Press, 1954), p. 49.

Her assignment was to introduce the new kindergarten procedures she had used in Louisville under the sponsorship of Anna Bryan. One of her first tasks was to alternate with Susan Blow in presenting a series of lectures on the kindergarten. Of these lectures Russell wrote, "It is to the lasting credit of Patty Hill that she dared meet the champion on her own ground and in fair combat won the victory." [25] Always a popular lecturer, Miss Hill earned an international reputation as people traveled from all over the globe to hear her. In these lectures she expressed her breadth of familiarity with the contemporary scene—she had studied with G. Stanley Hall, Francis Parker, and John Dewey; William Kilpatrick and Edward Thorndike were co-workers at Teachers College. Of all the forces acting upon her thinking, that of Thorndike is most evident in her proposed program—dramatic testimony to the influence of the growing scientism on the kindergarten. From her strategic position as head of the kindergarten–primary department at Teachers College she wielded a vast influence on the changing kindergarten curriculum. She was one of the first to promote the unification of kindergarten and first grade education. The period of Patty Hill's greatest impact on the kindergarten culminated with publication of *The Conduct Curriculum*.

Alice Temple

At the University of Chicago, Charles Judd had taken over the reins of Dewey as head of the School of Education. It was during his régime that Alice Temple was made chairman of the Kindergarten–Primary Department, leaving her position as principal of the Chicago Free Kindergarten Association to join the University faculty.[26] Her early training had been with Alice Putnam in Chicago, after which she had served as assistant, then supervising teacher, and finally principal of the Free Kindergarten Association. This was the kindergarten association that had been supervised by Anna Bryan after she had left Louisville and that maintained a close connection with the laboratory school at the University of Chicago.

---

[25] James Earl Russell, *Founding Teachers College* (New York: Bureau of Publication, Teachers College, Columbia University, 1937), p. 62.

[26] "Alice Temple," *Leaders in Education* (New York: Science Press, 1932), p. 916.

One has only to read Alice Temple's speeches and remarks to the International Kindergarten Union to recognize that the dominant impact upon her educational life was the thinking of John Dewey. Time and time again she restated the concepts of purposeful activity, of psychological continuity, and of the social nature of education as they applied to the kindergarten. Uncompromising in her standards of education for the young child, she presented her views with clarity.

Among Alice Temple's co-workers at the University of Chicago were Charles H. Judd and Franklin Bobbitt. Judd himself considered the University of Chicago laboratory school as a pioneer in the movement to coordinate the work in kindergarten and primary grades.[27] The unified kindergarten–primary organization was tested there for eleven years before recommended procedures were published in *Unified Kindergarten and First Grade Teaching.*[28]

[27] Charles H. Judd, "Introduction" in Samuel C. Parker and Alice Temple, *Unified Kindergarten and First Grade Teaching* (Boston: Ginn and Co. 1925), p. xiii.

[28] Alice Temple, "Preface," in *ibid.*, p. vi.

8
CURRICULAR INNOVATIONS
OF THE TWENTIES

From the various streams of change with their myriad cross-currents, a reconstructed kindergarten began to emerge. By 1925 Thorndike's S→R connectionist psychology, measuring devices, and Kilpatrick's project method had been added to Hall's child study information and Dewey's social organization as directive influences in curriculum design. The programs that resulted were a long way from the experimental attempts at revision in the early 1900's.

As university professors turned to "scientific study" of the kindergarten, they put their curricular recommendations into written form. By the early 1920's the competing colleges of education presented their proposals for kindergarten programs. In commenting on the leadership of Patty Smith Hill and Alice Temple, Lucy Gage, an assistant professor at George Peabody College, stated, "To these women scientific criticism continues to be an open door to further progress for the kindergarten." [1]

New publications employed differing terms depending upon the aspect of the larger educational scene to which priority was given. Stimulus-response psychology, which emphasized the plasticity of the child, was the foundation of the curriculum developed at Teachers College and set forth in *A Conduct Curriculum for Kindergarten and First Grade* compiled by teachers at the Horace Mann School. *Unified Kindergarten and First Grade Teaching,* written jointly by

---

[1] Lucy Gage, "Kindergarten Progress During the Past Twenty-Five Years," *Journal of Proceedings and Addresses of the National Education Association,* 1925, p. 481.

Alice Temple and Samuel Chester Parker, two faculty members of the University of Chicago, suggested procedures that reflected the emphasis on "scientific" curriculum building through analysis of its components.

Other books echoed the trends toward placing behavioral outcomes at the core of the kindergarten program and developing standards of achievement.[2] But not all kindergarten programs reflected the changed view of the child that behaviorism entailed; there is evidence that the dynamic nature of the child was exalted as extensive opportunities for free play were provided for him.[3]

A CURRICULUM FOR BEHAVIORAL CHANGE

To comprehend fully the conduct curriculum as it was presented in 1923, one needs an understanding of the evolution of the program. Charged with the responsibility of bringing newer kindergarten practices to Teachers College, Patty Hill began immediately to sponsor program revision. As director of the department of kindergarten and first grade education she supervised experimentation at Speyer School in New York City and later at Horace Mann School, where innovations were gradually introduced to test their effectiveness.[4] Pragmatic in nature, the studies brought about a patient overhauling of all procedures, with each part of the program gradually moving away from idealistic antecedents.

Evolution of the Conduct Curriculum

It was at Speyer School that the Patty Hill blocks were developed and tested over a period of twelve years. They represented a complete change from the blocks in the Froebelian gifts. The new

[2] See, for example, Staff of the Training School of the Southern Branch of the University of Los Angeles, *An Activity Curriculum for Kindergarten and the Primary Grades* (San Francisco: Harr Wagner Publishing Co., 1924); Margaret Canty, *et al.* (compilers), *Kindergarten Activities* (Milwaukee: Board of School Directors, 1925).

[3] Lalla Pickett and Duralde Boren, *Early Childhood Education* (Yonkers-on-Hudson, New York: World Book Co., 1925).

[4] Patty Smith Hill, "Introduction" in Agnes Burke, *et al.*, *A Conduct Curriculum for the Kindergarten and First Grade* (New York: Charles Scribner's Sons, 1923), p. xi.

blocks were large enough for children to erect structures that they could get into—a playhouse, a store, or a post office. The type of building created depended on the children's interest and purpose at the time. Over twelve years of testing and observing children's reactions went into the development of the Patty Hill blocks. A large variety of housekeeping toys and tools, a sandbox, large gymnastic apparatus, and materials for experimentation in science were among the play materials utilized in the kindergarten.[5] New songs were written that were considered to be more childlike, and rhythmic procedures were created that involved no dictation of steps.[6]

But to Patty Hill these changes in materials and methods were transcended by attempts to apply "the principles of democracy to school organization." She believed children could be trained in self-government by having wide opportunities "for learning from each other, and through their own experience." This was especially true when children's experiences were initiated by "their own purposes and plans." To achieve this it was necessary "to work out a technique of teaching, built upon a new conception of the teacher as a guide rather than a dictator." [7] As children were put into a classroom where greater freedom prevailed, teachers began to be more aware of the natural characteristics of growing children. At Speyer School they observed small, spontaneous groups of children drawn together by some shared interest. Changes in classroom organization furnished evidence that children were indeed capable of acquiring the techniques of democratic living; observers were especially pleased to find that increasing self-government on the part of the child decreased the necessity of teacher-administered discipline.

When John Dewey and his daughter Evelyn published a survey of promising educational practices in 1915, they found the Hill kindergarten, which was then housed in the Horace Mann School at Teachers College, to be in harmony with the broad stream of reform

---

[5] Charlotte G. Garrison, *Permanent Play Materials for Children* (New York: Scribners, 1926). (This book and the next reference were part of a Series on Childhood Education edited by Patty Smith Hill.)

[6] Alice G. Thorn, *Music for Young Children* (New York: Scribners, 1929).

[7] Hill, "Introduction" in *A Conduct Curriculum*, p. xi.

in education.[8] The kindergarten as a laboratory of democratic citizenship was in keeping with Dewey's pragmatic policy of expanding the school's social responsibility. He condoned efforts to discover which of the aimless activities of children could be used as points of departure for ends of recognizable worth. And, of course, the elevation of the child's own purposes coincided with one of his basic tenets.

Just about the time Dewey lauded the attempts to put democratic principles into operation in the classroom, experimentation in the Teachers College kindergarten moved into a direction dominated by connectionist psychology. The new experimentation involved defining desired behavioral changes and suggesting the means for their attainment. The ostensible reason for moving in this direction was to alert educators to the learning possibilities inherent in a flexibly organized kindergarten. Miss Hill wrote, "Even in 1915 this form of social organization impressed the more conservative pedagogical minds as radical and wasteful." [9] The mere enthusiasm of those who were conducting the experiment was not convincing to others, so, in search of evidence to support their program, teachers recorded what they considered to be typical outcomes in individual and group behavior. This was the beginning of translating the program into the specifics of habit formation. The process involved a precise definition of kindergarten objectives in order to provide the teacher with "a clearer consciousness of what she and the children must seek and achieve," [10] which led the experimenters directly into connectionist psychology.

Habit Formation as the Goal of Education

Insistence on the importance of habit formation in the kindergarten was certainly not an innovation. As we have seen, Thorndike had interpreted the meaning of behaviorist psychology for the formation of concrete habits as early as 1903. Five years later, Earl Barnes reinforced this conception of learning when he stated, "The directive work of the kindergarten, so far as guiding activity is concerned, must

---

[8] John and Evelyn Dewey, *Schools of Tomorrow* (New York: E. P. Dutton, 1915), pp. 110-116.
[9] Hill, "Introduction," in *A Conduct Curriculum*, p. xii.
[10] *Ibid.*, p. xix.

be mainly in the direction of organizing the tyrannical but necessary reflexes we call habits." [11] At the Ethical Culture School in New York City an outline for the study of habits was used as the basis of a kindergarten training course for normal students in 1911. The automatizing of certain forms of behavior recommended in this outline was believed to contribute to the economy of class procedure and future efficiency in the lives of children. It was assumed that when children learned to follow the leader in line, to wait quietly while material was distributed, or never to interrupt others, time would be freed for more purely expressional work. [12]

But it was at Teachers College, under the direction of Patty Hill, that the import of habit formation for the structure of the curriculum was pushed to its ultimate conclusions. As the shaping of specific habits of behavior became the problem under consistent study, the kindergarten curriculum was inevitably affected by the drive for an efficiently scientific education. As it developed, the inventory of habits became not only a set of kindergarten goals but a means of measuring change in behavior, however, the building of an inventory of habits that could be stated in measurable form was not readily accomplished. The captions on early record sheets developed at Teachers College proved too vague and indefinite to warrant attempts at scientific measurement. The services of Dr. Agnes L. Rogers of Goucher College were secured to direct the process of breaking up the large categories into the more specific abilities and habits involved. The first product of the study was a "Habit Inventory" that included such sample items as "responds instantly to signals," "does not give up easily," "comprehends when first addressed," and "ties shoe strings." [13]

The next step was using the "Habit Inventory" for curriculum reconstruction beginning with the analysis of the possible stimulus-

[11] Earl Barnes, 'Fundamental Factors in the Making of a Kindergarten Curriculum," *Journal of Proceedings and Addresses of the National Education Association,* 1908, p. 505. (Earl Barnes was a specialist in Child Development at Leland Stanford University and later a lecturer on education at Philadelphia, Pennsylvania.)

[12] Catherine J. Tracy, "Outline for the Study of Habits," *Kindergarten Review,* XXII (December, 1911), 238-241.

[13] Agnes L. Rogers, *A Tentative Inventory of Habits* (New York: Bureau of Publications, Teachers College, Columbia University, 1922).

situations that would elicit the desired responses. Taking seriously Thorndike's dictum that "the task of education is to make changes in human beings," [14] the investigators were as concerned with the *process* of change as with the desired outcomes. They had no desire to use arbitrary, verbal insistence to promote the establishment of certain modes of conduct. They did expect, however, that as the appropriate social situation was provided, the inevitable response would be a "changed nervous system which leads to habits of behavior, finally culminating in character." [15] *A Conduct Curriculum* resulted from uniting the desired outcomes with what were considered to be appropriate stimulus situations. Written with a singleness of purpose, this small volume presented the curriculum in behaviorist terms.

The actual compilation of the stimulus experiences and the desired responses was the work of kindergarten and first grade teachers at Horace Mann School, who acknowledged Professor Hill as the initiator of the task. In the fifteen-page introduction Patty Hill explained the origin and rationale of the curriculum. The organizing foci of the curriculum were the environmental situations that were carefully selected to elicit desired responses and to provide the practice necessary for reinforcing the bond. Typical activities were listed around such headings as sandplay, blockbuilding, woodworking, hygiene, safety, music, or language. This was accompanied by a parallel list of prescribed changes in thought, feeling, and conduct. An excerpt from the list of activities and desirable changes through paper work will illustrate the specificity of the designated outcomes.

PAPERWORK [16]

Typical Activities	Desirable Changes in Thought, Feeling, and Conduct.
	Group I
Cutting paper.	Pleasure in activity. Learning how to use scissors.

[14] Edward L. Thorndike, "Measurement in Education," *Teachers College Record*, XXII (November, 1921), 371.

[15] Hill, "Introduction" in *A Conduct Curriculum*, p. xvi.

[16] Agnes Burke, *et al.*, *A Conduct Curriculum for the Kindergarten and First Grade* (New York: Charles Scribner's Sons, 1923), 44-45.

Group II

Cutting paper— (experimental).

Folding paper— (experimental).

Pasting—interest in using paste rather than fastening pieces of paper together.

Pasting pictures.

Cutting out pictures.

Cutting paper into small pieces and pasting on sheets of paper.

Making paper flowers.

Making ornaments for Christmas tree.

Making baskets, paper hats, caps, wreaths, valentines, invitations, box wagons, and pinwheels.

Learning:
to get out and put away materials,
to hand scissors to another person,
to cut,
to carry scissors properly,
to paste edges of paper securely—using right amount of paste,
to fold and crease,
to take care of scraps and wipe off tables.

Pleasure in activity and in using product.

Group III

Further experiment with paper, paste, and scissors, usually with the idea of making some definite thing.

Making scrapbooks, houses— cutting windows and doors, wreaths, crowns, paperdolls, dresses, fairy wings, invitations, place cards, cards for special days, fans, paper cups, etc.

Same as Group II, also learning:
to put paper products where they will not be crushed,
to measure and cut papers in right proportions,
to be critical of product,
to find out how and where to get help.

Pleasure in originating.

Pleasure in making things to wear.

First Grade

Making most of things made by Group III.

Repeating unit of design of cut paper for special decoration.

Spontaneous cutting and folding paper leading to making stencils.

Pleasure in personal adornment.

Learning much better technique and more detail in planning.

Beginning to show decided originality in making designs.

Making pictures of cut paper,
  animals, scenes, peep shows,
  etc.
Making paperdolls and dressing
  them.

Through specific directions the "Habit Inventory" became not merely an appendix to the curriculum but a gradual transformer of it. Miss Hill wrote that as the inventory was used, supervisors and classroom teachers "began to think of all instruction in terms of desirable changes in thought, feeling or conduct; in other words, in terms of changed behavior due to a changed nervous system." [17] She believed it was natural to appreciate changes in behavior first in the realm of moral and social conduct, but that ultimately the study must include all types of responses. An analysis of the desired traits listed in the *Conduct Curriculum* shows them to be heavily weighted on the side of social and moral behavior. Each area of the curriculum refers to conduct reflecting sharing, responsibility, cooperation, polite responses, and respect for people and supplies. Growing dexterity and skill in the manipulation of tools and materials was another recurring value.

Subject Matter in the Curriculum

Perhaps the preoccupation with social conduct helped to minimize the content in the curriculum that would result in increased factual knowledge. Suggested social studies activities were related to holidays: Columbus Day, Halloween, Election Day, and the like. Nature study was quite closely related to seasonal changes. Even many of the explicitly stated desired outcomes for these activities were social or emotional rather than cognitive in nature. No rationale was presented for the selection of curricular content related to specific knowledge. The identification of materials for children's use seemed to outweigh a concern for content. As many of the stimuli to improved behavior were materials (i.e. sand, blocks, paint, clay, wood), such materials assumed a major role in curriculum building.

[17] Hill, "Introduction," in *A Conduct Curriculum*, p. xiv.

Unification of Kindergarten and First Grade

Continuity was a major objective of the *Conduct Curriculum's* program for both kindergarten and first grade. Typical activities were listed for kindergarten children of three different age levels (two and one-half to four years, four to five years, and five to six years of age) and for first graders. For the youngest, group experiences were simple and manipulative, while the desired behavioral changes were pictured at initial stages of development. Continuous growth was postulated until first grade children were expected to engage in activities demanding greater cooperation and increased skill. Many of the same experiences were suggested for children of all ages with the expectation that children's interests, skill, and participation would attain new levels of growth. Reading, writing, and number work were gradually added with the kindergarten child participating in a few pre-reading activities: repeating verses, telling stories, using signs in block building, or recognizing pictures and names in books. The first grade children were expected to grow gradually into reading in books through chart stories about daily experiences.

Assessment of the Conduct Curriculum

A propelling force behind the compiling of this curriculum was the idea that kindergarten teachers needed a practical guide for putting the reconstructed program into daily practice. The writers endeavored to present a curriculum that "a teacher of average ability and training could use," [18] with the assumption that precisely designated goals would clarify the teacher's task.

In many ways the Hill program appeared to reflect John Dewey's theories with an emphasis upon social interaction and problem solving. But, as habit formation came to dominate curricular plans, individual and group problem solving became a means for instilling prescribed conduct through experiences that had meaning for children. Such stress upon behavioral goals with fixed values for all children is out of line with Dewey's reconstruction philosophy. It is clear that by the time the *Conduct Curriculum* was published the emphasis was placed on Thorndike's psychology.

[18] "New Studies in Education," Including a Review of *A Conduct Curriculum*, unsigned, *Teachers College Record*, XXV (May, 1924), 246.

The incompatibility of elevating a fixed set of habits as goals of the kindergarten program with expounding the concept of individual purpose and psychological continuity of growth apparently went unrecognized by those closely involved in the experimentation. Some outspoken critics feared, however, that a curriculum concentrated on habit formation and governed by set goals would lead to stereotyped and rigid teaching. Agnes DeLima expressed the possibility of the *Conduct Curriculum's* becoming not a "means of wider freedom but of more repression," shortly after its publication.[19] Kilpatrick was equally skeptical about the use of a list of trait objectives.[20] The great danger, he argued, was that teachers starting with a list of traits would be too easily deflected from the primary objective of education—the reconstruction of experience.

A Conduct Curriculum for the Kindergarten and First Grade, which appeared to be the inevitable result of the demand for a curriculum wedded to the scientific movement, was referred to extensively in contemporary kindergarten publications. One measure of the impact of this curriculum upon succeeding kindergarten programs is to be found in records and reports still in use. Items on present day kindergarten report cards are very similar to those on the habit inventory.

SYSTEMATIC CURRICULUM BUILDING

In contrast to the brief, direct *Conduct Curriculum,* the kindergarten publication from the University of Chicago, *Unified Kindergarten and First Grade Teaching,* was the most inclusive and monumental of the decade. Patty Smith Hill considered it encyclopedic in scope, yet scientific in its methods and materials.[21] The authors, Samuel Chester Parker and Alice Temple, demonstrated a

---

[19] Agnes DeLima, *Our Enemy the Child* (New York: New Republic, 1926), p. 133.

[20] William H. Kilpatrick, "How Shall Early Education Conceive Its Objectives?" *Childhood Education,* II (September, 1925), 12.

[21] Patty Smith Hill, review of *Unified Kindergarten and First Grade Teaching,* in *Childhood Education,* II (March, 1926), 352-353. The same opinion was expressed by Winifred E. Bain, *An Analytical Study of Teaching in the Nursery School, Kindergarten and First Grade* (New York: Bureau of Publication, Teachers College, Columbia University, 1928), p. 11.

breadth of understanding both of contemporary educational thought and of the complexity of teaching and learning. They pictured the education of the young child as embracing a variety of learning processes: problem solving, skill development, imitative activities, habit formation, and expressive acts.

Scientific Basis for the Curriculum

One suspects that Samuel Parker and Alice Temple were influenced by the measurement movement and by the experimental work at Teachers College. A discussion of the "Inventory of Habits" was included in the chapter on "Civic-Moral Ideals and Habits," although the kindergarten teachers in the University Elementary School at Chicago devised their own form for recording the progress of children according to such attributes as adaptability, leadership, inquisitiveness, or responsibility.[22] These were the years under the influence of Charles Judd at the University of Chicago, years when efficiency was a highly prized attribute of any educational plan. The respect for Thorndike's psychology was such that early childhood educators could hardly offer a curriculum that ran counter to it.

While Parker and Temple were influenced by the measurement movement and habit inventories, the emphasis given in their book to the scientific curriculum building of Bobbitt and Charters constitutes its unique link to the general efforts to build a science of education. A conscious effort was made to determine the components of the curriculum and to clarify the bases on which curricular decisions were made: goals were identified, the selection of content discussed, and the appropriate experiences illustrated. Objectives, Parker and Temple maintained, were both individual and social and as such were not incompatible for, "it [could] be shown that almost every feature of social life for which it is necessary to prepare children corresponds to certain strong interests which they possess by nature." [23] The formula for objectives was derived partly from Herbert Spencer's broad social goals—for example, good health, and the harmless enjoyment of leisure—and partly from Thorndike's spe-

---

[22] Samuel Chester Parker and Alice Temple, *Unified Kindergarten and First Grade Teaching* (Boston: Ginn and Co., 1925), pp. 424-25.
[23] *Ibid.*, p. 32.

cifications—skills, habits, ideals, and interests. Thus the unified program was planned to advance training for recreational activities, which included games and festivals, music and literature, as well as the skills of reading and number work.

Content for Kindergarten Classes

Information and understanding were given a prominent place in the curriculum plans of Parker and Temple to counteract the neglect of these goals, which the authors believed existed in early childhood education. They expected children's lives to be definitely enriched by knowledge, though they realized that many kindergartners "maintained that the information which kindergarten pupils acquire is of no importance so long as they are enjoying themselves and are being given practice in thinking, expression, etc." [24] Content was essentially derived from the study of social life, which might include such aspects of community life as the grocery store, the post office, or the railroad station—thus remaining close to Dewey's idea of the reconstruction of experience. First-hand experiences with nature were also recommended.

After the abandonment of the Froebelian program the problem of the selection of experiences for kindergarten children continued to plague kindergartners. Patty Hill had avoided the issue by putting her faith in prepared materials and in situations to stimulate learning. Parker and Temple, however, developed a rationale for the selection of topics and activities, their selective criteria were similar to the rules designated by Charters in his book published ten years earlier. Three rules were proposed: "(1) build curriculum around important, well-defined social needs; (2) adapt the curriculum to pupil maturity; (3) select topics and activities having the largest relative values." [25] The writers illustrated the use of these criteria in selecting experiences for kindergarten children in the laboratory school at the University of Chicago. Reading, writing, arithmetic, and spelling were categorized as essential social skills and were then examined to determine their appropriateness to the developmental level of the kindergarten child. Handwriting was given little place in

24 *Ibid.,* p. 38.
25 *Ibid.,* p. 51.

the kindergarten program because of the young child's lack of muscular coordination. For kindergarten children who had achieved a mental age of six years, however, reading was found quite in keeping with their delight in nursery rhymes and stories. The third principle of relative value was illustrated in social studies material; since the organ grinder or balloon man played a minor part in community life, only a small place could be accorded to their work in the school program.

Although earlier she had been the exponent of purposeful activity, at this time Alice Temple did not stand for individual need as the guiding principle in the selection of problems. She joined Parker in stating forcefully, "We do not believe in the extreme contention that the pupil's felt need is the most important factor in curriculum making." [26] While they considered interest to be the basis of economical learning, they nevertheless concluded with Thorndike that the teacher could decide what was to be learned and then activate interest. Here again, these contentions seem to have stemmed as a protest against a "do-as-you-please" kindergarten curriculum. Writing a little later, Alice Temple protested that teachers were justified in planning at least the outline of a course of study in advance so long as specific experiences were then selected and organized with reference to the children concerned.

The Complexity of Curriculum Planning

Parker and Temple expected both habit formation and problem solving to be incorporated into one curriculum plan; they also proposed to have both a psychological continuity of growth and systematic sequences of learning skills as integral parts of the program. An understanding of social life might well progress around pupil-initiated projects, but they believed systematic sequences of instruction to be requisite for growth in reading and arithmetic.

In the opinion of these authors, curriculum planning was further complicated, by the need to provide for differences in individual capacity. The suggested practical provisions for differentiated instruction ranged from homogeneous grouping to supplementary assignments for gifted pupils. Toward the end of the year, some of

[26] *Ibid.*, fn. p. 56.

the more mature kindergarten children in the laboratory school at the University of Chicago were grouped to begin reading instruction, a procedure made possible because there were two teachers for the class of forty children.

Effective education, as outlined by Parker and Temple, demanded a balance between a number of complex elements. In order to determine the amount and direction of various parts of the curriculum there was a need for more "mathematically precise, scientific measures of educational objectives and learning processes." [27] Unification of work in the kindergarten and first grade was carefully explained and promoted. The general atmosphere of the room was to be free, informal, and homelike at both levels.[28] The theme of community life prevailed in order to promote a gradual, but parallel, advance in children's power to use ideas and to develop skills.

Effect of This Publication

The theoretical nature of the book was mitigated by many illustrative records of classroom experiences, but no simple, direct answer was presented to the teacher in order to solve her problems, rather, it was implied that each teacher must make many curricular decisions independently on the basis of the underlying principles presented. The impact of this book is difficult to assess. One finds it referred to sparingly in other kindergarten literature, and some of its precise recommendations found little general acceptance. By the thirties, as we shall see, kindergarten children were increasingly viewed as a homogeneous group. There is no evidence that children in other kindergartens were grouped for reading instruction on the basis of mental age or any other criteria. The recognition given to individual differences was apparently not shared by other kindergarten leaders. Perhaps the very theoretical nature of Parker and Temple's recommendations made them difficult for a kindergarten teacher to follow in practice. Perhaps, also, the prevailing concern for conduct goals and their measurement made this aspect of the book the one most frequently selected for discussion.

[27] *Ibid.,* p. 592.
[28] *Ibid.,* p. 559. See also: Alice Temple, "The Kindergarten-Primary Unit," *Elementary School Journal,* XX (March, 1920), pp. 498-509.

Read with retrospective insight, the book impresses the reader by its evident recognition of the multi-dimensional aspects of learning and by its grasp of the diversity of learners' capabilities and needs. One can only speculate whether, if the emphasis of the authors on the importance of intellectual development in the early years had found more followers, it might have prevented some of the dilemmas of the kindergarten curriculum today.

FREE PLAY AND PROJECTS

The two major efforts to promote a reconstructed curriculum for kindergarten and first grade were by no means the only publications of the early twenties. Vying with the scientific spirit, which emphasized behaviorism and a means-end relationship between goals and procedures, was Kilpatrick's project method as a way of organizing the kindergarten curriculum. Illustrative projects were proposed and described in a number of kindergarten publications.

The Project Method

Kindergarten teachers of the Milwaukee Public Schools compiled a volume setting forth the projects carried out in various schools of their system.[29] According to Lalla Pickett and Duralde Boren, writing as members of the East Texas State Normal College, projects were accepted as an integral part of the kindergarten curriculum, but only as a group problem was expanded from an individual or small group interest.[30] The term "activities' was given to what were equivalent to projects in *An Activity Curriculum,* a product of the staff of the training school of the Southern Branch of the University of California.[31]

The term "project" was given a great range of interpretation in these writings, from a loose equating of a project with any ex-

[29] Margaret Canty, Joanna A. Hannon, and Grace M. Campbell (eds.), *Kindergarten Activities* (Milwaukee: Board of School Directors, 1925), pp. 65-130.

[30] Lalla H. Pickett and Duralde Boren, *Early Childhood Education* (New York: World Book Co., 1925), pp. 73-109.

[31] Staff of the Training School of the Southern Branch of the University of California, *An Activity Curriculum for Kindergarten and the First Grade* (San Francisco: Harr Wagner Publishing Co., 1924).

perience demanding activity on the part of the child to one requiring that the purposes and plans be those of the children and not of the teacher. It is clear that in *An Activity Curriculum* and in *Kindergarten Activities* projects were intended to be the means for establishing habits of accomplishment, improving skills, and enriching the child's accumulation of knowledge. The trends toward scientific efficiency were apparent in the demands for well-developed habits, for standards of promotion, and for the measurement of outcomes. The designation of specific learnings and precise goals for all children drew the project method away from Kilpatrick's own definition, which set "wholehearted purposive activity" at the heart of his plan. The similarity of described projects is striking and invariably weighted on the side of holiday and seasonal activities.[32] One suspects that the point made by Kilpatrick was not captured in many kindergarten project curricula and that teachers were insensitive to the fact that, as kindergarten projects became stereotyped and similar throughout the country, there was little chance for original purposive action on the part of the child.

Free Play

Closer to Kilpatrick's notion of projects originating from the child's purposive acts were those described in the program from the East Texas State Normal School.[33] Knowledge and skills entered the program only as they enhanced the meaning of children's play life or carried projects to a successful completion. The emphasis in this curriculum was really on the child's unique capacities for construction and expression with little emphasis given to standards of achievement.

Actually, this program could be considered the logical successor to the earlier free play program sponsored by Frederick Burk in California. Although the proponents of the earlier program felt called upon to justify free play in the recess period, it had now been elevated to the most significant period of the day. Moreover, this particular free play curriculum suggested the possibility of extending freedom

---

[32] See for example: "An Easter Sale," and "Giving a Thanksgiving Party," in *An Activity Curriculum*, pp. 53-56, 87-89.

[33] Pickett and Boren, pp. 73-109.

of choice throughout the entire morning so that a child vitally interested in a personal project might work on it as long as he chose. He then joined group activities only as they drew his interest. As friend, guide, and counselor to "the small, active busybodies in her care," the teacher was "not in the schoolroom to tell the child what he needs to know, but to help him to discover these things for himself." [34] Originality and initiative were qualities highly regarded in this program. The children responded to the opportunities for self-selection and self-direction: they moved to rhythmic stimuli in their own way; drew pictures to represent their own thought images; told stories to give their thoughts verbal expression. As this curriculum placed such major emphasis on children's impulses and interests it may have been one of those considered lacking in direction to the point where it permitted planlessness, recalcitrance, and chaos to pass for spontaneity, individuality, and education.

As Kilpatrick continually reiterated that project teaching demanded that the purposes and plans must be derived from children and not from teachers, he shifted the balance of education to a child-centered emphasis. One suspects, however, that much of the confusion in utilizing the project method at the kindergarten level stemmed from a failure to grasp Kilpatrick's intent and from an unclarified view of the nature of the child.

The Nature of the Child

We can know the kindergartners' views on this subject only from the programs formulated by them for they did not write directly in these fundamental terms. Nor were their curricula clearly distinguished by competing views, for they characteristically contained elements of more than one perspective. On the one hand they insisted on viewing the child as an inherently active being with natural tendencies to construct, to investigate, to create, and to communicate with others. The development of these individual impulses was expected to result from the interaction of the child with his cultural environment. The individual, as well as all other living organisms, was in continual interactive adjustment with his surroundings. Individuality was a product of the human organism's participation in

[34] *Ibid.*, p. 14.

a social situation; therefore, education must provide those social situations most conducive to self-development.

Interwoven with this essentially Deweyan stance were the assumptions that the primary impulses to behavior came from physiological sources. This resulted in thinking of the child as a response mechanism subservient to the control of selected stimuli. Basic to this view was the emphasis upon the plasticity of the individual, which connoted his more passive or receptive role in the acquisition of responses. The mingling of these two views of child nature and learning resulted, of course, from the kindergartners' ready application of new scientific thinking to the solution of their curricular problems. In their haste to derive clues for new practices from available disciplines they seldom took time to sort out disparate beliefs.

THE RECONSTRUCTED KINDERGARTEN PROGRAM

In spite of the differing rationales one suspects that by the end of the first quarter of the twentieth century the reconstructed kindergarten programs were startlingly similar in actual practice. Several forces tended to mold a fairly homogeneous program, for example, the basic assumption that the child's natural proclivity for play was the perfect agency for learning at this stage of development continued to undergird all kindergarten programs.

The Needs of Early Childhood

The young child's developmental characteristics and interests were considered to be the point of departure for much curriculum planning and were recognized in a number of ways.[35] If child study had not provided a wealth of answers for deciding what should be

[35] For some of these ways see: Nina C. Vandewalker, "The Kindergarten Curriculum as Modified by Modern Educational Thought," *Proceedings and Addresses of the National Education Association,* 1919, pp. 171-175; Edna Dean Baker, "The Balanced Program," *Proceedings of the Thirtieth Annual Meeting of the International Kindergarten Union,* 1923, pp. 131-137; "The Kindergarten in Relation to Preschool and Parental Education," in Guy Whipple (ed.), *Preschool and Parental Education,* Twenty-Eighth Yearbook of the National Society for the Study of Education, Part I (Bloomington, Illinois: Public School Publishing Co., 1929), 252.

done in kindergarten, it at least demonstrated some of the kinds of learning within the capabilities of the young child. The child's interests and background experiences were considered in selecting and offering materials and projects. Young children's natural love of manipulating and experimenting with objects was given due recognition.

A concern for proper health, so lacking in early kindergarten programs, was now evidenced in many aspects of curriculum planning. Diet, rest, cleanliness, and muscular development were duly provided for as a healthy body was recognized as essential for sound development. Quiet times were scheduled to break the strain of demanding and challenging play. Short periods were provided for stories, singing, and conversation in order to keep them within the child's ability to pay attention and to sit quietly. A mid-morning lunch and a rest period were part of the plans to maintain healthful conditions and maximize growth.[36]

The core of the new kindergarten program was the work–play period. This was a sizeable portion of the kindergarten day, characterized by individual freedom, during which the child used available materials to fulfill his own interests, to work out a designated problem through his own efforts, and to carry out projects. Ample opportunity was provided for a child to engage in expressional activities in a manner consistent with his own stage of development.

Guiding Behavior

By 1925 the major battle over the teacher's function was settled, at least in theory. No longer was she described as the director of each movement or product of the child; the revolt against direct teacher control had been effective. But though the suggested regime was less rigid and the teacher's control less direct, the teacher did not abdicate her authority. Control assumed a different form; it was asserted by careful manipulation of the environment and by the quiet reinforcement of norms of behavior.

While free social interaction and democratic procedures continued to be advocated as a part of classroom organization, the

[36] See programs specified in: Hill, *A Conduct Curriculum,* p. 9; Parker and Temple, *Unified Kindergarten and First Grade Teaching,* pp. 110-111; Pickett and Boren, p. 110; *Preschool and Parental Education,* pp. 253-256.

reasons for their recommendation moved away from Dewey's basic intent of using democratic procedures to promote skills in problem solving that would eventually enable individuals to evaluate and work in a changing society. In the reconstructed program, the freer organization was utilized primarily to inculcate prescribed attitudes and behavior in an environment interesting to the children. Confidence was placed in the kindergartners' ability to influence child behavior. It is clear that while leaders of experimental programs still held to many of Dewey's tenets, Thorndike's psychology held the highest priority in designing the program.

Standardized Programs

One element that encouraged standardization of the curriculum was the similarity of equipment and materials found in all kindergartens: housekeeping equipment in the doll corner, tools and a workbench for construction, large blocks for building, an easel and paints, clay and crayons for expression.[37] These materials took on great significance as they constituted stimulus centers for the promotion of behavioral goals. By 1920 the appearance of the progressive kindergarten had changed completely from the days of the dictated Froebelian program. Toys were no longer locked away to be doled out by the teacher, the formal tables with one-inch grooves disappeared, large equipment for vigorous activity—see-saws, slides, and swings—were frequently used indoors. A second generalized element producing program conformity was the similarity of content material in kindergarten curricula. Holidays and seasonal activities formed the one consistent choice of subject matter for discussion and for projects. The home, the school, the grocery store, and other community enterprises found in the child's social environment formed the other major source.

Unification of Programs

The over-arching concern to provide a curriculum fostering continuous growth in the early childhood years found expression in

[37] Jean Lee Hunt, *A Catalogue of Play Equipment* (New York: Bureau of Educational Experiments, 1918); Hill, *A Conduct Curriculum,* pp. 7-8; Parker and Temple, pp. 83-94. (This is apparent also in the illustrations in books on kindergarten curricula.)

the programs that were presented in the 1920's. Recommendations were based upon the informal social organization of the kindergarten. In the first grade, the program was an extension of the kindergarten with the gradual addition of more skill development in reading, writing, and arithmetic. First grade programs, previously academically utilitarian, were modified as programs that combined "the development of skills in 'tool' and 'graphic' subjects with the development of children's social and intellectual behavior," and provided "adequate opportunities for creative expression of children's interests." [38]

Changing Emphasis on Social Reform

As kindergartens originally supported by individual philanthropy became a part of public school systems, the zeal to elevate the community by starting the young child on the "right path in life" declined. The major purpose of many free kindergarten associations was fulfilled as they helped to establish kindergarten as a part of the educational system in their community. Ostensibly the behaviorist curricula were closest to the character training, which gave impetus to the earlier philanthropic kindergartens. The goal of character training remained unchanged; however, the means for achieving it differed. The proliferation of precise habits, selected not only as essentials for democratic living but also as the Christian ethics of the teachers of the period, brought rigidity to the curriculum and an inability to adjust to social change. By formulating a code of ethics as goals for kindergarten programs, the kindergartners expected to contribute positively to American society. Individual growth may well have been modified to conform to stated goals, but the method of social change they suggested was inflexibly tied to their middle class values. Avenues for adjusting the curriculum to social change in the future were closed.

The habits that were elevated as goals formed a class-associated value system based on perceptions of the teachers who selected them. Because teachers emphasized punctuality, cleanliness, responsibility, and sharing, they were institutionalizing a form of cultural imperialism. Influential kindergarten leaders had been involved in the kin-

---

[38] Mary Dabney Davis, *Nursery-Kindergarten-Primary Education in 1924-1926*, U. S. Bureau of Education Bulletin, 1927, No. 28 (Washington, D. C.: Government Printing Office, 1927), 12.

dergarten at the turn of the century when the social emphasis was paramount. They projected the lady bountiful attitude of the 1900's in terms of the behaviorist psychology of the 1920's. Unconsciously they embodied in the new program a force for cultural leveling; values were set up as goals, and the curriculum was geared toward conformity.

To the degree that programs stressed individual problem solving, they had their origins in the Deweyan idea of social reform in tune with changing social conditions. This view assumed that the teacher could not anticipate the demands made on the individual by society. The best solution, then, would be to foster the ability to meet problems in everyday living effectively, which would serve the cause of social reform by the very flexibility of its relationship to specific problems.

Though some of the remnants of social reform remained in the general outlook, the tremendous zest to spread the kindergarten movement and to embrace all children within its benevolent grasp was gone. The "new education" as an accepted (or in some cases a rejected) part of public school systems no longer received its former general attention.

Behaviorism and the Curriculum

Several factors converged to cause the behavioral emphasis to dominate in succeeding kindergarten programs. Patty Smith Hill was an able lecturer and Teachers College was, at this time, training a substantial number of American teachers. In her brilliant career spanning forty years she articulated the growing scientific emphasis to a generation of teachers. Equally important was the fact that the conduct curriculum provided ready answers for the teacher's problems. Goals were made specific; evaluation became a possibility. Although the experimenters at Teachers College may never have intended to have each child achieve every objective listed, the door was opened for an evaluative procedure that used the behavioral goals as standards of accomplishment. Conduct stated in measurable terms seemed to be the answer to the "widespread desire to determine standards for kindergarten procedures." [39] The results,

[39] Julia Wade Abbot, *Kindergarten Education 1918-1920*, U. S. Bureau of Education Bulletin, 1921, No. 19 (Washington, D. C.: Government Printing Office, 1921), p. 10.

described in terms of desirable habits, became standards for promotion.[40]

As the reconstructed program bound to specific objectives gave the teacher new directives for kindergarten planning, the impetus to experiment with new procedures declined. In spite of warnings against the crystallization of the new curriculum, the pragmatic overhauling of each part of the young child's school day was considered complete. The experimentation that had brought about a revision of the Froebelian program was dropped as the new practices were endorsed by a new set of kindergarten leaders more conversant with the form of the changed curriculum than with the rationale that supported it.

THEORY AND RESEARCH

The usual gap existed between newly evolved theory and general practice. A comprehensive survey of kindergarten practice made in cooperation with the Research Committee of the Department of Kindergarten Education of the National Education Association revealed that some teachers still maintained separate periods for "each of the traditional play materials, e.g., the gifts and occupations," both implying the use of teacher direction.[41] Other teachers continued one period to develop some special skill in handling materials through specific directions, but they provided freedom of activity in the second period; by 1925, however, an increasing number of teachers were beginning to favor one work period in which activities were not confined to the use of materials, but included "apparatus, domestic duties, the care of pets and plants as part of the work." [42] As teachers accepted the values of the single work period they were able to move more freely into the role of guide rather than director of activities.

This survey, conducted by Mary Dabney Davis, also serves to illustrate the application of the new methods of science to the study

[40] See, for example, Hill, *A Conduct Curriculum*, pp. 121-123; *An Activity Curriculum*, pp. 97-108; *Kindergarten Activities*, pp. 164-166.

[41] Mary Dabney Davis, *General Practice in Kindergarten Education in the United States* (Washington, D.C.: National Education Association, 1925), p. 44.

[42] *Ibid.*, pp. 46, 48.

of kindergarten. Surveys, rating scales, and experimental techniques were utilized by advanced students of kindergarten education with the expectation that the kindergarten would profit from scientific analysis. Rating scales developed to measure the degree of teacher guidance of such aspects of growth as habits of cleanliness, emotional adjustment, creative use of play materials or language expression revealed the kindergarten ranking high in the provision of healthful conditions and creative use of materials.[43]

Efforts to ascertain the effect of kindergarten experience on the progress of children in subsequent grades probably drew the most attempts at scientific measurement. A study made by W. J. Peters will serve to exemplify the work of others.[44] Using two groups of children of matching intelligence, Peters compared the progress of a group with no kindergarten training to another with extensive kindergarten instruction. On the basis of evidence gathered through the fifth grade, Peters proclaimed that the kindergarten was a saver of both life and money. A check on the list of doctoral dissertations and master's studies concerning early childhood education in the twenties shows a vast enthusiasm for scientific topics.[45]

It had taken about thirty years for a reconstructed kindergarten curriculum to evolve; general acceptance was even more delayed. Even as kindergarten leaders were focusing upon the problem of clarifying and disseminating the new curricula, several leading educators were giving the progressive movement a new emphasis. The growth of the doctrine of self-expression was destined to make the curriculum child-centered to an even greater degree.

[43] Winifred E. Bain, *An Analytical Study of Teaching in Nursery School, Kindergarten, and First Grade* (New York: Bureau of Publications, Teachers College, Columbia University, 1928), p. 75.

[44] W. J. Peters, "The Progress of Kindergarten Pupils in the Elementary Grades," *Journal of Educational Research*, VII (February, 1923), 117-126. Cf. W. D. Commins and Theodore Shank, "Kindergarten Training and Grade Achievement," *Education*, XLVIII (March, 1928), 410-415; Faye Risser and Harry E. Elder, "The Relation Between Kindergarten Training and Success in the Elementary School," *Elementary School Journal*, XXVIII (December, 1927), 286-289.

[45] See listings in *Preschool and Parental Education*, Twenty-Eighth Yearbook of the National Society for the Study of Education, Part I (Bloomington, Illinois: Public School Publishing Co., 1928), 273-274.

9
EXPRESSIONISM AND THE RELEASE OF POTENTIAL

The dramatic reshaping of the kindergarten in the twenties was the outgrowth of continual discussion among leaders in the annual meetings of the International Kindergarten Union. Those who proposed the new programs at teacher training centers were also ardent workers within the organization of the kindergarten movement. To the kindergartners involved, the reconstructed program seemed to enable them to be "progressive" and to focus on the needs of the child, while at the same time to utilize the precision of science.

Outside the organizational framework, however, other educational innovations developed, which were not tied to a connectionist psychology or the analysis of curriculum components, but to the doctrines of self-expression and individual adjustment. Prominent among the schools that ultimately shifted the emphasis from "scientific education" to a confidence in strengthened individualism as a means for social reform were the City and Country School, organized by Caroline Pratt, and Walden School, promoted by Margaret Naumberg.

CAROLINE PRATT'S PLAY SCHOOL

Caroline Pratt defied the concern for habit formation, which she considered lazy pedagogy and a means of covering up a multitude of teaching sins.[1] Miss Pratt understood teaching to be a creative act

[1] Caroline Pratt and Jessie Stanton, *Before Books* (New York: Adelphi Co., 1926), p. 18.

and, in her opinion, the insistence upon habit formation failed to recognize the creative artistry necessary for superior teaching. Rather than viewing the child as a passive, plastic organism, Miss Pratt envisioned a seeking, expressive individual and built her curriculum around him. Of the ventures to mold the conduct of young children she wrote, "Habit formation or the training of special abilities sets aside this seeking quality and substitutes mechanical forms through which individuals tend to become standardized." [2] Building conformity of behavior was completely opposed to the credo of expressionism which dominated the Play School.

Origin of the City and Country School

Indeed, Caroline Pratt had consistently rebelled against conforming to any educational formula. After teaching in a one-room school at the age of sixteen, in 1892 she was given a scholarship to Teachers College where she was exposed to the Froebelian kindergarten training of that period. She labeled the Froebelian doctrines "mystical fol-de-rol" and was steered into manual training work. Though trained in industrial education at Teachers College and given instruction in *slöjd* (handwork, usually in wood) in Sweden, she objected to the graded order of learning one manual operation after another in a manner that skirted all practical application. After a period of teaching manual training in a Normal School for girls in Philadelphia, which she found constraining, she moved to New York. In three subsequent teaching positions, one in a private school and two in settlement houses, she was given the freedom she wanted from any set system of instruction. The children's response to the opportunity to construct whatever they pleased was dramatic. The constructed objects were crude but satisfying to the children, and a single rule, "Work or leave this shop," insured discipline. [3]

Caroline Pratt's interest returned to preschool education, however, as she speculated about a new way of working with young children. When, at the age of eighty, she wrote the story of her early teaching career, she attributed this renewed interest to the inspiration she received as she watched a friend's child busy at play in his nurs-

[2] *Ibid.*
[3] Caroline Pratt, *I Learn From Children* (New York: Simon and Schuster, 1948), pp. 14-20.

ery. The six-year-old boy was deeply engrossed in manipulating his miniature railroad system, which he had imaginatively created from building blocks, old boxes, and other available scrap material. Miss Pratt related her impressions of the absorption, ingenuity, and realism of the child's play; this seemed to be a perfect picture of child learning. Play could remain play to the child, while at the same time it could be directed toward gaining knowledge about the environment.

The Play School, which Caroline Pratt opened in New York City in 1913, occupied quarters successively in Hartley House Settlement, Fourth and Twelfth Street, MacDougal Alley, and West Twelfth Street. The Greenwich Village community was an ideal place to combine her early interest in social reform with a burst of attention to play as a combination of creative imagination and constructive manipulation. But according to Miss Pratt's own account she knew little about the area when the school first opened. The compelling factors that led to locating the school in the Village were the low rents and a humanitarian desire to do something for the poor. The first class of six preschool children included the daughter of a German-born carpenter, the son of an Italian writer, and the son of an Irish fireman. As the school expanded to add six-year-olds, the working-class parents were skeptical of a school built around play, but the artists and writers who were moving into the Village in increasing numbers were willing to take a chance with their children and were pleased with an educational program that permitted them to be imaginative in recreating and learning about their environment. The school eventually included children from three to thirteen. When the older children objected to the original name, it was changed to City and Country School, for at that time the school also maintained a summer camp at Hopewell Junction.[4]

The welcome given the school by the Greenwich Village intelligensia intensified the early importance given to expressionism and colored the subsequent growth of the enterprise. In interpreting the directive influence of the clientele of the school, Cremin has written that what began "as an effort to build a richer life for slum children

---

[4] Pratt and Stanton, pp. viii-ix.

was slowly transformed into a classless experiment in creative education." [5]

Blending Impression and Expression

From the beginning the program was based on a rich variety of first-hand experiences. Even the four-year-olds made excursions to see the butcher, the barber, or the roofers at work in order to gather vital information to feed their dramatic play and to help them organize their facts. In their life at school the children reconstructed these experiences in spontaneous play and realistic action. Although realistic experience was a vital part of the educational plan, the child's re-creation was not considered as only a mirroring of his encounters with life, but as an "interpretation, a personal expression of the environment-as-felt." [6] What the child built in his construction of the harbor he had recently visited was the outcome of his efforts to deal with the whole experience within the limits of his understanding. The result was a blending of impression and expression in the children's work in school that resembled the mode of work of the artists in the surrounding area. It is easy to appreciate the willingness of the Village artists to patronize the school.

Miss Pratt argued that education in the past "regarded the child [as] a product"—a product molded to preconceived goals. Reversing this conception, she proposed that children be considered incipient artists, each with an eagerness to externalize his own perceptions of reality. [7] Materials that the young child could dominate and work with were essential to this individual expression.

To the information gained through vital contacts with the surrounding community, the child's imagination must propel him to clarify old relationships and to build new ones. Imagination was an added mode of discovery. Miss Pratt was concerned to get imagination operating to its fullest, and she believed that the process of re-

[5] Lawrence A. Cremin, *The Transformation of the School* (New York: Knopf, 1961), p. 204.

[6] Robert H. Beck, "Progressive Education and American Progressivism: Caroline Pratt," *Teachers College Record,* LX (December, 1958), p. 133.

[7] Pratt and Stanton, p. 6.

leasing imagination proceeded step by step as the child developed a conscious relationship to his environment.[8]

The "Here and Now" in Learning

Since re-creation evolved from highly sensitive impressions dependent upon first-hand experiencing, the interest of the children was considered to be focused on the present. The effect of this was to extend concern for the immediate aspects of the child's life into all learning areas. It was while the school was situated in MacDougal Alley in the converted garage behind the Mitchell home that Lucy Sprague Mitchell wrote stories for the younger groups about the common things in their everyday world—the steam shovel, the lost spoon, the child's walk with his father.[9] These stories inaugurated a new trend in literature for the young child, in the direction of "here and now" awareness books. The excessive use of fairy tales as emotional stimuli was not recommended, instead the emphasis was on the present so that children would "have a solid base of related facts to work out from." [10] As second-hand knowledge was not thrust upon the child before he had a chance to gather facts and relate them for himself, so fantasy was postponed until he had the opportunity to come to grips with the real world.

Foundation Learnings

Believing that education begins with life and that books are only a small part of the total learning enterprise, the City and Country School teachers postponed study of the 3 R's until the age of seven. This did not mean that no attention was given to the rudiments of subject matter. A geographical orientation to their environment was begun with three- and four-year-olds as they learned to go about their school building independently. The orientation of the fives extended beyond the doors of the school as they learned the names of streets and the location of their homes in relation to the school. The sixes began map-making by tracing their excursions

[8] Caroline Pratt and Lula E. Wright, *Experimental Practice in the City and Country School* (New York E. P. Dutton, 1924), p. 42.

[9] Lucy Sprague Mitchell, *The Here and Now Storybook* (New York: E. P. Dutton, 1921).

[10] Pratt and Wright, p. 32.

on a map; map interpretation became an initial excursion into symbolism.

Number work was begun with the recognition of small groups of objects in play or in preparation for mid-morning lunch. The foundations of reading and writing, however, were not as carefully worked out. The concept of reading readiness was not yet available for their use, but the many opportunities children had for oral expression helped prepare the way for books.

It was always through the instrumental value of play that the tool subjects were learned. As the eight-year-olds ran the supply store for the school they had many reasons to increase their mathematical proficiency; as the nine-year-olds managed the post office, skills in spelling and writing were called into practical use. Pleasure and satisfaction in learning were more highly valued than efficiency. In this educational plan individual, first-hand research provided the factual relationships; individual and group work projects put the information into practical use; finally, competency in the 3 R's increased as the skills contributed to the larger endeavors of the pupils. All possible support was given to the children as they carried out their plans. Besides many excursions out into the community, specialists were provided in music and rhythms, cooking and sewing, shop work, and language.[11] As the school expanded it included a manual training shop, pottery room, kitchen, library, gymnasium, science laboratory, and print shop.

Education for Individualism

The experiences were planned for the children to draw out their creative power. The teachers' interest was focused on what children did, how they acted, what use they made of their environment; underlying motives and emotional makeup were discussed less than the child's overt behavior. The assumption was made that children who learn to understand their world can take their place in it, and this understanding involved both impression and expression within the limits of the child's potentials.

Unfortunately, as artistic self-expression became the educational objective it opened the way for all manner of shoddiness in

[11] Pratt and Stanton, pp. 138, 338.

learning. Under the best circumstances the artist-teacher who was skilled in framing a curriculum around this concept of learning might well aid the child in the development of necessary skills as well as first-rate art. Indeed, Agnes DeLima, in her survey of progressive schools, indicated that children in Caroline Pratt's Play School showed up well on standardized achievement tests.[12] But the extended freedom could easily degenerate into license and the broad general plans into planlessness. The Play School gave support to the idea that the teacher must take the "lid off" and free children to learn for themselves.

Miss Pratt's educational plan was uniquely her own, a plan she built around the belief that, "The answer which the child has found out for himself has meaning for him." [13] The influence in favor of individualism, the stress placed on release of the driving desire "to know" contrasted sharply with the basis for the "scientific" programs of the era. Her observation of children and her pragmatic testing of procedures formed the base for the program she developed, rather than her dependence on the theoretical propositions of others. Beck summarized her achievement in the following way: "It was not a school of Dewey or of Rousseau or of anyone else. Practice was altered as experience and imagination suggested the modification. So careful was this consideration of revision and practice that the school became a laboratory whose research activity was the beginning of the Bureau of Educational Experiments." [14] Now known as the Bank Street School, the Bureau of Educational Experiments, has continued to emphasize experimental practice.

MARGARET NAUMBERG AND WALDEN SCHOOL

While Caroline Pratt was promoting an educational scheme singularly her own, another experimental school developed that stressed creative self-expression, but drew its rationale from one distinct psychological theory. In 1915, in an audaciously radical enterprise, Margaret Naumberg organized her school in order to

[12] Agnes DeLima, *Our Enemy the Child* (New York: New Republic, 1926), p. 154.
[13] Pratt, p. 45.
[14] Beck, p. 137.

search for an educational plan conducive to the growth of an integrated personality: her inspiration was derived from Freudian theory. "I started the school," she explained, "with the purpose of applying the principles of analytic psychology to the education of normal children. I welcomed psychoanalysis as an educational technique, as soon as I came in contact with it. I believed in it as a means of helping both individuals and groups in a modern school to gain fresh orientation according to their innermost needs." [15] To strike out so unreservedly for the development of personality through an understanding of depth psychology was to be on the cutting edge of educational reform in 1915.

Margaret Naumberg had been exposed to the usual educational developments of the period. Acting under the impetus of the common concern for social reform, she went to London after her graduation from Columbia University in 1910. The English labor problem she had intended to investigate held her attention only briefly, and she traveled on to Italy to learn about the Montessori method. Her one attempt to utilize Montessori's teaching techniques and material convinced her that the materials were unimaginative and the method limiting to children's creative endeavors. So it was to the teachings of Freud that Miss Naumberg turned as she founded her school. Having undergone a period of analysis with the Jungian practitioner Dr. Beatrice Hinkel, she was convinced of the need for all individuals to be freed from the restraints that limited the expression of feelings; she urged all teachers to be analyzed.

The Role of the Unconscious

Certain psychoanalytic concepts dominated the purposes and program of the Walden School. As psychoanalysis was concerned with the "deep and internal mechanisms of all human beings," so teachers needed to become "aware of the role of the unconscious in their lives or in those of their children." [16] Believing that the dynamics of human behavior included emotional and instinctual as well as mental responses, Miss Naumberg drew attention to the primacy of the emotions. In her plan, one of the major functions of the school

[15] Margaret Naumberg, *The Child and the World* (New York: Harcourt, Brace, 1928), p. 45.
[16] Naumberg, p. 135.

was "to create the right type of environment for the release of the unconscious emotional life of children into positive and personal expression." [17]

Miss Naumberg's picture of the child included the analytic image of an organism that was a bundle of conflicting wishes, instincts, and desires. In order to function harmoniously, the power buried deeply within needed to be channeled into positive forms of work and personal expression. Thus the process of sublimation, proposed in Freudian psychology as a method of reducing personal conflict, became a major technique of education at Walden School. As children were freed from inhibiting, unconsciously held defense mechanisms and were helped to channel their conflicting impulses into more productive paths, healthy, harmonious, individual functioning was the expected result.

The founder of Walden School rejected behaviorist psychology with its concern for objective data because she believed it denied the inner life of feelings, which should be one of the mainsprings to action. Mind, body, and emotions should be allowed to function together, and educational plans, in Miss Naumberg's opinion, could best promote integrative functioning when they recognized that "bodies and minds function more completely in a state of pleasure than in one of pain." [18] The pleasure principle of analytic psychology became a recognized consideration in her definition of learning experiences; this, in Freudian terms, would be held in check by the reality principle as the limits of sublimation were set by the environment.

Accepting the psychoanalytic argument that personality structure was largely determined in the early years, the Walden School began with children of two and three years of age. Miss Naumberg was convinced that the usual school procedure reduced "successive generations of human animals to sheep-like docility," and she expected to reverse this process by elevating personality as the objective of all classroom endeavor. Effectiveness in reaching this goal demanded starting with children at a very early age; her hope was to begin with "a nursery group for six-month infants as well as a group

17 *Ibid.,* p. 46.
18 *Ibid.,* p. 224.

of year-old youngsters." If initiative and independent functioning were fostered in the very young, she believed that by kindergarten age they "would astonish all observers by the originality and independence of their work." [19]

Individualism vs. Group Responsibility

The individualism in personal development envisioned by the founder of Walden School was in sharp contrast to the social emphasis of the reconstructed kindergarten of the twenties. Whereas the usual kindergarten program promoted interest in cooperative group work, Miss Naumberg aimed to strengthen the obvious variations of individual children by encouraging "such differences in type and temperament as form the base of each personality." As a Jungian, Miss Naumberg was *not* *un*concerned with "the psychology of the group"; she held that each human group, including a classroom group, evolves its own emotional life. Even a classical Freudian would have been forced to give primary attention to the nexus of affective relations in which the child was reared. Nevertheless, Miss Naumberg considered the kind of "group-consciousness" emphasized by other educators, including Dewey, a dangerous sort of "herd psychology" that was destructive to the personality of the individual.

Margaret Naumberg became an outspoken critic of the "herd psychology," which she believed placed "emphasis on the individual's living for the group rather than for himself." [20] Rather than placing her hope for social reform in Dewey's plan of social responsibility, Miss Naumberg looked to the release of the potential energy she believed was too often thwarted or locked within the child as the one possibility for building a better future for society. To sacrifice the individual to group interests, as she felt Dewey's educational proposals did, was to maintain cultural mediocrity. It was in the individual's failure to know himself that she found "the cause of his ineffectual adaptation to a positive and adequate social existence." [21] Kilpatrick's project method likewise suffered from excessive group orientation. She opposed the "group minded" approach of American

19 *Ibid.*, p. 15.
20 *Ibid.*, p. 60.
21 *Ibid.*

schools in general for their systematic submergence of the individual in the process of socialization.[22]

Dewey's response was a castigation of schools that "indulge pupils in unrestrained freedom of action and speech, of manners and lack of manners." [23] Fostering creativeness was well worth while, Dewey agreed, but it was not the totality of education. He reasoned that "true progressive education" included a searching study of society, as well as study of the child, as one of its moving forces.

The Curriculum of Walden School

The curricular experiences planned for children at Walden School focused upon individual growth. Creative activities seemed to be the answer for they constituted "the key to the nature of man." As Miss Naumberg expressed it, the "language of the unconscious does not manifest the ordinary logic of word and phrase. It may, however, express itself in speech, in gesture, in tones of the human voice, in daydreams, night dreams and all types of artistic expressions." [24] On this basis, self-expression was pushed to first place among things to be sought in education. The energy of the libido, if channeled appropriately, was expected to rush forth in a burst of creativity. Children painted what they felt impelled to paint with the result that pictures were a reflection of feelings. Children as young as four and five were found to have an intense interest in form and color, which resulted in quite abstract designs, and a child's choice of color was believed to be related to his feelings about objects. Drama was creatively produced in order that children might build self-knowledge through sensitively expressed gesture, tone of voice, or bodily stance. As they grew older, creative writing was another medium for the reflection of feelings.

No attempt was made to define syllabi. For older children, tool subjects were to be learned in pursuit of larger interests. Every subject, according to Miss Naumberg, needed to be "taught as freshly

[22] Margaret Naumberg, "The Crux of Progressive Education," *The New Republic,* LXIII (June 25, 1930), p. 145.

[23] John Dewey, "How Much Freedom in New Schools?" *The New Republic,* LXIII (July 9, 1930), p. 205.

[24] Naumberg, *The Child and the World,* p. 202.

and as creatively as the so-called arts." True standards of work were to develop, not from the demands of the teacher, but out of the discipline of the creative process. The great necessity for teachers who were responsive to the needs of individuals and yet able to keep their hands off the creative enterprise led to the employment of men close to the arts, Lewis Mumford, Hendrik Van Loon, Ernest Bloch. There is ample evidence that first-rate art resulted from this educational program. In the various forms of expression, Agnes DeLima found good clues to the inner states of each child's mind.[25] She considered the environment that enabled children to work without restraint responsible for this end result.

The Kindergarten and Freudian Psychology

Although Freudian psychology provided the theory for curriculum planning at Walden School, Cremin writes that, during this period, psychoanalytic theory "made a direct impact upon a relatively limited circle of educators." [26] The doctrines of connectionism were so prevalent in educational circles that most teachers remained ignorant of the intricacies of depth psychology. This was eminently true of the kindergartners of this period; not only were the new kindergarten curricula based upon connectionism, but the kindergartners had embraced Deweyan philosophy for a long period of time. The debates within the International Kindergarten Union recorded between 1892 and the early 1920's, when the new curricula were presented, were utterly devoid of Freudian influence either in terminology or intent.

Dewey's talk of a kindergarten classroom as an "embryonic community" had stimulated initial kindergarten reforms. This concept, at the heart of Dewey's social reformism, was one of the reasons for the wide acceptance of Deweyan practices among kindergartners. Through their discussions ran, also, the strains of Deweyan rationalism, which seemed to echo his explicit denial of the significance of the emotions in learning. As part of his educational creed, Dewey had written "if we can only secure right habits of action and thought, with reference to the good, the true, and the beautiful, the emotions

[25] Agnes DeLima, *Our Enemy The Child* (New York: New Republic Inc., 1926), p. 213.
[26] Cremin, p. 214.

will for the most part take care of themselves." [27] In the 1920's kindergarten theory was as far from analytic psychology as it had been from connectionism in 1900. Dewey's social philosophy of education and Thorndike's connectionist psychology were exclusively commanding the attention of kindergarten leaders at this period of time.

THE EXPANSION OF EXPRESSIONISM

Few people in the twenties made their rationale for expressive activities as explicit as Margaret Naumberg, but concern for the release of individual creative potential spread. When Harold Rugg surveyed educational innovations in the late twenties, he wrote about schools whose purpose was individual growth through self-expression in contrast to those that employed the scientific study of education and statistical fact-finding techniques.[28] Finding the initial impetus for progressive schools in the work of Parker, Dewey, and Kilpatrick, Rugg pointed to the educational procedures at the City and Country School, Walden School, and Lincoln School at Teachers College as demonstrating the second step in the sweeping evolution that brought about the child-centered school. "We are in the midst of a vigorous and widespread reform movement in education," he wrote. "The second stage in the educational revolution is thoroughly launched. There is no going back now." [29] In Rugg's view, this second stage had for its aim nothing less than the production of individuality through "physical, rhythmic and emotional, as well as intellectual growth." Thus, Rugg found in creative self-expression the very essence of progressive education.

When Rugg's interpretive survey of progressive schools was published he was a professor at Columbia University's Teachers College. As Director of Research for Lincoln School he was brought into contact with such artist-teachers as Satis N. Coleman and Hughes

[27] John Dewey, "My Pedagogic Creed," *The School Journal,* LIV (January 16, 1897), p. 80.

[28] Harold Rugg, "The Reconstruction of the American School System," *The New Era,* XI (April, 1929), pp. 82-83.

[29] Harold Rugg and Ann Shumaker, *The Child-Centered School* (Yonkers-on-Hudson,- New York: World Book Co., 1928), p. 53.

Mearns. They were representative of a group of Lincoln School teachers who were evolving a creative approach toward all subjects and evaluating the effect of each upon the creative power of children.

Satis N. Coleman and Musical Expression

Satis N. Coleman encouraged children to feel the joy of creating in music. In her search for forms of musical expression to let all children realize "they have music in their soul," she experimented with unique procedures in singing, rhythms, making simple musical instruments, and composing music.[30] The teacher's aim was always the release of the child's power to feel, to experience, to create. Miss Coleman thought this goal could never be reached by early emphasis upon technique, but only through "musical training that permeates the heart." [31] Spontaneity of expression and depth of feeling needed to be fostered before any attention was given to technique, which followed only as the child's natural enthusiasm for music required skill development.

While music in the mass of public schools consisted chiefly in drill in group singing and musical notation, Satis Coleman included in her creative musical experiences everything rhythmic and tonal: dancing, song, pantomime, rhythmic language, and instrumental sounds. Her program was organized on a dynamic, active, music-making basis through which the child could portray his feelings and emotions. The goal was always child growth through musical experiences.

The preservation of the child's natural enthusiasm for rhythm, sound, and movement meant exposure to a rich pattern of musical experiences at an early age. According to Miss Coleman, satisfying experiences that guarded his natural tendencies and directed his "emotional force into channels of wholesome expression" would build an early intimacy with music that would serve him well as a means of happiness all his life. During the early years, Miss Coleman felt, the child should sing and dance and play simple, elementary

[30] Satis N. Coleman, "The Creative Music Experiment in the Lincoln School of Teachers College," *The New Era,* VIII (January, 1927), p. 7.
[31] Satis N. Coleman, *Creative Music for Children* (New York: G. P. Putnam's Sons, 1922), p. 169.

instruments. Drums, rattles, tambourines, and trumpets were used to provide joyous experiences with tone and rhythm.[32]

Hughes Mearns and Creative Writing

Creative writing flourished under Hughes Mearns's sympathetic encouragement and stimulation of older children at Lincoln School.[33] But Mearns did not limit his philosophy of self-expression to creative writing alone; rather he expanded it to embrace the entire curriculum. He counted himself among those "who believe that the way to wisdom and enlarged living is through a broad cultivation of spiritual and creative powers"; he opposed curricula "conceived in practice as a body of information or as skills based upon the use of such information." [34] He argued that curriculum regarded as the development of creative power made for great artists, great scholars, and thinkers; it produced distinction. In powerful language Mearns described the creative curriculum as one in which, "Personality develops with the springing certainty of a dry seed dropped onto moist earth." [35]

The methods Mearns offered for promoting the creative spirit were directed toward releasing "the torrential force that comes unbidden out of the mysterious recesses of personality." The key word, so far as Mearns was concerned, was environment rather than curriculum, and Rugg considered Mearns a master in the cultivation of a "drawing-out" environment. Mearns believed that the creative impulse was most observable in young children and most readily flourishing in play. The spirit of play—unrestrained, out-pouring, genuinely engrossing—was very close to creativeness and needed cultivation. The curriculum for children would vary with individual needs and be "used simply as food for the spirit." [36]

Education Through Creative Expression

These curricular enunciations signify the triumph of self- expression in education as well as in art. The over-arching goals were

[32] Coleman, "Creative Music Experiment," p. 8.

[33] See Hughes Mearns, *Creative Youth* (Garden City, New York: Doubleday, Doran and Co., 1925).

[34] Hughes Mearns, "The Curriculum and the Creative Spirit," *The New Era,* X (April, 1929), p. 113.

[35] *Ibid.,* p. 116.

[36] *Ibid.,* p. 113.

the discovery of latent powers and the liberation of reserves of artistic emotion. It was not for the sake of the creative product but for the purpose of producing creative children that this liberation was cultivated. The results could be measured only in terms of the unfolding personalities of children. In a burst of enthusiasm for the production of superior persons through education in the creative process Harold Rugg wrote, "The truly creative act in the school leads to the discovery of new powers within one's self and brings about a widespreading sense of release. This leads in turn to new flashes of insight, the steady enlargements of attitudes of confidence, and the step-by-step obliteration of inferiorities." [37] The quintessence of education was creative power.

An emphasis upon the creative arts was not new in the kindergarten; art, music, movement plays, and construction had been a part of the kindergarten curriculum from its earliest days. More and more time for free play was built into the program; but at this period, kindergarten leaders were preoccupied with the educational implications of habit formation and Dewey's social philosophy. Though Hall had alerted them to some of children's emotional needs in the 1890's, they were not yet ready to accept the analytic insistence upon the primacy of the emotions. The influence of Freud was delayed until the psychoanalytic image of the child gradually gained acceptance in child development literature. Frequently the effects of psychoanalytic thinking seeped into the education of young children with no explicit acceptance of the supporting rationale.

When Margaret Mathias wrote about art experiences for young children in 1924, she used Dewey's writings on art to support the program she proposed. The emphasis was on the child's growing ability to depict his own imagery. "A child starts with an idea to express," wrote Miss Mathias. "As he draws, the idea grows." [38] The stages in the development of the artistic process Miss Mathias outlined were just as they had been presented years before to the International Kindergarten Union. First, the manipulative stage provided opportunity for the child to become acquainted with materials. Second, in the stage of symbolism the child presented many of his

[37] Rugg and Shumaker, pp. 285-286.
[38] Margaret E. Mathias, *The Beginnings of Art in the Public Schools* (New York: Charles Scribner's Sons, 1924), p. 48.

ideas, but they were not recognizable to others; his drawings were mere symbols that stood for objects to him. The child, however, was concerned with conveying an idea. Finally, in the realistic stage, the child's efforts were directed toward actual representation of objects; he was ready to "return to original form." It was not until the child had arrived at this state that his technique became a problem to him.

The kindergarten child, of course, was considered to be in the first or second stage and to need no techniques. His "mistakes" in color were attributed to an undeveloped color sense. Following the pattern set by the *Conduct Curriculum* desirable attitudes, knowledges, habits, and skills were designated for the use of each media. The social habits of responsibility and respect for the rights of others were expected outcomes related to a number of different media.

When Alice Thorn wrote about music for young children it was largely from a developmental, reasoned point of view.[39] The young child's interest in sound and movement were recognized as the fundamental elements in building musical experiences. Rhythmic activities were valued partly for the large muscle movements and the complete relaxation they provided. They also were expected to foster such desirable social habits as taking turns, giving help to others, and developing a tolerant attitude toward others. Miss Thorn considered appropriate music to be the greatest stimulus to rhythmic activity, though "the child's instinctive desire for muscular activity" accounted for a large amount of his clapping, skipping, or jumping. Singing provided a pleasurable experience with tone, and musical instruments furnished variety in experimenting with sound. Though Alice Thorn worked with Satis Coleman in originating a book of simple melodies for young children to sing, her theoretical premises were not fraught with the expressionism that permeated the Coleman text.[40]

Rugg believed that the rational view of child art, which emphasized the child's ability to depict his expanding concepts, left "out of consideration the inner drives of the child—his desire to use color, to set down in his own crude and naïve way the primitive outpourings

[39] Alice G. Thorn, *Music for Young Children* (New York: Charles Scribner's Sons, 1929).

[40] For the songs for children see: Satis N. Coleman and Alice G. Thorn, *Singing Time* (New York: John Day, 1929).

of his imagination." [41] To Rugg it mattered little whether they drew realistic sparrows and robins; the crucial factor was to let their "inner enthusiasm and expressiveness have a continuous outlet."

PSYCHOLOGY IN THE NURSERY SCHOOL

The kindergartners were at the forefront of the progressive education movement as long as it reflected the cultivation of social insight and interest, but when one group of progressive educators turned to an extreme emphasis upon individual self-expression based upon Freudian psychology, their response was more delayed. It was another decade before the kindergartners began to talk about emotional release.

Nevertheless, a new movement embracing the nurture of very young children gained momentum in the United States in the twenties. Nursery schools, according to one United States Office of Education bulletin, increased from 3 to 262 in the decade between 1920 and 1930.[42] Among the leaders of the nursery school movement, which was only beginning to build its theoretical structure, there was greater acceptance of analytic psychology.

English Origins

The primary concern of Rachel and Margaret McMillan, as they launched the twentieth century nursery school movement in England, was to provide adequate physical care for young children. Appalled by the prevalence of disease among the children of the poor, they started the Deptford School Clinic in 1909 as a private philanthropy. The McMillan sisters' vision of education was nurture that would provide healthy conditions and skilled physical care beginning with infancy.[43] Careful attention was given to right food, clothing, personal habits, and healthy surroundings, as well as early

---

[41] Rugg and Shumaker, p. 222.

[42] Mary Dabney Davis, *Nursery Schools: Their Development and Current Practices in the United States,* U. S. Office of Education Bulletin, 1932, No. 9 (Washington, D. C.: Government Printing Office, 1932), 1.

[43] Margaret McMillan, "The Nursery School in the Old Country," *Progressive Education,* II (January-March, 1955), 22-23.

diagnosis and correction of defects and disease in order to raise the health standards of the whole nation.[44]

The aims of the English Nursery School were soon broadened to include "an education in harmony with our modern knowledge of psychology." [45] Psychological as well as physical nurture became an objective of nursery schools, and the whole effort grew to become not just a substitute for home care among children of the poor, but an extension of home life from which all children could profit. It thus became the responsibility of the nursery school to provide an opportunity for full expression of feelings and ideas in an atmosphere of love and sympathy.

Views concerning discipline, among some leaders of the nursery school movement in England, had a large component of psychoanalytic thinking. "We are only just beginning to realize, largely through the work of Freud and Jung and other psychoanalysts, how great is the danger of the repression of appetites and instincts—the dynamic forces of the mind—and how appalling are the disasters that result from it," wrote Olive A. Wheeler.[46] The nursery school could provide an environment free from over-repressive discipline that "drives impulses below the threshold of consciousness" where they may organize antisocial tendencies. Opportunity for free expression was considered an insistent demand of childhood by some nursery school teachers; and while this did not mean that the child was unguided, it did mean lack of repression and ample opportunity for freedom of movement and expression.

The belief gained credence that behavior is caused and that the causes may be largely emotional; nursery school teachers were admonished to study the motives underlying action. Children's free drawings were deemed a sure guide to understanding the real feelings of the young child. Play, also was believed to be a primary revealer of feelings, "For through his play much may be learnt of the influence

[44] Margaret McMillan, *The Nursery School* (New York: E. P. Dutton, 1919), pp. 50-62, 138-144, 264-268.

[45] Grace Owen (ed.), *Nursery School Education* (New York: E. P. Dutton, 1923), p. 11.

[46] Olive A. Wheeler, "The Mind of the Child" in Owen, *Nursery School Education* (New York: E. P. Dutton, 1923), p. 34.

the home has already brought to bear on his life, of the experiences which have interested him. It is important that ample opportunity should be allowed for the child to re-live his actual experiences," wrote Grace Owen, concluding that through play the child would express the fullness or barrenness of his early years.[47]

The work of Emile Jacques Dalcroz influenced the procedure of those early nursery schools. As a teacher in Geneva, Switzerland, he devised a program of rhythmic bodily training to reinstate the relationship between music and bodily expression. It was built on a plan to coordinate the muscles, nerves, senses, and emotions into a harmonious, integrated response.[48] It was, however, not Dalcroz's systematic scheme of bodily training that the nursery school advocates found useful, but his belief in a rhythmical order to life. In the nursery school alternating periods of rest and activity, sound and quiet, food and fasting could bring about a consciousness of rhythm in human development.

Expansion of Nursery Schools in America

Research in child development, parent education, philanthropy, research in curricula and method, and teacher training were among the various interests that stimulated the expansion of the nursery school movement in the United States.[49]

The Ruggles Street Nursery School in Boston exemplified philanthropic interest organized by the Women's Education Association of Boston in 1920. It was housed in Ruggles Street Neighborhood House, one of the charities of Mrs. Quincy Shaw, who had supported early kindergartens throughout Boston. The directors of Ruggles Street Nursery School sent Abigail Adams Eliot, a student at Radcliffe, to England to study at the Rachel McMillan Nursery School

[47] Margaret E. Eggar and Grace Owen, "Education of the Nursery School Child," in Owen, *Nursery School Education* (New York: E. P. Dutton, 1923), p. 75.

[48] Adolph E. Meyer, *An Educational History of the American People* (New York: McGraw Hill, 1957), pp. 131-133.

[49] Mary Dabney Davis, *Nursery-Kindergarten-Primary Education in 1924-1926,* Bureau of Education Bulletin, 1927, No. 28 (Washington, D.C.: Government Printing Office, 1927), 3.

and Training Center. On her return Miss Eliot opened the nursery school for children of the working class.[50]

By 1926 nursery schools were established as part of research centers at Teachers College, Cornell, Iowa University, Johns Hopkins, Minnesota, Yale, and the Merrill-Palmer School of Homemaking in Detroit.[51] An early interest in curricula and methods for children under kindergarten age led to a nursery school class at Teachers College. As head of the Kindergarten-Primary Department at Teachers College, Patty Hill became a supporter of the nursery school movement and brought Grace Owen from England to lecture at the college during the summer session of 1921.

The Iowa Child Welfare Research Station at the State University of Iowa was established for the purpose of the scientific study of the child and for the dissemination of that knowledge. By 1928 five preschool groups of about one hundred children each were maintained. "These five preschool divisions are essentially laboratories for scientific observation and experimentation with young children," wrote the founder, Dr. Bird T. Baldwin "but the child is safeguarded in every respect, and his best development is the prime consideration at all times." [52]

In Detroit the Merrill-Palmer School for Homemaking, endowed by Senator and Mrs. Palmer "for the creation of a school for homemaking and motherhood," added a nursery school as a laboratory to study the management of children.[53] Following the pattern for recruiting kindergarten teachers, Merrill-Palmer School sent to England for Miss Emma Henton, a graduate of the Gypsy Hill Training School in London, who conducted the nursery school where college girls could have practical experience with young children as a preparation for motherhood. Nursery schools rapidly became a

[50] Elizabeth Winsor Pearson, "The Ruggles Street Nursery School," *Progressive Education,* II (January-March, 1925), pp. 19-21.

[51] Davis, *Nursery-Kindergarten-Primary,* p. 4.

[52] Bird T. Baldwin, "Preschool Laboratories at the Iowa Child Welfare Research Station," *Preschool and Parental Education,* Twenty-Eighth Yearbook of the National Society for the Study of Education, Part I (Bloomington, Illinois: Public School Publishing Co., 1929), 212.

[53] Helen T. Woolley, "Preschool and Parental Education at the Merrill-Palmer School," *Progressive Education,* II (January-March, 1925), 35.

part of the home economics department of numerous land grant colleges.[54]

In summarizing the growth of the nursery school in the early twenties, Mary Dabney Davis considered parent education an important aspect. "Parenthood is becoming a real profession," she wrote in explaining the need for parents to understand more about the emotional well-being of children.[55] Indeed, this was a period of rapid organization of parent education as exemplified by the growth of the National Congress of Parents and Teachers.

The Chicago Cooperative Nursery School was of interest because of the pattern for nursery school organization it established. In 1915 a small group of faculty wives of the University of Chicago banded together to develop a nursery school as a cooperative venture. A working relationship was established with the University, not only for physical space and maintenance, but for advisory contacts with a nutritionist from the home economics department and with the head of the kindergarten department, Alice Temple.

Ages of Nursery School and Kindergarten Children

The kindergartners, ever concerned with the nurture of young children, welcomed the nursery school movement. Patty Hill, for example, was a vigorous leader in promoting this cause. Though early kindergartens had included children from three to seven years of age, by the twenties the age-range of children was more limited. As kindergartens had become part of public schools rigid age-grade standards were applied, and kindergarten education was extended to children one or two years younger than those in first grade. In many areas by the early twenties, kindergarten children entered at the age of four; if it was impossible to care for all children, the five-year-olds were given preference and a one year curriculum was followed.[56]

---

[54] "History of the Movement in Preschool and Parental Education," *Preschool and Parental Education,* Twenty-Eighth Yearbook of the National Society for the Study of Education, Part I (Bloomington, Illinois: Public School Publishing Co., 1929), 28. Cornell, Iowa State College, and Ohio State University rapidly added nursery schools.

[55] Davis, *Nursery-Kindergarten-Primary,* p. 2.

[56] *Organizing Kindergartens in City School Systems,* United States Bureau of Education Bulletin, 1923, No. 2 (Washington, D.C.: Government Printing Office, 1923), 1.

During this period the nursery school accepted very young children—some as young as eighteen months to two years of age. A survey of nursery schools in operation a little later stated the average entering age as two years five months.[57] Expressing enthusiasm for this downward extension of education into infancy Arnold Gesell wrote, "The historic notion of school entrance must be steadily replaced by a more dynamic conception of school education, and in actual practice by a policy of developmental supervision which will extend the strands of national education down to the nursery." [58]

Psychological Rationales

The nursery school in the United States did not by-pass behaviorism; indeed, it drew specialists who were engrossed in the science of behaviorism. Out of studies made in the nursery school at the psychological clinic at Yale, norms were established in relation to motor development, adaptive behavior, and personal habits. These normative studies were cited by Gesell, once a student of G. Stanley Hall, as evidence of the marked influence of early conditioning environments. "It is almost dismaying to note how promptly and how relentlessly the conditioning process begins. It begins literally at birth," he concluded.[59]

Even when the purpose of nursery school was related to emotional growth it occasionally referred to the conditioning process. Mary Dabney Davis attributed the expansion of nursery education partly to the concern to help individuals "start life fortified with adequate emotional controls and social adjustments that may obviate many of the present difficulties in adolescent and adult life." [60] This was possible, she believed, through techniques for the conditioning of behavior, and she drew on John Watson's work on the emotional responses of infants. Other kindergartners who wrote about nursery education reflected the behavioral emphasis. E. Mae Raymond, an instructor at Teachers College, described the nursery school as an

[57] Mary Dabney Davis, *Nursery Schools,* p. 21.

[58] Arnold Gesell, "The Downward Extension of the Kindergarten," *Childhood Education,* II (October, 1926), 55.

[59] Arnold Gesell, "Significance of the Nursery School," *Childhood Education,* I (September, 1925), 13.

[60] Davis, *Nursery Schools,* p. 1.

opportunity for growth in social efficiency.[61] Luella A. Palmer, Supervisor of Kindergartens in New York City, wrote about the emotional adjustment of children in terms of the stages of development as proposed by Gesell.[62]

A manual for *Nursery School Procedure* written by two members of the faculty of the University of Minnesota presented a normative picture of the child from two to five and described nursery school education as habit training.[63] They considered the good nursery school to be the one that fostered in the child desirable habits of personal hygiene, eating, sleeping, and attitudes toward himself and others.

Aspects of psychoanalytic thinking, however, also formed an appreciable part of the theoretical background of the nursery school movement in the United States, raising warnings against the danger of too rigid an emphasis upon habit-building. In proposing a program of nursery education Rose Alschuler believed habits and routines could be means for enriched living but not ends in themselves. The ends could only be "strong young bodies, sound emotional make-ups and the freedom for the individual that will come through a sense of security and that can express itself through generally developed strengths." [64] For a substantial number of nursery school teachers, emotional factors played an important role in the development of the children's habit responses. Harriet Johnson, Director of the Nursery School for the Bureau of Educational Experiments in New York City, wrote that back of all activities "lies the driving force that directs them," and she designated this force as "an affective component which is just as much a part of the physiological picture as the working of a muscle, though not so obviously." [65] Miss Johnson

[61] E. Mae Raymond, "The Nursery School as an Integral Part of Education," *Teachers College Record,* XXVII (May, 1926), 786.

[62] Luella A. Palmer, "Emotional Needs of the Pre-School Child," *Childhood Education,* II (January, 1926), pp. 230-236.

[63] Josephine C. Foster and Marion L. Mattson, *Nursery School Procedure* (New York: D. Appleton and Co., 1929).

[64] Rose M. Alschuler, "The Franklin School Nursery of the Chicago Public Schools," *Preschool and Parental Education,* Twenty-Eighth Yearbook of the National Society for the Study of Education, Part I (Bloomington, Illinois: Public School Publishing Co., 1929), 158.

[65] Harriet M. Johnson, *Children in the Nursery School* (New York: John Day Co., 1928), p. 11.

also pointed to the value of loosely organized play in giving children freedom from pressure and coercion.

The articles in an issue of *Progressive Education* devoted to nursery education in 1925, together with a chapter on "Nursery Education" in the Twenty-Eighth Yearbook of the National Society for the Study of Education, provide an interesting contrast of the two prevailing psychological trends.[66] Here one can read about the more behavioristic nursery schools at the Yale Psycho-Clinic or at Iowa State College in Ames, Iowa, and compare them with accompanying accounts of the nursery school at Walden School or the one conducted by the Bureau of Education Experiments, which revealed analytic leanings. There is ample evidence during this period to conclude with Ilse Forest that "psychoanalysis, whatever may be the final judgment concerning its real worth as a means of interpreting behavior, is at the present time influencing preschool education, both in England and in the United States." [67]

As Arnold Gesell pointed out the very term, preschool, was new at this period.[68] In many instances it was coterminous with nursery school, but eventually denoted the years from two to six. Due to this development publications for nursery schools and kindergartens became less distinct over the following years and some publications began to consider education for the whole preschool span. This became, ultimately, another means for the effects of Freudian psychology to be felt in kindergarten education. Gradually the psychoanalytic stress on the danger of repression gained credence among kindergartners. An over-zealous emphasis on the formation of desirable habits was accepted as the possible cause of later unfortunate reactions. Repressive practices in feeding and toilet training gave way to a freer consideration of the child's own bodily rhythm. A sense of security came to be considered necessary for a well adjusted personality. The belief in behavior as caused gained increasing accep-

[66] *Progressive Education*, II (January, February, March, 1925); *Preschool and Parental Education*, Twenty-Eighth Yearbook of the National Society for the Study of Education, Part I (Bloomington, Illinois: Public School Publishing Co., 1929), 137-246.

[67] Ilse Forest, *Preschool Education* (New York: Macmillan, 1927), p. 223.

[68] Arnold Gesell, "The Changing Status of the Pre-School Child," *Progressive Education*, II (January, February, March, 1925), 8.

tance; with explanations in terms of past experiences, remembered or forgotten, but nevertheless forming the unconscious motives of conduct. In the nursery school movement these Freudian insights gained much more complete and rapid acceptance. The kindergartners were more restrained and delayed their acceptance of even these analytic conceptions.

In summary, Freud's pedagogical significance at the kindergarten level did not result from a conscious acceptance or understanding of the doctrines of psychoanalysis. Its impact in succeeding years was gradual and can be traced through changing conceptions of discipline and the literature relating to expression in the creative arts. The common concerns of kindergarten and nursery school teachers made it possible for a new generation of kindergartners to accept some basic analytic beliefs without having an understanding of psychoanalytic theory. The kindergarten had always accepted play as a medium for learning, for example, so kindergarten teachers were not immune to the analytic insistence on the need for freedom in play, even though they lacked a clear idea of the total theoretical structure behind this demand. To a later generation of teachers, who had not lived through the process of transforming the curriculum, the Freudian interpretation of the sublimating function of expressive activities may have been as reasonable as the Deweyan interpretation of art as the imaging forth of expanding concepts. At least the possibility was open for teachers to draw upon psychoanalytic theory to explain their practices and to inextricably mix behaviorism with some analytic postulates.

10
THE CHILD DEVELOPMENT
POINT OF VIEW

Extensive revision of the curriculum is frequently followed by a period for disseminating new theory and putting it into practice. This was true of the kindergarten in the decades that followed the curricular upheaval of the nineteen-twenties. Some modifications of program occurred, as we shall see, and gradual changes in point of view destroyed some original vitality, but the form of the curriculum remained essentially the same. For this reason these decades, at least until Sputnik again turned the thought of the nation to education, can be considered as a whole.

The methodology of child study set in motion by *The Origin of Species,* which encouraged confidence only in scientifically observable data, reached a high point of application in the normative studies of this period. G. Stanley Hall's evolutionary hypothesis as well as his methods, were passed on to his students. Hall's concept of recapitulation held that each stage of behavior was essential to the behavior patterns to come: it followed that knowledge of the developmental characteristics of each stage was important. Arnold Gesell, one of Hall's students, capitalized on this approach. Hall's faith in recapitulation was based on a predetermined unfolding of behavioral patterns; Gesell's normative approach was based on a similar concept of inherent or genetic predetermination. Through Gesell this became known as maturational theory, which denied the malleability of behavior highlighted by Watson. Watson had placed awesome responsibilities in the hands of parents and teachers for shaping behavior; Gesell erected theoretical limits.

Modifications were also taking place in Freudian theory. As

historians have pointed out, "the almost exclusively biological approach of Freud, who neglected the role of culture in behavior, has been modified by greater attention to the culture as a source of the dynamics and the desires of behavior." [1] The search for the societal sources of anxiety and frustration produced a movement of great consequence in these decades—the concern for mental health or the total personality adjustment of individuals. Increased knowledge about the mechanisms of adjustment widened the concerns of educators to include the concept of the whole child.

Four strands of psychological thought were making a combined impact on the kindergarten: Thorndike's stimulus-response theory, Watsonian conditioning, Freudian analytic postulates, and the maturational theory of Gesell. What strikes one as especially significant in these decades is the trust that kindergarten leaders placed in child development data as the only basis for making curricular decisions. The child development point of view was articulated during this time.

NORMATIVE RESEARCH

The scientific study of the child expanded rapidly as researchers sought reliable knowledge of how children grow and develop. The Iowa Child Welfare Research Station, which opened in 1917, was followed by others across the country such as the Child Welfare Institute at Teacher's College, Columbia University (1924) and similar institutes at the University of California (1927). During the nineteen-twenties a great foundation, The Laura Spelman Rockefeller Memorial, guided by Beardsley Ruml and Lawrence K. Frank, furnished money to support research in child development, thus assuring the scientific study of all phases of child growth. A steadily enlarging pool of research information became available to support more effective instructional methods and materials. The decades of the twenties and thirties were characterized by specialized studies of different capacities or traits of the child.[2] Normative in nature,

[1] R. Freeman Butts and Lawrence A. Cremin, *A History of Education in American Culture* (New York: Henry Holt, 1953), p. 506.

[2] Robert I. Watson, *Psychology of the Child* (New York: John Wiley and Sons, 1961), p. 15; cf. John E. Anderson, "Child Development: An Historical Perspective," *Child Development*, XXVII (June, 1956), pp. 193, 195.

the studies charted the measurement of some segment of behavior by age or by sex.

Arnold Gesell

Having received his Ph.D. from Clark University, Arnold Gesell went on to the Clinic of Child Development at Yale where he led a search for normative data. He presented the results of his work in the form of growth gradients since age was regarded as the most important developmental dimension. The publication of the companion volumes *Infant and Child in the Culture of Today* and *The Child From Five to Ten* came as part of a series of influential contributions by Gesell and his co-workers.[3] The population of children studied from nursery school on were of "high average or superior intelligence" and came from homes of "good or high socioeconomic status."[4] Standardized procedures for measurement and observation were supplemented by "naturalistic observations, stenographically recorded."

From the data collected "norms" of growth were presented age level by age level in chapters that became known for their designation of "ages and stages." Traits, the authors claimed, were *"not* to be regarded as rigid norms nor as models"; they were simply intended to "illustrate the kinds of behavior—desirable or otherwise—which tend to occur at this age."[5] While Gesell did stress the importance of individual differences, the very organization of his publications in "ages and stages" promoted their interpretation as normative material and led to a disregard of his other points of view.

As Gesell went on to consider the "progressive morphogenesis of patterns of behavior" he linked them to "the innate processes of growth called maturation," which he considered fundamental and powerful.[6] Addressing himself to parents and teachers, Gesell wrote of development, "The total ground plan is beyond your control. It is too complex and mysterious to be altogether entrusted to human

[3] Arnold Gesell and Frances L. Ilg, *Infant and Child in the Culture of Today* (New York: Harper, 1943); Arnold Gesell and Frances L. Ilg, *The Child From Five to Ten* (New York: Harper, 1946).

[4] Gesell and Ilg, *The Child From Five to Ten,* p. 3.

[5] *Ibid.,* p. 72.

[6] Gesell and Ilg, *Infant and Child in the Culture of Today,* p. 41.

hands. So Nature takes over most of the task, and simply invites your assistance." [7] In Gesell's maturational theory, the child was no longer viewed as an amorphous bit of behavior to be shaped, but as an individual depending on inner regulation in the growth process. Accepted as an educational postulate, inner regulation meant more reliance upon innate growth and less emphasis upon environmental stimuli. It reinforced the earlier analytic "hands off" program; it also included mental growth and gave support to the assumption of fixed intelligence.

A whole new literature of scientific, descriptive data was developed during this period. Researchers, intent upon establishing a large body of reliable facts about the details of human development, allowed descriptive data to prevail over abstract constructs and processes. A considerable amount of data was added from all spheres of growth—physical, intellectual, emotional and social—as it applied to the genetic period under investigation. In retrospect, the emphasis seems largely on the quantitative and objective—motor performance, sensory capacity, language attainment—in a rather segmented or compartmentalized approach.[8] But from the normative data categorized by age, the characteristics, interests, and abilities of the kindergarten child were derived and rapidly put to use in kindergarten literature.

Depth Psychology

An increasing volume of literature began to view the dynamics of individual behavior from the point of view of depth psychology. Freudian theory was not only serving as a frame of reference for empirical work in human behavior but was also affecting beliefs about socioemotional development.[9] The work of Lawrence K. Frank and Daniel Prescott exemplifies the concern for mental health or total personal development. Like others involved in the mental

---

[7] Gesell and Ilg, *Child From Five to Ten,* p. 6.

[8] Watson, p. 16. Cf. C. Murchison (ed.), *A Handbook of Child Psychology* (Worcester, Massachusetts: Clark University Press, 1931).

[9] Urie Bronfenbrenner, "Developmental Theory in Transition," *Child Psychology,* Sixty-second Yearbook of the National Society for the Study of Education, Part I (Chicago: University of Chicago Press, 1963), pp. 524-525; See also: John E. Anderson, "Child Development: An Historical Perspective," *Child Development,* XXVII (June, 1956), p. 194.

hygiene approach, they looked to the nonrational motivations in behavior and learning that have their origin not only within the individual himself but also in external conditions originating in the culture.

Lawrence K. Frank

Lawrence K. Frank was a convincing interpreter of the implications of depth psychology for the early socialization of the child. He explained that the gradual molding of behavior to conform to accepted societal patterns inevitably held frustrations and anxiety.[10] The fundamental need of the child during this process was for sympathetic understanding, patient support, and tenderness so that he could accept the process of socialization without becoming resentful, hostile, or overly aggressive. Discarding the dualistic concept of human nature postulated by Freud, Frank had faith that if they were given affectionate reassurance and tolerance for individual, temperamental differences during the early years, children would grow toward "friendliness, cooperativeness, gentleness, and genuine group or social activity." Thus guided, they would be free from the mechanisms of adjustment that foster aberrant behavior. Frank stated his conviction when he said this was preschool education's "immense opportunity and responsibility for the future course of our culture." [11]

This strong statement on the function of preschool education was made by Frank at the conference of the National Association for Nursery Education held in Nashville, Tennessee, on October 22, 1937, and later published in *Mental Hygiene* magazine. At a time when educational organizations exerted strong leadership, nursery school teachers had formed their own association. Requests by nursery school educators for opportunities to exchange experiences and to develop statements of essential standards for programs led to informal meetings in New York City in 1925. Chaired by Patty Smith Hill, these meetings formed the nucleus from which the na-

[10] Lawrence K. Frank, "The Fundamental Needs of the Child," *Mental Hygiene*, XXII (July, 1938), pp. 353-379.
[11] *Ibid.*, p. 372.

tional organization grew.[12] At a conference in Chicago in 1929, members voted to maintain an autonomous organization rather than to affiliate with any other existing group.

Daniel Prescott

In the early nineteen-forties Daniel Prescott was head of the Division on Child Development and Teacher Personnel for the American Council on Education. A collaboration center established in quarters provided by the University of Chicago, soon became a focal point for field work that helped to spread ideas of human development to teachers and principals. Later Prescott became a member of the Institute for Child Study at the University of Maryland and was involved in continuous field work to promote the understanding among educators that he believed necessary to guide the personal development of each child.

Two profound contributions of psychoanalytic theory were basic to Prescott's teachings: (1) all behavior is caused, and the search for causes is essential in working with individuals; (2) mind and emotions do not operate in a vacuum, but are a function of the complex and interrelated aspects of development. Prescott agreed with Frank that most children face a number of adjustment problems that complicate achievement in learning in the traditional school and successful accomplishment of their own developmental tasks. He considered the climate of affection, social background, and self-defensive and adjustment processes as essential factors needing consideration when educational decisions about the child were made.[13] This implied the necessity of educators' dealing with all facets of behavior—with the "whole child."

[12] Mary Dabney Davis, "How NANE Grew," *Young Children,* XX (November, 1964), p. 106.

[13] These ideas were abbreviated for use by Viola Theman in "Emerging Concepts of Child Growth and Development: What They Suggest for Classroom Practice," Harold Shane (ed.), *The American Elementary School,* John Dewey Society Thirteenth Yearbook (New York: Harper, 1953), p. 60. She derived them from Daniel Prescott, "A Statement of Ideas About the Child," written for the Educational Policies Commission (mineographed form). One can find a similar development in the book *Helping Teachers Understand Children* (Washington, D.C.: American Council on Education, 1945).

Prevalence of the Depth Psychology

An assessment of emerging concepts of child growth and development made by Viola Theman in 1953 uncovered a genuine agreement between the ideas about the child expressed by Prescott and those of Arthur D. Hollingshead and John E. Anderson, two other child development specialists writing during this period.[14] Dr. Theman's article helps to clarify the pervasiveness of this point of view. Such commonality, however, she considered rare. In general she found child development data loaded with difficulties in terminology, lacking a cohesive point of view, and holding few clearly structured or generally accepted concepts. Consequently, although research changed concepts about the development of children, the absence of coordinated efforts by researchers and theorists forced those who would utilize new insights to depend upon available segments of theory.

What kindergarten specialists selected from child development data, however, seemed to imply a tender nurture for the child. A healthy personality required patient support. Guidance of the powers that maturation permitted to unfold called for following evidence of the child's readiness as an indication for offering educational experiences.

Stating the Point of View

Arthur T. Jersild, Professor of Education at Teachers College, Columbia University, laid down the basic definition of the child development point of view:

The child development approach to the curriculum means an effort to apply to the education of children the lessons learned from the study of children themselves. Research in child development has provided many findings which have implications for education. . . . But the child development approach does not represent merely a collection of facts. It represents also a point of view.

Basic to this point of view is a spirit of inquiry—a desire to learn

[14] *Ibid.,* pp. 58-61.

about the ways of children. . . . With this spirit of inquiry goes an attitude of respect for children at all stages of their growth.[15]

Both the attitude of respect for children and the collection of facts then available were transferred to curricula. Normative, objective data formed the foundation of Jersild's recommendations for children during infancy, preschool years, and the elementary school period. Similarly based were the suggestions to be found in the Thirty-eighth Yearbook of the National Society for the Study of Education, *Child Development and the Curriculum,* which related the developmental process to the various subject matter areas of the curriculum.[16] A later explanation of the child development point of view added the concepts of socioemotional development presented by Frank and Prescott.[17] James L. Hymes, Jr., described the manner in which teachers could "build good feelings into children" in order to promote mental health and emotional strength, which he designated as the goal of the child development point of view.[18] Both explanations held implications for practice.

RELIANCE ON CHILD DEVELOPMENT
FOR CURRICULAR DECISIONS

Eager as always to utilize new information about the child, kindergarten leaders welcomed the child development point of view. Their trust in child study reached its ultimate point during this period, for child development understandings became the dominant referent in all curricular decisions. In actual influence, the child development point of view seemed to support the curriculum already evolved, so it confirmed more than it innovated in kindergarten practice.

[15] Arthur T. Jersild, *Child Development and the Curriculum* (New York: Bureau of Publications, Teachers College, Columbia University, 1946), p. 1.

[16] National Society for the Study of Education, *Child Development and the Curriculum,* Thirty-eighth Yearbook, Part I (Bloomington, Illinois: Public School Publishing Co., 1939).

[17] James L. Hymes, Jr., *A Child Development Point of View* (Englewood Cliffs, New Jersey: Prentice-Hall, 1955).

[18] *Ibid.,* p. vi.

The accumulated normative data was rapidly put to use in kindergarten literature. *Education in the Kindergarten,* whose authors were members of the Institute of Child Welfare at the University of Minnesota as well as recognized leaders in kindergarten education, opened with a chapter describing the characteristics of the five-year-old child.[19] The first significant book on kindergarten for over a decade, it established a practice that was followed by most kindergarten books through the nineteen-fifties. Statements about five-year-olds depicted their physical growth, language ability, play interests, competence in routines, and similar traits easily measured by objective standards. The writers suggested that as developmental characteristics were thoughtfully considered, a program could be planned appropriate to the child's "stage of development" that would "be satisfying to him in the present" and "prepare him for the years immediately following." [20] This normative view of the kindergarten child became standard practice.[21] A picture of the "average" or "normal" kindergarten child was presented as a guide to the teacher.

Normative data *was* utilized to define those conditions that would foster growth organismically—including physical, intellectual, social, and emotional development. These were developmental needs conceived by adults who then used them to formulate a program. Children need protection against fatigue by the provision of a rest period,[22] they require equipment and time for big muscle play,[23] and freedom from pressure that would encourage them to talk.[24] It was in this developmental sense that the kindergarten became a

[19] Josephine C. Foster and Neith E. Headley, *Education in the Kindergarten* (New York: American Book Co., 1936), Chapter I.

[20] *Ibid.,* p. 33.

[21] Clarice D. Wills and William H. Stegeman, *Living in the Kindergarten* (Chicago: Follett, 1950); Hazel M. Lambert, *Teaching the Kindergarten Child* (New York: Harcourt, Brace and Company, 1958); Helen Heffernan and Vivian E. Todd, *The Kindergarten Teacher* (Boston: D. C. Heath, 1960).

[22] Charlotte G. Garrison, Emma D. Sheehy, and Alice Dalgliesh, *The Horace Mann Kindergarten for Five-Year-Old Children* (New York: Bureau of Publications, Teachers College, Columbia University, 1937), p. 8.

[23] Foster and Headley, *Education in the Kindergarten* (1936 edition), p. 61.

[24] Wills and Stegeman, p. 49.

"needs curriculum" and its purpose, the nurture of all the child's potentials with careful recognition given to appropriate environmental conditions. The concept of need seemed to imply that "a series of natural or spontaneous needs" appeared in spite of social or economic restrictions[25] and that a teacher familiar with child psychology could identify them for the individual or the group.

A proliferation of articles gives evidence to the strength of this trend to view the kindergarten program as a needs curriculum. The behavior of the kindergarten child and the needs arising from them have been continuously extolled as the basis of curriculum planning.[26] It seemed to again provide kindergarten leaders with the opportunity to focus on the child and at the same time to utilize the objective data of science. In actuality the normative view of child development tended to paint an increasingly homogeneous picture of five-year-olds and to deny uniqueness arising from differing environmental backgrounds.

Providing for Socio-Emotional Development

Encouraged by child psychologists like Prescott and Frank, some kindergarten teachers placed great stress upon the socio-psychological climate in the classroom. New insights replaced previous ignorance of the relationship between emotional stresses and the ability to adjust and to learn. Again, the changes are most evident in the authority pattern of the classroom and in the opportunities for freedom of expression. The early swing to extreme permissiveness that existed in some nursery schools abated as the theme "free the

[25] John E. Anderson, "Changing Emphasis in Early Childhood Education," *School and Society,* XLIX (January 7, 1939), pp. 1-9. (Dr. Anderson was director of the Institute of Child Welfare at the University of Minnesota).

[26] Cf., Maycie Southhall, "Meeting the Needs of Children," *Childhood Education,* XIV (April, 1938), pp. 339-340; Laura Hooper, "Trends in the Modern Kindergarten," *American Childhood,* XXIV (November, 1938), pp. 51-52; James L. Hymes, Jr., "A Newcomer: Early Childhood Education," *Peabody Journal of Education,* XXVII (March, 1950), pp. 266-269; Betty Ann Roth, "Promising Practices in Kindergarten Education," *Midland Schools,* LXXIV (March, 1960), pp. 18-19.

child" was replaced by "freedom through self-imposed controls." [27] The purpose was to strengthen the ego, to make it more independent of the superego—that is, the demands of parents, teachers, and society. "Self-discipline," "self-regulation," and "self-control" became familiar words used to describe this revised distinction.[28] Although continual blocking and frustration were believed to place heavy psychological burdens on the child, complete permissiveness implied lack of concern for individual development. The real goal was a sense of personal responsibility fostered not through rigid controls but through gradual growth in self-regulation. The parents' and teachers' task was not only to maintain limits to social behavior firmly and kindly but also to strengthen the individual ego so that it could cope with both inner drives and outer pressures.[29]

Ego strength grew under conditions that indicated to the individual that he was adequate, appreciated, and respected. It was believed significant that the child felt secure in his school situation, accepted by his teacher and other pupils, positive about himself in the new school surroundings. As one kindergarten teacher stated, "It is, therefore, important to help a child gain the inner security which comes of feeling welcomed and wanted—he needs to feel that he BELONGS." [30] Love supplanted fear as a means of control in order to avoid the emotional problems resulting from denials, forc-

[27] Cf. Harold Rugg, "Contrasts in Culture and Education," *The New Era*, XXXVII (February, 1956), pp. 52-53; Sadie D. Ginsberg, "Changing Attitudes About Children," *Partners in Education*, Forty-fifth Annual Schoolmen's Week Proceedings (Philadelphia: University of Pennsylvania Press, 1958), p. 338.

[28] Cf. Lawrence K. Frank, "Discipline in Our Time," *Childhood Education*, XX (September, 1943), p. 7; May Hill Arbuthnot, "Transitions in Discipline," *Childhood Education*, XV (November, 1938), p. 107; Howard A. Lane, "Discipline in Today's Education," *Childhood Education*, XX (November, 1943), pp. 104-106.

[29] Lawrence K. Frank, "Discipline of the Child," *Child Study*, XV (January, 1938), p. 98. For a longer explanation of this view of discipline, see Dorothy W. Baruch, *New Ways in Discipline* (New York: McGraw-Hill, 1949).

[30] Elizabeth Campbell, "Kindergarten Shape Up," *Progressive Education*, XXIII (May, 1946), p. 265.

ing, and harshness.[31] The feeling tone in adult–child relationships was considered as important as overt actions.

Following Prescott's recommendations, teachers searched for causes of behavior and turned to unconscious determinants—the emotional drives. In the search for cues to the child's motives, play was considered a revelatory mode for inner feelings and drives. An extensive compilation of children's play episodes supplied evidence that play was "a fairly good indicator of how life is going" for them.[32] Dramatic play was of inestimable therapeutic value for the young child: a child could spank the baby, act like a dog and bite all the children, or raid the refrigerator with enormous zest, and in general relieve feelings in a manner that was impossible in normal interaction.

During this time, kindergarten teachers wholeheartedly accepted artistic expression as an important means of giving continuous outlet to inner enthusiasm and expressiveness. The effect of this concern for emotional release was to center attention on the process of creation rather than on the end product; the child was more important than the picture. In the words of Natalie Cole, "How infinitely worthwhile, helping a child to find inner harmony through new means of expression." [33]

It was Viktor Lowenfeld who tied together the earlier emphasis on conceptual growth through art expression and the newer concern for emotional outlets.[34] He explained the developmental stages from the scribble to full, mature artistic expression in terms of emotional as well as mental growth. The child brought not only increased perception to the creative act but a continually altered "subjective relationship with man and the environment." [35] When the child could attach meaning to an apparently undefined scribble, it meant that he

[31] Ginsberg, p. 341. See also: Aline D. Auerbach, "Discipline Through Affection," *Child Study*. XXII (Summer, 1945), pp. 102-103.

[32] Ruth E. Hartley, Lawrence K. Frank and Robert M. Goldenson, *Understanding Children's Play* (New York: Columbia University Press, 1952), p. 19.

[33] Natalie Cole, *The Arts in the Classroom* (New York: John Day, 1940), p. 10.

[34] Viktor Lowenfeld, *Creative and Mental Growth* (New York: Macmillan, 1947).

[35] *Ibid.*, p. 7.

no longer thought in terms of motion but in terms of mental pictures.[36] This was a big step forward, but if he "continuously attempts to relate all his experiences such as thinking, feeling, perceiving (seeing, touching, and so on), to one another, it must also have a unifying effect on his personality." [37] The great contribution of art to education and to society was the power it contained to integrate harmoniously all the components of growth.

Creative rhythmic movement came under similar influence and was an additional release of feeling and imagination. Expressive movement was believed to grow from imagination and emotional impulse, while rigid movement stemmed from self-consciousness and a mechanical application of learned steps.[38] The child's instinctive enjoyment of motion—twisting, turning, wiggling, squirming—could be utilized for creative growth. As Emma Sheehy expressed it, children's "movements spring from feelings and needs that are strong within them. The expression of these in movement has vitality and, if we give it encouragement and support, its own unique form evolves." [39]

It became easy to justify activities carried on in the kindergarten for years through the reasoning of depth psychology. To many new kindergarten teachers, play, as an expression of deep seated concerns and feelings, may have been just as comprehensible as the Deweyan explanation of play as the reconstruction of experience. There was never a period in the history of kindergarten when creative expression was not deemed important: to its earlier value as a reflection of conceptual refinement was added the belief that it also reflected emotions. Thus the symbolism of the child might reflect distortions due to idiosyncratic perceptions.

The gradual espousal of modified Freudian doctrines was implicit in discussions about practice, though no effort was made in theory to plumb the implications it held for the curriculum. Already

[36] Viktor Lowenfeld, *The Meaning of Creative Expression for the Child* (New York, Bank Street Publications, n.d.), p. 12.

[37] *Ibid.*, p. 6.

[38] Maria Bird, "Rhythmic Movement in Schools," *The New Era,* XV (May-June, 1934), pp. 141-143.

[39] Emma D. Sheehy, *Children Discover Music and Dance* (New York: Henry Holt and Company, 1959), p. 154.

firmly established concerns for emotional stability and effective social relationships were reinforced until they became the dominant aspect of some kindergarten classrooms—at least in those moving in the direction of closer alliance with the philosophic thought of nursery school leaders.

ORGANIZING THE CURRICULUM

The concern for individual needs had stemmed from child development proposals; this same information led kindergarten teachers to question prevailing means of organizing the program. In defining the organization, what had earlier been called projects were later designated as units of work, centers of interests, or even an activity program. These organizing procedures were used in connection with many of the familiar phrases of the period: "developing the whole child," "education through activity," "building social living." The voluminous output of literature on the activity program in the thirties included the kindergarten level. The hallmarks of the activity program were "learning in a life-like setting," "flexibility of program planning," "learning by doing," and "developing skills in group living" [40]—all characteristic aspects of the kindergarten program since the twenties.

"Units of work," which could be built into an activity program, were emphasized by some writers. They were recommended as "the vehicle for bringing activity into the classroom and carrying knowledge out of the classroom," by Foster and Headley.[41] The appropriate number of units per year was specified, the length of time to be devoted to each made clear, and certain precise units suggested. These suggestions were highly weighted with seasonal and holiday units. The unit organization, presented in great detail, characterized

[40] See for example: Henry Harap, "Trends in Early Elementary Education," *Childhood Education,* XIV (October, 1937), pp. 53-57; M. Julia Detroz, "A Critical Analysis of the Activity Curriculum in the Elementary School," *Childhood Education,* IX (January, 1933), pp. 198-200; Mary L. Hickey and Dolores Saum, "The Kindergarten Activity Program," *American Childhood,* XVII (February, 1932), pp. 10-11.

[41] Foster and Headley (1936 ed.), p. 112. This type of organization was also recommended in the two subsequent editions of the book in 1948 and 1959.

the plans in the *Curriculum Records of the Children's School* gathered together by members of the staff of the Children's School of the National College of Education in Evanston, Illinois.[42]

As early as 1938, however, one group of writers repudiated units of work for implying "a group interest too complete and too closely integrated for kindergarten children." [43] There was an increasing belief that the unit was too highly structured for the young child. In place of units, other authors recommended "centers of interest." Wills and Stegeman described flexible centers of interest based upon the experience level of the group—centers of interest that the teacher stimulated as she could, but without coercion: if "the center of interest the teacher had in mind does not 'take' with the children, she must be willing to drop the idea and work toward something else." [44] The centers of interest suggested were the home, a grocery store, a post office, a circus, holidays—all very similar in content to the earlier units. The distinguishing feature seemed to be the flexibility imputed to centers of interest both in time-span and number of children included.

Still another concept of the center of interest equated it with available materials, which gave variety to experience and allowed for choice.[45] Centers included separate ones arranged for housekeeping, block building, art materials, books and puzzles, science, and one where a work bench, tools, and wood were available. As here described the "center of interest" placed extreme reliance upon materials as a means of organizing the curriculum.

The words had changed somewhat, but essentially they stood for the same experiences provided for children in the twenties—block building, sand play, easel painting, celebration of holidays, studies of seasonal changes, learning more about the home and community helpers.

[42] *Curriculum Records of the Children's School* (Evanston, Illinois: Bureau of Publication, National College of Education, 1932). See also: May Hill Arbuthnot, "The Unit of Work and Subject Matter Growth," *Childhood Education,* IX (January, 1933), 182-188.

[43] Garrison, Sheehy and Dalgliesh, p. 5.

[44] Wills and Stegeman, pp. 217-218.

[45] Mamie W. Heinz, *Growing and Learning in the Kindergarten* (Richmond, Virginia: John Knox Press, 1959), pp. 65-66.

Providing for Intellectual Development

The empirical work of the behaviorists, with its emphasis on observable variables and its dismissal of the ellusive concepts of "consciousness" and "mind," treated the child more as a reactor than a knower and led away from the study of intellectual growth. The psychoanalytic study of personality with its concern for inner drives stressed problems of motivation, impulse, conflict, conscience; thus emotional rather than mental growth was central. The intellectual aspects of development simply did not become a subject for intensive study by kindergarten leaders during this period. They followed developments in child study closely, and did not make cognitive growth a fundamental concern: in retrospect this becomes important.

Relying upon insights from child development to form the foundation for major curricular decisions, kindergarten leaders ran into difficulties when they tried to use this data as a means for selecting intellectual content for classroom activities. Among the mental characteristics of the five-year-old, derived in normative research, were his eagerness for information, his curiosity, and his desire to investigate and examine.[46] As desirable as it might be to encourage curiosity, to allow children to investigate and examine, these recommendations gave the teacher little guidance about the "what" of learning. They related to process goals and were not directly helpful in the selection of content. The absence of conceptual goals posed a serious problem.

An integration of more content into the curriculum, however, seemed to be called for both in keeping with the mental abilities of five-year-olds and in answer to criticisms that kindergarten was barren of intellectual stimulation. To provide for intellectual needs, chapters organized around subject matter areas appeared in kindergarten literature. As we have seen, there was an earlier tendency to categorize areas of the kindergarten curriculum around literature, art, music, and nature study. Foster and Headley's *Education in the Kindergarten* had chapters on natural and social science, the arts, language work, and literature.[47] They credited the kindergarten

---

[46] Foster and Headley, p. 6; Wills and Stegeman, p. 18.
[47] Foster and Headley, Chapters V, XII, XVII, XVIII.

teacher with the ability to select the content appropriate to the needs of her group of children; but there was no rationale presented to aid the teacher in choosing those experiences related to the needs of the particular children under her care.

As a result of the studies of children's interests there was an increasingly large component of the "here and now" in the content of the curriculum. This had its beginnings in the Dewey sub-primary program, which drew problems from the child's interactions with his immediate environment. It was reinforced when the use of the *Here and Now Storybook* by Lucy Sprague Mitchell revealed children's delight in the details of their everyday life.[48] This book, growing out of the work at Carolyn Pratt's Play School, replaced fantasy literature for young children with stories of common experiences in which the child could envision his own daily activities. Child development research also described the child's world as comprised of what was 'here-and-now," [49] and these notions formed the background for the idea that social studies units must start with "the home" and gradually move out in time and space only as children grow older. Interests were thought to originate from a stimulating environmental set-up. It was never expected that the teacher would "pour-in" information, but that she would provide experiences that would enable the child to absorb information through first-hand manipulation and encounter.

Implicit in all the discussions was the belief that the first screen in selecting experiences was the developmental needs of the group as revealed by normative data. This was, of course, an adult view of children's needs. According to theory, a needs or emerging curriculum requires teacher-pupil planning in order to identify the "felt needs" of the learner; however, the ability to make group plans was considered limited in the five-year-old child. Wills and Stegeman wrote that the teacher should not expect any form of extensive group planning in the kindergarten year.[50] Lambert agreed that at first the kindergarten child lacked the maturity and experience for detailed

[48] Lucy Sprague Mitchell, *Here and Now Storybook* (New York: Dutton, 1921).

[49] Gessell and Ilg, *Child From Five to Ten*, p. 63.

[50] Wills and Stegeman, p. 87.

planning, but that later in the year planning in groups of three or four children becomes possible with the guidance of the teacher.[51]

There was no recognition of any other basis for the selection of activities than "need," which raises several questions. Are needs in a developmental sense a sufficient basis for determining kindergarten experiences? Can the learner's needs be determined in a group of kindergarten children whose language facility is limited and whose skills in group planning are undeveloped? With the procedure for selecting experiences so indefinite, one suspects that teachers who worked well intuitively and who readily exercised creative imagination developed challenging and interesting kindergarten programs, but that undoubtedly there were classrooms in which the emotional climate was exemplary and democratic social interaction was fostered but that were sterile in intellectual content. Rising dissatisfaction brought demands for other kinds of learning experiences.

[51] Lambert, pp. 81-82.

11
PRESSURES FOR CHANGE

While researchers continued their attempts to tunnel their way into the nature of the child, societal pressures were shaping the kindergarten. One particular conflict agitated the equilibrium during these years: on the one hand were pressures to follow the values of the conventional elementary school with its emphasis on the development of skills and concern for knowledge; on the other hand the kindergarten shared with the nursery school an emphasis on the development of the whole child, the role of the emotions in learning, the importance of a positive self-image, and non-authoritarianism. Kindergarten was squeezed between two sets of values. Mabel Louise Culkin stated this dilemma emphatically, "There is a tendency . . . to regard its activities as somewhat tenuous beside the red corpuscular attainments of the nursery school, or the amazing achievements of the primary school in teaching reading without tears in a miraculously short time." [1]

Effects of Economic Depression

When America fell into the Depression in 1929, many kindergartens were faced with budgetary cuts that threatened their very existence. A high point of public school kindergarten enrollments had been reached in 1930 when almost three-quarters of a million pupils were enrolled; by the early nineteen-thirties the number declined to

[1] Mabel Louise Culkin, "The Contemporary Kindergarten," *Educational Record,* XXIV (October, 1943), 345.

a little over six hundred thousand.[2] While nursery schools flourished through the federal funds of the Works Progress Administration, kindergartens had to rely on local financing or occasional state financial aid, both of which were curtailed during this period. As emergency nursery schools proliferated, the five-year-olds seemed to be left in an educational no-man's land.

"With the widespread and positive recognition of the value of the institution, friends of the kindergarten have been amazed, almost aghast, at the catastrophes impeding its progress during the past four years," wrote Winifred Bain.[3] Not only were kindergartens in some cities abandoned in order to relieve school budgets, but in others the teaching staff was reduced and the number of kindergarten–primary supervisors decreased. This meant crowded classrooms where teachers were faced with two large classes a day and little expert leadership. It seemed all too easy to cut off this lower rung of the educational ladder; in one school budget meeting kindergarten was referred to as "a boom time luxury." [4]

Writers speculated that there may have been factors other than the financial depression that accounted for the slowing down of the kindergarten movement in the 1930's. It appeared to be difficult to interpret the basic values of kindergarten to certain administrators and to some segments of the general public. To many taxpayers the objectives of the public kindergarten seemed vague and the results nebulous.[5] As late as 1954 it was stated that kindergartens had not increased adequately because people "failed to recognize their value." [6] This statement was written during a later period when children were swarming into kindergarten classrooms. The population explosion at the end of World War II resulted in some kindergartens

[2] Emory M. Foster, *Statistics for Public School Kindergartens and Primary Grades 1930-1934-1938* (Washington, D. C.: U. S. Office of Education, n.d., p. 1. The figures given for enrollment are 1930—723,443 and 1934—601,775).

[3] Winifred Bain, *Parents Look at Modern Education* (New York: D. Appleton-Century Co., 1935), p. 53.

[4] Fred Engelhardt, "How to Save the Kindergarten," *Journal of the National Education Association,* XXIII (April, 1934), 114.

[5] Culkin, *Educational Record,* XXIV, 346.

[6] Sarah Lou Hammond, "What Happens to the Five-Year-Olds?" *Educational Leadership,* XII (October, 1954), 9.

having as many as fifty children in a class, or sometimes fewer sessions per week for each child, but more distinct groups of children for the teacher. Crowding and heavy responsibilities for the teacher in the kindergarten were not considered as deleterious to learning as they might be in the primary grades.

Despite the movement to coordinate the work of the kindergarten with that of the primary grades, there was, in many cases, a relative separatism, which emphasized the differences in outlook.[7] Finally, it was suggested that the reconstructed curriculum had already become fixed and rigid. The learning opportunities in classes of forty-five or fifty pupils were considered too meager; some projects were called masterpieces of teacher-pupil coercion.

Explaining the Kindergarten

If administrators and the general public did not understand the values and the rich experiences kindergarten could provide for children, it was not because teachers and supervisors did not try to interpret them. Explanations appeared regularly in periodical literature of the thirties and forties, especially in *Childhood Education,* the official journal of the Association for Childhood Education, the organization that was an outgrowth of the International Kindergarten Union. As the kindergarten-primary unit became a part of teachers colleges and influenced the literature of early childhood, the several professional organizations moved in the direction of becoming an association that included these age-grade levels. The Kindergarten Department of the NEA became the Department of Kindergarten-Primary Education in 1927, but was relatively inactive for a period of years. By 1930 the International Kindergarten Union and the National Council of Primary Education had merged to become the Association for Childhood Education. Since leaders of the organization believed that children between the ages of two and eight had common needs, they wished to promote the coordination of work

[7] Bess Goodykoontz, Mary Dabney Davis and Hazel F. Gabbard, "Recent History and Present Status of Education of Young Children," *Early Childhood Education,* Forty-sixth yearbook of the National Society for the Study of Education, Part II (Chicago: University of Chicago Press, 1947), 59. (These authors were members of the U. S. Office of Education.)

in nursery schools, kindergartens, and primary grades.[8] They continued the journal that supplanted the International Kindergarten Union yearbooks as a forum for current opinion. Friends of the kindergarten used it continually to interpret kindergarten philosophy.[9]

After the wave of books published in the mid-twenties, it was a decade before any significant new volumes on the kindergarten appeared, but there was no lack of articles in periodical literature.[10] Many of the articles were devoted to explaining the value of kindergarten. Over and over again supporters interpreted kindergarten goals in terms of the specifics of habit formation: such as learning to wait for a turn, to respect the property of others, to share with friends, to take part in group enterprises, to obey the rules of the group.[11] Attitudes of unselfishness, courtesy, fair play, perseverance, and consideration were the expected results of kindergarten experiences.[12] The democratic virtues of being able to plan together, to share responsibilities, and to think through problems as a group were also extolled. It is obvious that, stated in this manner, the goals were a residue of the habit training developed under the auspices of Patty Smith Hill.

When these goals were generalized, the function of the kindergarten was revealed as fostering the individual, personal growth for each child. The rhetoric changed gradually: the discussions were no longer in terms of "character training," but of providing "wholesome, happy living for each child," or "social and emotional adjustment." In 1940 a study showed that "no aim was more consistently accepted

[8] Edna Dean Baker, "Report of Conferring Committee on Reorganization, International Kindergarten Union," *Childhood Education,* VI (June, 1930), 469.

[9] See for example: Elinor Lee Beebe, "Entering Kindergarten and What it Means to the Child." *Childhood Education,* XII (October, 1935), 23-28; Rebecca M. Coffin, "Independent Work and Play Periods," *Childhood Education,* XIV (January, 1938), 218-222; Dorothea McCarthy, "Guiding Children's Social Development," *Childhood Education,* XV (November, 1938), 113-117.

[10] In every two-year period there were over forty articles listed in Education Index; usually there were over fifty with the high point of 95 in 1957-1959.

[11] Edna Dean Baker, "Interpreting the Kindergarten," *Journal of the National Education Association,* XXII (April, 1933), 122.

[12] Ruth G. Strickland, "The Contribution of the Kindergarten," *Journal of the National Education Association,* XX (March, 1931), 77.

than the socialization of the child;" [13] indeed, social adjustment has become the one kindergarten goal accepted and understood by the public at large. More recently the major function of the kindergarten has been referred to as "individual personality development." [14] This one broad purpose was designated by large numbers of kindergarten teachers in both public and private schools and seemed to reflect psychoanalytic views; but always, when the specifics behind these general statements are analyzed, a large component of habit formation remained.

Professional Detachment

The early interest in kindergarten included a community of laymen in close contact with professionals. The free kindergarten associations of the early years were made up of non-professionals concerned with the welfare of young children but who depended on trained teachers to work directly with the children. However, as the training of kindergarten teachers became more professionalized and as kindergartens became part of the bureaucratic structure of public schools, the place for the concerned layman diminished. Since articles appeared essentially in the "house organs" of early childhood education they became filled with a specialized educational terminology lacking meaning and appeal to powerful laymen; leaders were protesting the values of kindergarten only to themselves. They were talking more to each other than to the public at large or even to other professional educators. Effective dialogues were not carried on with the professionals on either side of the kindergarten—neither with the nursery school educators on the one hand nor with the administrators and teachers of the elementary grades on the other hand. The conflicting values of these groups blocked communication. While the curriculum in the primary grades had been responsive to some of the values cherished by early childhood educators, their curriculum rationale was different enough to deter effective dialogue. Instead of

[13] Dorothy Koehring, "Kindergarten Contributions to Present Day Elementary Education," *Childhood Education*, XVIII (May, 1942), 401.

[14] *Kindergarten Practices, 1961*, Hazel Davis, Project Director (Washington, D. C.: Research Division, National Education Association, 1962), Research Monograph 1962-M2, p. 25.

moving to close the gap during this period, the kindergarten increased its support for the child development point of view. Administrators, who neither understood nor accepted the rationale of the kindergarten, demanded other kinds of learning experiences. One answer was to push some of the work of the first grade down into the kindergarten. Programs of reading readiness or even of reading instruction appeared.

READING READINESS

The pressures to bring the kindergarten in line with the primary grades were felt in efforts to begin the skills of literacy early. William S. Gray, an authority in the teaching of reading, had insisted that kindergarten should share the responsibility of the first grade in preparing children to read. "Since pupils entering the first grade, who are prepared for reading, make satisfactory progress in learning to read; kindergarten teachers should adopt as one of their aims the development of those attitudes and habits which make for reading readiness." [15] This recommendation was made with the full recognition that the chief purpose of kindergarten was "to help the child adjust to school life"; very directly this included preparing him "to make rapid progress in learning to read." [16]

To administrators unable to understand or to accept what they considered to be the vague goals of kindergarten, the function of preparing children to read was welcome. One outspoken administrator stated, "Curriculum planning on the kindergarten level has in the past been approached in a very impractical fashion. . . . My own philosophy and objectives would be that kindergarten is a readiness program for the first grade." [17] From the literature of the period it is impossible to tell how many shared this opinion, but judging from the vehement responses of the leaders in the field of kindergarten education, the opinion must have been widespread.

[15] William S. Gray, "Training and Experiences That Prepare for Reading," *Childhood Education*, III (January, 1927), 213.

[16] *Ibid.*, p. 214.

[17] Harry Bowen, "A More Meaningful Kindergarten," *Ohio Schools*, XXXIII (April, 1955), 28, 31.

Positions Regarding Reading Readiness

The concept of readiness gained credence and became pivotal in discussions of the curriculum for young children. Attached to the reading process, the alliterative term "reading readiness" was applied —and given a variety of meanings over the years. As Thorndike had originally used it in educational psychology, readiness was a synonym for "set" or that condition in an organism for which to act is "satisfying" and "not to act is annoying." [18] Thus readiness referred to a condition at a given moment and constituted an effective predisposition to one particular kind of activity.[19] It was thought possible for a teacher to facilitate readiness by assisting in the acquisition of vital adjustments and getting rid of conditions that interfered with the proper mental set. This concept of readiness also proposed that the teacher develop strong motives for reading, which resulted in replacing storytelling by direct reading from books so that children would recognize books as the source of intriguing stories and thereby desire to learn to read.

The concept of maturation, however, suggested that there was an optimum time for learning to read and that attempts to teach before this stage was reached were laborious and unsuccessful. According to Gesell, in the achievement of any skill, the development of function is preceded by certain structural developments. Studies were made of the physical maturity of children's eyes in order to prevent giving reading instruction before eyes were ready to carry the strain.[20] Gesell extended the description of the active physiological process of maturation as equally applicable to mental processes.[21] The belief became established that a mental age of six-and-a-half was essential

[18] Edward L. Thorndike and Arthur I. Gates, *Elementary Principles of Education* (New York: Macmillan, 1929), p. 89.

[19] Arthur I. Gates, *Psychology for Students of Education* (New York: Macmillan, 1923), p. 106.

[20] Winifred Bain, *Parents Look at Modern Education* (New York: D. Appleton – Century Co., 1935), p. 85. Cf., Olive S. Peck, "Eye Hygiene in Reading," Marjorie Hardy (ed.), *Reading Emphasis in School Activities* (Washington, D. C.: Association for Childhood Education, 1933), p. 7.

[21] Arnold Gesell, "Maturation and the Patterning of Behavior," in Carl Murchison (ed.), *A Handbook of Child Psychology* (Worcester, Mass., Clark University Press, 1933), p. 210.

before a child could profit from systematic reading instruction. This implied that the teacher must respect the individual readiness of each child; there was little she could do to hurry it along.

Nevertheless, it was still believed that an experiential readiness or the development of a background of certain experiences would make subsequent intellectual content more meaningful.[22] The idea grew that children who had concrete experiences with objects and materials could absorb the symbols related to them more readily than those who lacked such experience. This had great meaning for kindergarten teachers, who were eager to think of the kindergarten as a place where the child could secure informally the type of concrete experiences that would prepare him for reading in first grade. They had been saying for a long time that the rich, first-hand experiences of the kindergarten provided an excellent background for later work of a more formal nature.

M. Lucile Harrison's small volume published in 1936, a classic exposition of reading readiness, included activities to promote experiential readiness.[23] Following a discussion of factors of physical and personal development, a chapter was devoted to the kinds of vital experience children should have in order to build the generalized abilities considered important. To foster the desired skills, informal, first-hand experiences were suggested, such as excursions, dramatizations, construction work, and games—many of the activities kindergarten children had engaged in for some time, but here their meaning for the reading process was clarified. The chapter concluded with the statement that one of the most important contributions of the kindergarten year was training in readiness to read. Miss Harrison's recommendations for experiences were meaningful and acceptable to kindergarten teachers. The idea caught on and evoked a continuous stream of literature explaining the building of experiential readiness. The concept was so broad, however, that it eventually lost its definitive aspects in such statements as: "In a well-rounded kin-

[22] John E. Anderson, "Changing Emphasis in Early Childhood Education." *School and Society,* XLIX (January 7, 1939), 5.
[23] *Reading Readiness* (Boston: Houghton Mifflin Co., 1936).

dergarten program almost everything a child does leads toward reading in some way." [24]

While one group placed their emphasis on the word *experience* and interpreted reading readiness as resulting from experiences valuable in the present and possessing deferred values for the time when children would have to deal with the abstract symbols of reading, another group placed the emphasis on the word *reading* and brought reading readiness closer to the mechanics of the formal reading process. These included such abilities as seeing likenesses and differences in form, hearing differences in sound, and knowing the left to right, top to bottom progression in reading. Using these specific skills, it was possible to introduce more formal ways of building reading readiness. Workbooks were frequently recommended for first grade, but their use in kindergarten programs expanded as well.[25]

Eventually reading readiness came to mean a composite of these discrete points of view: an expression of interest and purpose in reading, a general state of maturation including social and emotional maturity as well as visual equipment, and an experiential background that could be developed through kindergarten activities. Opinion divided, however, on how closely reading readiness should be related to the mechanics of learning to read. Kindergarten specialists had welcomed the broad concept of experiential readiness, but they rebelled at the use of narrowly conceived pencil-and-paper exercises as a part of the kindergarten curriculum. Especially they opposed the view of readiness as the primary function of the kindergarten; the deferred values of a readiness program simply did not square with "the child development point of view."

Protests grew increasingly vigorous. A program that insured that a five-year-old "goes through a reading readiness book, does eye-perception exercises, learns to stay within lines when he colors, learns to share, and above all, learns to sit still" was sterile and failed

[24] Edwina Deans, "Is There a Reading Readiness Program?" *Viewpoints on Educational Issues and Problems,* Thirty-ninth Annual Schoolmen's Week Proceedings (Philadelphia: University of Pennsylvania Press, 1952), p. 96.

[25] Marion Monroe, *Growing Into Reading* (Chicago: Scott, Foresman and Company, 1951), p. 224.

to see the child in all his developmental aspects, according to Celia Stendler.[26] The greatest threat to the kindergarten was the misconception of purpose; as Millie Almy put it, "there are at least some instances in which children are going to kindergarten because the adults are placing a premium on 'reading readiness.' " [27] Kindergarten had to be more than preparation for first grade; five-year-olds needed a more challenging and flexible program. Anne Hoppock denounced kindergarten programs that were beginning reading by "using a purely mechanical system which crowds out the broad-based language experiences which are essential to success in reading." [28] Such a program not only denied children the right to explore, to create, to stretch their minds; it tended to "rob children of childhood."

During the decades between the twenties and the sixties two very strong positions developed. There were those who believed that unless kindergarten included a more or less formal reading readiness program it asked too little of children and featured only play. A survey published in the early sixties reported that many principals held that formal reading readiness work was expected to supply the "intellectual" stimulus of the kindergarten program.[29] A second group firmly opposed this position on the grounds that it asked too much of young children in a way that ran counter to their developmental needs. When a premium was placed upon reading readiness, children were denied full, rich living at the five-year-old level. The question of reading readiness, loaded with an academic or a limited connotation, caused more "good kindergarten teachers to 'do battle' than any other single question bearing on kindergarten education." [30]

[26] Celia Burns Stendler, "Let Them Be Five," *Illinois Education,* XXXVII (April, 1949), 286.

[27] Millie Almy, "Programs for Young Children," *Educational Leadership,* VIII (February, 1951), 271.

[28] Anne Hoppock, "Danger to Kindergartens," *Journal of the American Association of University Women,* LII (May, 1959), 228.

[29] *Kindergarten Practices, 1961.* Hazel Davis, Project Director (Washington, D.C., Research Division, National Education Association, 1962), Research Monograph 1962-M2, p. 26.

[30] Neith Headley, *Foundation Learnings in the Kindergarten,* (Washington, D.C.: Department of Kindergarten-Primary Education, NEA, 1958), p. 1.

Determining Readiness

The habit inventories of the twenties became the trait rating scales of the thirties and were firmly established as part of kindergarten report cards. Children were rated on such characteristics as cooperation, courtesy, self-reliance, promptness, and orderliness. Parents were informed whether children were performing in a satisfactory or unsatisfactory manner. But the new directions of evaluation were related to reading readiness. Since mental age was considered an important criterion in determining readiness, it was necessary to ascertain the IQ of each child. The use of individual Stanford Binet tests was recommended,[31] but there was also a search for a satisfactory group test to determine mental ability.

By 1936, Emmett Betts, Murray Lee and Willis Clark, Marion Monroe, M. J. Vanwagenen, Gertrude Hildreth, and others had developed readiness tests to be used at the kindergarten level.[32] These tended to focus upon such reading mechanics as auditory discrimination, seeing likenesses and differences, ability to remember visual forms, and ocular-motor control. Like all systems of evaluation, the tests had an impact upon the goals of the program. "Pressures inherent in the reading-readiness program compel teachers to depend upon drill so that the children will give satisfactory performance on the test at the end of the year," commented one writer.[33]

MAJOR DEVELOPMENTS OF THE PERIOD

Obviously in the past decades much of the theory of the kindergarten had been based upon the doctrines of behaviorism. The picture of the child presented in kindergarten literature was largely in terms of the normative data of the period. The concept of a "needs" curriculum was based on a concept of developmental needs derived from child study. Faith in an instinctual process of matura-

---

[31] Harrison, *Reading Readiness*, p. 62. Cf., "Training Kindergarten Teachers to Give Binets," *School and Society*, XLVIII (July 23, 1938), pp. 123-124.

[32] Harrison, pp. 63-64.

[33] Martha Seeling, "Education in a Democratic Society," in Jerome Leavitt, (ed.), *Nursery-Kindergarten Education*, (New York: McGraw-Hill Book Company, 1958), p. 34.

tion tended to support a belief in fixed intelligence and the possibility of determining a meaningful measure of that innate intelligence. Reliance on objectively determined scientific data was supreme.

The normative picture of the child, coupled with the standards set for conduct in the twenties, seemed to imply that one program could be equally effective for all kinds of children regardless of their background of experience. "A good school day" recommended for all five-year-olds could become a curriculum for conformity, especially when precise habits were the desired goals for all. The fallacy in the use of normative data developed through equating it with "normal behavior." It was all too easy to cover up the uniqueness of individual children or of groups.

Analytic permissiveness coupled with a belief in genetically regulated maturation induced teachers to remove direct restrictions and to withhold learning pressures. As a result the psycho-social climate of the kindergarten became more democratic, but little progress was made toward understanding or promoting intellectual growth. The swing toward emphasis on the child's socio-emotional growth was a beneficial one. It gave substantial encouragement to many aspects of the kindergarten program that teachers had been carrying out on an intuitive basis. The entirely proper but sometimes overwhelming concern for the physical, social, and emotional development of young children, however, often led to programs that were intellectually barren. A confusion of goals led some teachers to withhold intellectual challenge or guidance in the development of skills for fear they might inhibit the child's individual expression. In an effort to protect the child from repetitious rote learning, which is often meaningless, opportunities for mental growth were negated in some programs.

While some teachers held firmly to the child development point of view, others capitulated to the pressures to make kindergarten a direct preparation for formalized learning. One suspects that in these classrooms less attention was given to new information about the complex relationship between learning and the emotions. Undoubtedly there were schools where inappropriate formal workbook exercises were a major part of the kindergarten day.

The child development data of the period did accentuate the difference between effective and ineffective teaching-learning methods. It clearly supported the necessity for children's dealing with concrete aspects of their world before they could go into symbolization and abstractions in a meaningful way. It has left no doubt about the subtle links between feelings and learning. Though developmental psychology could not serve as a means for the selection of material to be learned, it has provided many answers to questions about the ways in which children deal with information and concepts.

To summarize the past forty years, the form of the curriculum itself remained relatively unchanged despite new ways of talking about it. One suspects that a kindergarten teacher from the twenties would feel comfortably at home in many kindergarten classrooms in the sixties. Even though it was called a "needs" curriculum, the content frequently centered around seasons and holidays, the home and community helpers. The equipment and supplies found in kindergarten classrooms were exactly those developed in the twenties. The organization of the curriculum remained essentially the same. Creative experiences, always deemed significant, were elevated to an even more conspicuous place in the curriculum. One of the major weaknesses of the "needs" curriculum was the failure to define or develop a rationale for determining children's intellectual needs. The kindergarten teacher was left with no criteria for selecting among experiences for her precise group of children.

Pressures for change in the kindergarten curriculum during this period came essentially from outside the leadership of early childhood education. Although there was gradual acceptance of some fundamental postulates of psychoanalysis, the leaders never really consciously espoused Freudian theory nor analyzed its implications for the curriculum. Had they done this, they would have recognized how much the analytic insistence upon individual meanings was at variance with standards accepted for all children.

As reading specialists and administrators advocated formalized reading readiness programs and exerted efforts to put them into practice, kindergarten teachers became defensive about the more flexible program that had such great meaning for them. Placed in a defensive position, which demanded their energies for maintaining the status quo, they were not as free to branch out into new channels of curriculum change. Certainly in the past forty years the changes in the kindergarten curriculum have been negligible compared to the vast reconstruction of the program during the forty years that immediately preceded them. Since the beginning of the decade of the sixties, however, the kindergarten has faced even sharper challenges to its most cherished convictions. There is an intensive drive for curriculum revision that can no longer be denied.

NEW DEMANDS FOR CURRICULUM RECONSTRUCTION

Early childhood education is obviously in ferment—a ferment comparable to that at the turn of the century. The issues, too long left unresolved, are plaguing kindergarten today. Never before has the education of very young children assumed greater importance in the eyes of the general public. Kindergarten is challenged to make its contribution to building a "Great Society" in a way never before contemplated. New programs for children of slum areas are being developed, not for 'building character," nor for "fostering social and emotional adjustment," but rather as a means of providing a "cognitive tooling up" to prepare children for subsequent school experiences. Francis Keppel, U. S. Commissioner of Education, expresses the belief that the greatest possibility for reaching culturally deprived children lies in early childhood.[34] As a result, educators not formerly concerned with early childhood have turned to designing programs for children under six. Throughout the country questions are raised about the effectiveness of early education for children who live in an increasingly complex and technological society.

Specialists in the field of early childhood education are themselves seeking solutions to perplexing problems. Elenora Moore writes that children in urban core sections of large cities should have school experiences different from those of children who live in suburbia.[35] Faith in a needs or emerging curriculum is questioned by three current writers: "Children's spontaneous interests, which at one time were advocated as a basis of selection for an emerging curriculum cannot be relied on to lead the child into all the areas of knowl-

[34] *Education Summary* (New London, Connecticut: Croft Educational Services, January 1, 1956), p. 1.

[35] Elenora Moore, *Fives at School* (New York: G. Putnam's Sons, 1959).

edge he will need to explore in order to interpret today's world." [36]
It has been suggested that the "here and now" of children is vastly
different from that of children growing up in the nineteen-twenties.[37]
Reliance on "manipulative materials" as adequate stimuli for learning has been criticized as not holding "the challenge for young
children that it formerly did." [38] The "blocks, paints and clay curriculum" has been found lacking in intellectual content.[39] These statements strip away some of the basic orientations the kindergarten has
followed in this century; they also evidence a new freedom in thinking about the curriculum that is unique to our time. Such criticism
seeks to retain what is valid in the program, to change what is no
longer useful.

Others, more impatient to construct an effective program, are
tending to disregard existent theory. Impatient parents, anxious for
their children to begin reading and writing, exert pressure for formalized approaches. The Montessori method, which promises early
skill development, is experiencing an extensive revival. Educators,
focusing sharply on cognitive aspects of growth and designing programs that rapidly immerse children in symbolic learning, tend to
disregard the vast body of knowledge about the young child that has
been collected over the past fifty years.

Some programs seem to take children by the tail, like comets,
and drag them into the space age. Dr. Omar K. Moore writes, for
example, "Modern society is evolving so dynamically that we can
no longer depend on child-rearing methods which were adequate
before. . . . We have no time. We can't stand pat. . . . A new kind of
person is needed to handle the rate of change." [40] He proposes that

[36] Kenneth D. Wann, Miriam S. Dorn and Elizabeth Ann Liddle,
Fostering Intellectual Development in Young Children (New York: Bureau of Publications, Teachers College, Columbia University, 1962), p. 99.

[37] Elizabeth Ann Liddle, *The Child's World Today: A Study of Information Concerning Selected Technological Advancements as Verbally Expressed by Five Year Olds With Implications for the Curriculum* (Un-
published Doctoral Dissertation, Teachers College, Columbia University,
1958).

[38] Kenneth D. Wann, "Children Want to Know," *Childhood Education,*
XXXVII (September, 1960), 11.

[39] Roma Gans, Celia B. Stendler and Millie Almy, *Teaching Young
Children* (Yonkers-on-Hudson, New York: World Book Co., 1952), p. 225.

[40] Quoted in Maya Pines, "How Three-year-olds Teach Themselves to
Read and Love It," *Harper's Magazine* (May, 1963), p. 64.

specially designed "talking typewriters" be used to teach three- and four-year-olds to read. Most radical in disregarding accumulated knowledge about child development is Carl Bereiter, who recommends "selecting specific and significant educational objectives and teaching them in the most direct manner possible, as is done in the intermediate and secondary school grades." [41]

The widespread discontent accentuates the need for concerted effort to reconstruct the kindergarten curriculum. In 1960 Ilse Forest, who experienced and wrote about the curricular reconstruction of the twenties, told the Pennsylvania Schoolmen's Week conference;

At the turn of the century, a group of kindergartners revolted, and, under the leadership of Patty Smith Hill and others, made of the kindergarten an excellent illustration of progressive education. The time is past due when kindergartners should again take hold of the situation, and recreate their thinking and procedures to meet the needs of today. . . . In 1960 we cannot afford to be less courageous. [42]

Such a reconstruction implies no simple relationship between socially derived goals and demands on children to perform, nor an ad hoc utilization of new educational knowledge. It signifies a look at all current issues and the synthesis of all relevant knowledge to determine supportable solutions.

No single arena for debating issues and determining new directions exists in the sixties as it did at the turn of the century. No one organization enlists the support of active early childhood specialists or serves as an effective voice for supportable program innovation. While the Association for Childhood Education International holds the membership of many public school kindergarten teachers and leaders, its interests embrace the education of children from two to twelve. The former Department of Kindergarten-Primary Education of the NEA has become the Department of Elementary-Kindergarten-Nursery Education exerting influence mainly through its

[41] Carl Bereiter, *et al*, "An Academically Oriented Pre-School for Culturally Deprived Children," in Fred M. Heckinger (ed.), *Pre-School Education Today* (Garden City, N. Y.: Doubleday, 1966), p. 106.

[42] Ilse Forest, "The Responsibility of the Kindergarten in the School's Readiness Program," *Education in Transition*, Forty-Seventh Annual Schoolmen's Week Proceedings (Philadelphia: University of Pennsylvania Press, 1960), p. 134.

publications. From a reorganization of the National Association for Nursery Education an enlarged association spanning the nursery, kindergarten, and primary years was voted by the membership in 1964.[43] Under the unwieldy name of the National Association for the Education of Young Children, the organization appears to have a strong forward thrust. All associations include the kindergarten level. The leadership of early childhood educators is divided among them.

Funding for experimental programs comes from large corporations and from the U. S. Office of Education, which may have an inestimable influence on curricular change. The fragmentation of leadership plus the diversity of points of view complicate the process of reconstructing the kindergarten program.

[43] Cornelia Goldsmith, "The Impact of a Growing NAEYC on Young Children," *Young Children*, XX (March, 1965), p. 209.

12
TOWARD NEW THEORETICAL POSITIONS

Of the fundamental assumptions that undergird the kindergarten curriculum some remain almost in their original form, others have changed with ideological changes. Theoretical positions that were conceived with a breadth of vision have proved serviceable over long periods of time; others, developed in accord with their contemporary culture, rapidly became useless in a changed society. With the kindergarten at the center of one vital educational debate, it seems appropriate to focus attention on the basic postulates that were built into the curriculum in its nearly one hundred and twenty years of existence in this country. The issues demanding resolution as we approach the last decades of the twentieth century arise from entrenched assumptions and points of view.

The pressures for change in the kindergarten curriculum are uncomfortably great. Change itself, however, cannot be the only criterion nor pressure the only motive. Constructive action must go beyond defense of the status quo; it grows as the educator faces challenges with the illlumination of historical perspective and with an integrity that becomes evident in future projections. As new theory and research are brought to bear on perplexing problems in kindergarten education, subsequent innovations will be a step into the future. By utilizing an understanding of past developments in the evaluation of emerging directions, early childhood educators will guarantee that past values will not be hidden or ignored. The future may then become more clearly perceived and more soundly based.

TRANSITIONS IN DEVELOPMENTAL THEORY

Two major assessments need to be made in connection with the child development data in use in kindergarten literature: the first is the adequacy of the collection of facts gathered in the thirties and forties, the second is its effectiveness as a basis for making curricular decisions. The normative description of the child must first be evaluated in terms of current beliefs about the nature of development.

When the first edition of *Education in the Kindergarten* appeared in 1936, the chapter on the characteristics of five-year-olds in objective, descriptive terms reflected the child development research at that time.[1] It represented the frontier of thinking about child growth during that period. A compendium of child development information published in 1931 reveals that in the data presented descriptions of molecular phenomena, anecdotal accounts of behavior and normative guidelines predominate.[2] As we have seen, the assumption underlying the description of five-year-old characteristics suggested a developmental growth pattern so powerful that it negated varying individual backgrounds: nature was conceived as prevailing over nurture in setting limits to growth. Intellectual growth was subsumed under this dominant theoretical position.

Although the use of child development data has generally remained frozen at this level, child development theory and research have moved toward the study of more abstract psychological processes and behavioral constructs. In assessing theoretical perspectives Urie Bronfenbrenner writes that, "the gathering of data for data's sake" has lost favor and that the major interest is now clearly with "inferred processes and constructs" such as autonomy, aggression, dependence, or anxiety.[3] The point of view has shifted from normative desecription to understanding the child as a total organism interacting in a milieu, from objective studies of motor development

[1] Josephine C. Foster and Neith E. Headley, *Education in the Kindergarten* (New York: American Book Co., 1936).

[2] C. Murchison (ed.), *A Handbook of Child Psychology* (Worcester, Mass.: Clark University Press, 1931).

[3] Urie Bronfenbrenner, "Developmental Theory in Transition," in Harold W. Stevenson (ed.), *Child Psychology*, Sixty-second Yearbook of the National Society for the Study of Education (Chicago: University of Chicago Press, 1963), p. 527.

or language growth to the recognition of forces which change human characteristics in broad perspective.

Illustrative of the new child studies which attempt to explain what is taking place in the functioning of the child as he progresses along the developmental path is Lois Barclay Murphy's concept of "coping." This study, based on data gathered over a twelve-year period, is an analysis of children's patterns of response to "new situations and challenges calling for responses not previously crystallized." [4] In this approach clues to the child's makeup and functioning are inferred from his patterns of coping with the obstacles, hazards, and series of active transitions that invade his life. This theoretical innovation leads directly away from the static view of trait development, which says that the child should grow consistently in independence. "On the contrary," writes Lois Murphy,

> if the child has some inner compulsion to be autonomous under all kinds of conditions, if he is not able to ask for help when his energy lags or when he is confronted with a situation which is too much for him, we can very likely expect trouble later. The branch that bends with the wind is less likely to break than a more rigid branch. [5]

Children's coping procedures were found to include regression as well as steady progress.

New Views of Intellectual Growth

The theoretical construct of "intelligence" has, of course, been a matter of intensive research for decades. The most profoundly striking shift in point of view is occurring as the impact of environment upon intellectual functioning is gaining recognition. Until recent years, the scientific study of behavior with its focus upon conditioning and the study of personality with its concern for motivation have viewed the child in a "state of mindlessness." [6] We are now

---

[4] Lois B. Murphy, *The Widening World of Childhood: Paths Toward Mastery* (New York: Basic Books, 1962), p. 6.

[5] Lois B. Murphy, "Self-Management Capacities in Children," in Alexander Frazier (ed.), *New Insights and the Curriculum* (Washington, D.C.: Association for Supervision and Curriculum Development, 1963), p. 119.

[6] William E. Martin, "Rediscovering the Mind of the Child; A Significant Trend in Research in Child Development," *Merrill-Palmer Quarterly,* VI (January, 1960), 67-76.

ready, William Martin believes, to perceive the child not only as a reactor and a purposer but also as a knower, for we are at the threshold of working out a cognitive theory of behavior and development.

Newer conceptions of intellectual development challenge the belief of fixed intelligence and suggest that an individual's encounters with his environment in the early years are the major determinants of his intelligence. The relevant work of Benjamin Bloom utilizes no original research but has extended the interpretation of older data through synthesis and new statistical analysis.[7] In *Stability and Change in Human Characteristics,* Bloom presents the proposition that variations in the environment are most potent during periods of rapid change. He then offers evidence that identifies the rapid change periods for selected characteristics: height, intelligence, school achievement, interests, attitudes, and personality. With the exception of school achievement, Bloom found the most rapid period for the development of the above characteristics to be in the first five years of life.

Following his thesis that characteristics are more amenable to change during the period of rapidly accelerating growth, Bloom summarizes evidence that "by about age 4, 50% of the variation in intelligence at age 17 is accounted for." [8] Thus, environmental impact upon intellectual growth is inferred to be the greatest in the early years; deprivation in these years is believed to have serious consequences. Bloom hypothesizes that nursery school and kindergarten can profoundly affect "the child's general learning pattern." [9] For personality characteristics, Bloom estimates that as much as one half of the variance of dependency and aggression at adolescence is predictable at age five.[10] The early years, then, are equally important for affective growth. Although Bloom's proposition that the early years hold great significance for personality development is in harmony with psychoanalytic literature, his proposal that the early years are most influential for intellectual growth is at variance with the tradition that put great faith in maturational theory.

[7] Benjamin Bloom, *Stability and Change in Human Characteristics* (New York: John Wiley, 1964).

[8] *Ibid.,* p. 68.

[9] *Ibid.,* p. 110.

[10] *Ibid.,* p. 177.

J. McV. Hunt demonstrates in his forcefully organized book, *Intelligence and Experience,* not only that the assumption of fixed intelligence is no longer tenable, but that the general notion which considers behavioral development to be an automatic aspect of anatomic maturation is also erroneous.[11] Hunt synthesizes the vast body of research and theory extant, including the studies of Jean Piaget. Research based on animal behavior as well as studies of human development are included. In Hunt's interpretation is a hint that the generalization of results from infrahuman species to human behavior may not be quite as completely applicable as Thorndike believed. In interpreting studies of the swimming behavior of salamanders, which appears to depend purely on maturational development, Hunt explicitly states that this "need not imply that encounters with the environment are unimporant for behavioral development in higher organisms." [12] This raises a question untouched since Thorndike's early studies were based upon an assumption that the path from infant rats to humans was a continuous one.

The crumbling concept of fixed intelligence is referred to by Samuel Kirk.[13] Marie Hughes moves from the conception of "unfolding" to the process of environmental interaction.[14] Ira Gordon explains the way in which new data lead to the extremely important inference of cognitive development as modifiable.[15] All this illustrates a major reversal in psychology from a notion that intelligence is fixed and immutable to the idea that we can do something about a child's intelligence by the nature of the richness of his environmental interactions both animate and inanimate. Experience thus becomes the crucial factor in cognitive development as the view prevails that intellectual structure is built through interactive transactions with the world. And a corollary to this increasingly accepted belief is the sug-

[11] J. McV. Hunt, *Intelligence and Experience* (New York: The Ronald Press, 1961).

[12] *Ibid.,* p. 360. See also, p. 353.

[13] Samuel Kirk, *American Psychologist,* XIX (April, 1964), 293.

[14] Marie Hughes, "Learning and Becoming—New Meanings to Teachers," in Walter B. Waetjen (ed.), *Learning and Mental Health in the School* (Washington, D.C.: Association for Supervision and Curriculum Development, 1966), p. 127.

[15] Ira J. Gordon, "New Conceptions of Children's Learning and Development," *Learning and Mental Health,* p. 56.

gestion that the early years of development are particularly significant for intellectual growth. For the literature discussed gives evidence that experience affects not only the age at which behaviors develop, but whether or not they will, in fact, develop at all.

Many new propositions about cognition reflect the influence of Jean Piaget, who for more than thirty years has been studying the development of intellectual functions in chldren. For Piaget, intellectual growth is a developmental process involving two interactive functions between the individual and his environment: (1) inward integration or organization, called *assimilation,* and (2) outward adaptive coping, called *accommodation.* Further development depends on these internal and external factors "equilibrating" each other through the self-regulation and self-correction of the person.[16] Equilibrium represents the point at which the processes of accommodation and assimilation achieve a fruitful balance.

The picture of the development of intelligence that emerges from the observations of Piaget and his collaborators is one in which there are periods of cognitive reorganization. One such reorganization is estimated to occur at about eighteen months of age and another between the years of five and eight. Millie Almy's recent replication of some of Piaget's work corroborates the transitional nature of the age period.[17] She finds that the results of her study argue in favor "of giving deliberate attention to whatever underpinnings of logical thought can be identified in the early childhood period." [18] Her findings also highlight the role of experiential factors and point to the significance of environmental encounters, including both the child's physical activity and social exchanges with his peers.

In order effectively to promote intellectual growth, according to Hunt, environmental transactions must contain a match between the inner integrative patterns a child has achieved and the external circumstances that will challenge him to accommodate himself to them without undue stress.[19] Teaching becomes the problem of "the

[16] Jean Piaget, "Foreword," in Millie Almy, *et al., Young Children's Thinking* (New York: Teachers College Press, 1966), p. vi.

[17] Millie Almy, *et al., Young Children's Thinking* (New York: Teachers College Press, 1966), p. 108.

[18] *Ibid.,* p. 127.

[19] Hunt, p. 357.

match." L. S. Vygotsky takes the position that intellectual structures are built through use; experiences provided for children must be "aimed not so much at the ripe but the ripening functions." [20] This implies a new concept of readiness for instruction. Almy concurs with Vygotsky's theory that learning can be "paced in such a fashion as to enhance and stimulate" development.[21] She further interprets Piaget's theory as implying that the nature of experiencing at each level of development determines not only the timing but the quality of thinking at the next level. Readiness can be achieved through educational experiences to a much larger extent than was believed possible when maturational theory dominated early childhood education. A fortuitous position on readiness can no longer be substantiated. In the case of children living in environments where appropriate experiences are unlikely to be available, waiting for readiness is unproductive, indeed.

At the very least the growing understandings of young children's thinking "open the door to mental territory so far largely unknown and uncomprehended." [22] New discoveries seem to open up unlimited possibilities for guiding children's learning. Yet the child is not completely manipulable. Certain developmental factors need recognition. Children have unique styles of learning as well as varying conceptual levels. Piaget's theory has been interpreted to show that there is a band of experiences within which the child can and must accommodate that will result in cognitive change; experiences too easily assimilated or those beyond the reach of assimilation do not lead to change. In the words of William Kessen, "The child can learn only in the range of the knowable unknown." [23]

In general, the research extends the efforts in the scientific study of growth that have dominated child development since the eighteen-

[20] L. S. Vygotsky, *Thought and Language* (Cambridge: Massachusetts Institute of Technology Press, 1962), pp. 104-105.

[21] Millie Almy, "Child Development and the Curriculum," In Dwayne Huebner (ed.), *A Reassessment of the Curriculum* (New York: Teachers College Press, 1964), p. 44.

[22] Irving Sigel, "Finding the Clue to Children's Thought Processes," *Young Children,* XXI (September, 1966), 345.

[23] William Kessen, "The Strategy of Instruction," in Jerome Bruner (ed.), *Learning About Learning* (Washington, D.C.: U.S. Government Printing Office, 1966), p. 102.

nineties. Although there is some distress over the extent to which research findings have been extrapolated, most psychologists are engaged in scientifically designed studies. A group of existentialist psychologists, however, repudiates the efforts to study man in terms of forces, drives, or developmental stages. To existentialists the human can never be explained in these fragmented terms; the more accurately the mechanistic aspects of functioning are described, the more readily is the existing "person" lost.[24] This group would de-emphasize "scientism" in the study of human development and encourage a "psychology of the fully evolved and authentic self and its ways of being." [25] To these psychological thinkers the issues still rest in the selection of acceptable means for obtaining data for understanding man's development.

But for the increasing number of educators who accept the importance of the early years for cognitive growth, the concept of modifiable intelligence, and the transactional view of learning, the issues concern the means for putting these new convictions into operation. The answers to a number of perplexing problems must be found. What experiences are crucial? How can these best be provided? How can we attain "the match" which might promote the optimum rate of intellectual functioning? Hunt suggests this need not imply "the grim urgency which has been associated with 'pushing' children." [26] Almy points out in fairness that the promotion of strategies that unravel the developmental process of ripening functions does not necessarily imply the judgment that certain learnings ought to be developed earlier.[27] Yet new programs bear witness to the fact that some American psychologists and educators have an interest in speeding up not only the cognitive processes but the learning of skills. Almy suggests further that experimental reports evidence "a degree of impatience with the playful, imaginative, highly personalized thought of the young child." [28]

Another major problem involves maintaining other values of

24 Rollo May (ed.), *Existential Psychology* (New York: Random House, 1961), p. 18.
25 A. H. Maslow, "Existential Psychology—What's In It for Us?" *Existential Psychology,* p. 59.
26 Hunt, p. 363.
27 Almy, *Young Children's Thinking,* p. 42.
28 *Ibid.,* p. 129.

growth while enriching intellectual development. Affective learning is equally significant in the early years. For many leaders in early childhood education, long term goals must include creative activity, spontaneity, and a positive self-concept. Early learning must not mechanize the child's impulses in a manner which sacrifices these values at their source. As we saw earlier, the child development point of view includes not only the construction of a curriculum based upon its tenets, but an attitude of respect for the developmental processes of children. While new psychological understandings supplant those of earlier periods, the point of view appears to be equally valid and to require thoughtful adherence.

Foundations for Curriculum Planning

This brings us back to the question of the effectiveness of child development as the sole basis for curriculum planning. It is doubtful whether all the data psychology can provide can furnish a complete foundation for curriculum development. On the kindergarten level teachers have not found it adequate for determining instructional practices involving intellectual content. Child psychology has been most successful in demonstrating what the child *can* learn and in answering questions of *when* and *how*. What the child can accomplish does not directly assist those making the decisions about what learnings *should* be fostered. Decisions concerning what to teach are philosophically and socially based. Growing interest in promoting creativity, for example, has its basis in a cultural value; the accellerating emphasis on science has expanded simultaneously with increasing technological advances. Sociological and philosophical orientations, as well as man's accumulated knowledge, form a significant substructure for curriculum building. To many educators, psychological data is an essential but not sufficient basis for prescribing instructional practices. Experiences in the past decades indicate that the theoretical rationale for the kindergarten must have a more pluralistic foundation. Evidence mounts that this point can no longer be at issue.

The Role of Play

One assumption proving serviceable over long periods of time is that children learn through play. The concept of what constitutes educative play has changed since Froebel's time, but the conviction that it provides for the dynamic qualities of the child's nature remains in full force. It is viewed as a major means of promoting growth organismically and is in complete accord with the developmental point of view. The advocates of play include growth in the intellectual realm; play activities set the stage for building language facility, enable the child to manipulate and experiment with objects and to develop powers of observation.

In spite of this acceptance of play as a vital learning force in early childhood evidenced by leaders in kindergarten education, it would nevertheless seem to be at the source of the disagreement with others in the educational scene. Because some educators and many parents view play as purposeless activity or as recreation and pleasure-seeking, they want to introduce "serious work" into the curriculum so children can get on with the "real business of learning." This constitutes a fundamental dichotomy in philosophy and value commitment that separates the two groups.

Clearly, some early childhood educators planning the program for young children hold the concept of play that Merle Borrowman has labeled "Hellenic-Romantic" characterized by experiences imbued with spontaneity, self-interest, and immediate satisfaction.[29] The kindergarten with its close alliance to the romantic influence of Rousseau and Froebel and the transcendental thought of Elizabeth Peabody is one of the direct heirs of this tradition. The effect of Dewey's kindergarten program was to reinforce the plan of initiating school tasks by using the child's immediate interests and promoting learning through pleasurable experiences. For present-day kindergarten specialists, Borrowman's statement of the Hellenic-Romantic attitude seems particularly appropriate: "unless students are 'playing' at school tasks—that is to say, approaching them with joy, spontaneity, self-direction and enthusiasm—the Hellenist would suspect that the student is being exploited in terms of someone else's interests."[30] Kindergarten teachers putting into practice the romantic

29 Merle Borrowman, "Traditional Values and the Shaping of American Education," Nelson B. Henry (ed.), *Social Forces Influencing American Education*, Sixtieth Yearbook of the National Society for the Study of Education (Chicago: University of Chicago Press, 1961), pp. 154-155.
30 *Ibid.*, p. 159.

view would protect children from a mechanistic approach to developing content or skills.

On the other hand there are those closer to the Hebraic-Puritan attitude Borrowman describes, who are suspicious of the relation between learning and fun. He uncovers their roots in Hebraic tradition and the New England Puritans to whom duty and obligation were the watchwords, reinforced by positive sanctions for work and success.[31] Some of these people would be drawn to the reading readiness approach in kindergarten to promote the development of designated skills; others might espouse the Montessori method with its promise of early writing and reading. Though Merle Borrowman has posed these two extreme points of view as abstract stereotypes, they are effectively illustrated in current views about the kindergarten and they promote an understanding of the emotion-laden attitudes attached to the curricular implications of each view. Though an individual's position might range anywhere between the two extremes, one suspects that many kindergarten teachers and specialists are very close to the Hellenic-Romantic end of the continuum—indeed, that they may have been drawn to the work with young children because they hold this point of view. With both attitudes toward work and play existing simultaneously, however, and with strong value commitments attached to each, one can begin to understand why the persistent literature about play goes unheeded by one group of educators. It seems that acceptance or rejection of the educative value of play is rooted in the Puritan ethic.

Aside from these two value commitments, many serious students of psychology support play as a means for promoting wholesome growth and learning. We have seen how the connectionists and psychoanalysts have incorporated play so that it appeared in curriculum recommendations with these orientations. Play allows for autonomy on the part of the learner to utilize his own drives, to solve problems, and to handle his environment—autonomy that Murphy considers essential to growth.[32] Many of the conditions E.

---

[31] *Ibid.,* p. 154.

[32] Lois B. Murphy, "Self-Management Capacities in Children," in Alexander Frazier (ed.), *New Insights and the Curriculum* (Washington, D.C.: Association for Supervision and Curriculum Development, 1963), pp. 107-120.

Paul Torrance lists as significant in fostering creative potential are readily available in play: oportunities to manipulate and explore, time for fantasy behavior, an avoidance of over-emphasis on verbal mechanics.[33] The "self-directing interest and curiosity and genuine pleasure in intellectual activity," which Hunt believes to be vital for optimum functioning, may be aspects of play skillfully utilized.[34] Encounters with physical objects, social interactions with peers, and the self-regulation in building new understandings considered essential by Piaget are possible in play. [35]

The emerging group of existential psychologists giving new weight to "identity," "choice," and "futurity" also sanction play.[36] George Kneller, one of this group, writes, "The function of play is one of personal liberation—personal release," and he unites play with new conceptions of art and science into a valuable means of self-expression and a necessary adjunct to the understanding of one's self in relation to other forms of being.[37]

Much that has been cited here supports the kindergarten leaders' faith in the efficacy of play in learning. It would seem that Froebel's concept of play is as fruitful today as it was one hundred and twenty-five years ago, but it may well be redirected to incorporate environmental transactions that promote cognitive growth more effectively. Though lay persons may look at play with misgivings, the art of teaching in the kindergarten still seems to involve the utilization of the young child's proclivity for play for educational purposes. It follows that teachers must learn to help the young child become deeply involved in his early encounters with the world of things and problems in a manner that insures against superficiality and indifference.

[33] E. Paul Torrance, "Factors Affecting Creative Thinking in Children: An Interim Research Report," *Merrill-Palmer Quarterly*, VII (July, 1961), 171-180.

[34] Hunt, p. 363.

[35] Piaget, in Almy, *Young Children's Thinking*, pp. v, vi.

[36] Gordon Allport, "Comment on Earlier Chapters," *Existential Psychology*, p. 95.

[37] George F. Kneller, *Existentialism and Education* (New York: John Wiley, 1958), p. 138.

A THEORY OF LEARNING

Learning is rather generally defined as a process of behavioral change moving in the direction of desired educational goals. Arthur Combs has categorized two dominant frames of reference applicable to promoting behavioral change that are in practice today: a stimulus-response approach in which the way people behave is understood as a direct outgrowth of the stimuli to which they are subjected, and a perceptual approach in which behavior is a result of how things seem to the behavor.[38] Our historical study demonstrated the dominance of stimulus-response theory in curriculum planning; it remains as an historic residue from the conduct curriculum of the twenties, which viewed the socialization of the child as compliance with a middle-class set of ethics and outlined the stimulus situations expected to foster such behavior.

The connectionist psychology of the nineteen-twenties, so helpful to the kindergarten leaders of the period, can hardly remain the sole learning theory for designing kindergarten curricula today. While certain essential learnings may need to be the outcome of stimulus-response methodology, it certainly does not include *all* kinds of learning at a kindergarten level. New developments in learning theory can no longer be ignored. Just as in Patty Smith Hill's era the incompatibility of a stimulus-response psychology with Dewey's flexible social framework of problem-solving went unrecognized, so today the incongruence between molding a child to a predetermined image and allowing for autonomy on the part of the learner and for individual differences remains to be perceived. Since at present no one theory accounts for all kinds of learning within its framework, decisions do not involve an either/or issue but rather the problem of fitting the stimulus-response methodology essential for some skill learning to the cognitive field theories, which emphasize problem-solving, understanding, and functional transfer. Each theory may

[38] Arthur W. Combs, "Personality Theory and Its Implications for Curriculum Development," Alexander Frazier (ed.), *Learning More About Learning* (Washington, D.C.: Association for Supervision and Curriculum Development, 1959), pp. 5-7.

have something to contribute to the educative process, but the problem of synthesis is a knotty one.

Until greater synthesis is achieved, issues in learning theory tend to relate to each other only to the degree that individual perceptual frameworks are recognized. Adherents of the stimulus-response theory give them less credence; supporters of perceptual psychology give them prime recognition. Some innovative programs for early childhood appear closely allied to stimulus-response theory. Automated teaching machines depend on conditioning with reinforcement—extensions of stimulus-response theory. A program that is planned to "concentrate fiercely on a few areas and drill the children like Marines for two hours a day," [39] relies entirely on the adhesion of desired responses to the offered stimuli.

Other learning theorists discard connectionist psychology as out of step with the transactional view of intellectual growth. They would utilize the cognitive, value and affective perceptions which the young child brings to school as the nucleus around which more meanings and concepts can be developed. In their opinion, it is the task of the skillful teacher to build a bridge from individually held perceptions to the extended realities of the child's world. A close relationship between the learner's perceptual concerns and the learning experiences available to them is required. "If this view of learning is valid," writes Donald Snygg, "learning is a process of exploration and experimentation." [40] The relevance of this view of learning to new conceptions of cognitive growth in young children is striking.

Learning that involves the person deeply again focuses on "the match." Barbara Biber states the problem well, "What can early education do to lead the young, groping mind toward the kind of intellectual potency that is represented by the capacity to deal analytically and synthetically with the ever widening world of objective knowledge and personal experience?" [41] This implies delving be-

[39] Maya Pines, "A Pressure Cooker for Four-Year-Old Minds," *Harper's Magazine* (January, 1967), p. 55.

[40] Donald Snygg, "A Cognitive Field Theory of Learning," *Learning and Mental Health in the Schools*, p. 91.

[41] Barbara Biber, "Preschool Education," Robert Ulich (ed.), *Education and the Idea of Mankind* (New York: Harcourt, Brace and World, 1964), p. 86.

hind all verbal façades to the personal meaning of perceptions and experiences. It also implies matching experiences to the conceptual repertoire of a particular child.

The match between the schemata of the individual and the circumstances of the environmental situation in determining whether accommodative modification will occur is a still poorly understood factor though it holds tremendous import for practice. Almy recommends an understanding of Piaget's theory as a powerful tool for assessing children's conceptual growth.[42] A knowing teacher may thus be equipped to select learning experiences appropriate to the conceptual abilities of a child and in this manner prevent meaningless verbalization and rote memorization.

When more sophisticated techniques for appraising the necessary match in both conceptual level and learning style are revealed, teachers will finally be able to provide for individual differences regardless of socioeconomic background. Some rapidly developing recent programs appear to require accommodation by young children that is out of line with their conceptual abilities. "The danger," writes Snygg, "is that the country is embarking on a great program of preschool education for disadvantaged children before we know what opportunities for experiences to give or how to give them." [43] At this stage of knowledge about development an extensive period of empirical trial and error is bound to ensue.

PROVIDING FOR THE ECONOMICALLY DEPRIVED

Societal concerns for the children of the poor are not new. Kindergartens in this country spread on a wave of philanthropic endeavor extended through Free Kindergarten Associations. The nursery school was originally conceived as one answer to the problems of disadvantaged populations. As we have seen, the reconstructed kindergarten program of the nineteen-twenties viewed character training, molding the child behavioristically to a predetermined image, as the way to help children get a better start in life. The behavioral image kindergarten specialists had in mind was grounded in middle-class virtues such as responsibility, industry,

[42] Almy, *Young Children's Thinking*, p. 136.
[43] Snygg, p. 94.

respect for property, sexual modesty, and decorum—not prime values at every socioeconomic level. The generation that drew up the code of behavior saw it as embedded in democratic values and suggestive for the teacher; the generation that followed adopted it as a ready-made set of habits each child must develop to become a conforming citizen in his kindergarten world.

That a middle-class code of values dominated the kindergarten scene for forty years is not surprising; this has been true at other educational levels as well. There is, however, growing evidence that children entering kindergarten from widely varying backgrounds have perceptual frameworks that make it difficult for them to become a part of a kindergarten where expectations differ greatly from those of their home. Martin Deutsch contends that children from lower socioeconomic levels entering the school situation go through a cultural trauma because they are unprepared to meet the middle-class standards required by the school.[44] To the young disadvantaged child, even the teacher's speaking in continuous sentences and anticipating the attention of children is a new phenomenon.

Attuned as the schools have been to the middle-class majority, children from home backgrounds that are at a lower economic and social level seem preconditioned to failure. Recognition of the importance of the early years for intellectual functioning, together with the facts of deprivation, has led to the argument that "an early start must be made to offset the lack of parental teaching, care and mind-molding." [45] This line of reasoning has produced a definition of goals in terms of helping the children "catch up" intellectually with middle-class children. As a result, recommendations for new programs emerge that are intended to provide systematically for intellectual development. Programs include those that would extend accurate language, develop the ability to pay attention for longer periods of time, and promote enthusiasm for learning through games, concrete

[44] Martin Deutsch, "Nursery Education: The Influence of Social Programming on Early Development," *Journal of Nursery Education,* XVIII (April, 1963), 191-197.

[45] Fred M. Hechinger, "Passport to Equality," in Fred M. Hechinger (ed.), *Pre-School Education Today* (New York: Doubleday, 1966), p. 6.

materials, and dramatic play,[46] as well as classrooms that would put children into a "highly task-oriented, no-nonsense" program geared to teach children "in the most direct manner possible." [47]

Highly task-oriented programs place a premium on early development of reading and mathematic skills. The implicit assumption underlying these recommendations is that the traditional program of the primary school is fixed and unyielding, that rigid grade standards are not to be adjusted to varying perceptual frames of reference. Instruction here consists not of matching educative experiences to the conceptual level of children but insistently demands rapid accommodation to school standards. In extreme instances the program takes the form of moving the bureaucratic requirements of inflexible school tradition down so that it hits children earlier.[48] The issue, which underlies numerous educational debates, is clear: should the school accommodate its program to the backgrounds of children or should children be forced to adjust to an outlined school program?

So long as it was assumed that intelligence was genetically fixed, the intellectual inferiority of children who tested below normal was generally accepted. There is sufficient evidence to prove now that economic and cultural differences do affect intellectual growth and put limits upon potential. The new transactional view, which suggests that the encounters the child has with his environment are significant in the building of potential, highlights the importance of the child's early experiences. The inference of development as modifiable holds great promise—a promise especially meaningful for certain segments of our population. The realization of intellectual power seems to demand more adequate growth producing stimulation in the early years—even

[46] Benjamin S. Bloom, Allison Davis, and Robert Hess, *Compensatory Education for Cultural Deprivation* (New York: Holt, Rinehart and Winston, 1965), pp. 17-18.

[47] Carl Bereiter, *et al.,* "An Academically Oriented Pre-School for Culturally Deprived Children," *Pre-School Education Today* (New York: Doubleday, 1966), pp. 106, 109.

[48] James L. Hymes, Jr., review of *Teaching Disadvataged Children in the Preschool* by Carl Bereiter and Siegfried Engelmann in *Educational Leadership,* XXIV (February, 1967), 465.

before kindergarten. The nature of effective stimuli is not readily understood and caution is essential in moving into new programs.

As intervention programs give increased attention to cognitive growth, questions arise. Can this goal be meshed with other long-range educational goals that lead to the good life? What safeguards are needed so that programs will maintain the essential element of humaneness? How can a program be planned that will have lasting effects on intellectual growth? For unless programs can be designed with a breadth of vision, this attempt at social engineering may have no more potent effect than the habit training of the twenties and thirties. "It seems doubtful," writes Millie Almy, "that early childhood education programs that are narrowly focused or designed primarily for acceleration in a particular area will have much beneficial effect on later intellectual development." [49]

The problem of "the match" that Hunt proposes is pertinent here. When school programs can be built around a valid match, not only between the child's past experience and the educational setting provided for him but also between his cognitive schema and the educative possibilities available to him, no child will experience a cultural trauma upon school entrance. Furthermore, schooling will automatically be relevant to the lives of learners. One significant message to be derived from the academic upheavals of the sixties is the necessity for learning to be relevant for individuals of all ages. Individualized learning is thus demanded, a demand that raises many issues concerning school organization.

[49] Millie Almy, "New Views on Intellectual Development in Early Childhood Education," A. Harry Passow (ed.), *Intellectual Development: Another Look* (Washington, D.C.: Association for Supervision and Curriculum Development, 1964), p. 24.

13
CURRICULAR ISSUES

Not only are there fundamental cleavages between the advocates of play and the promoters of a work regime, between behaviorist psychologists and those recommending a perceptual psychology, but there are also distinctive views held concerning the function of the kindergarten in the educational system. Three major purposes may be said to dominate the scene: (1) the promotion of social and emotional adjustment, (2) the development of intellectual power, and (3) the achievement of individual self-actualization.

THE FUNCTION OF THE KINDERGARTEN

The position of those who would highlight socialization is rooted in kindergarten tradition. Froebel protested that the kindergarten child must feel that he is part of a larger social whole. As we have seen, the early American kindergartens were overwhelmingly devoted to social adjustment. To Dewey, sub-primary socialization was considered an outgrowth of children's solving problems together in the school community. Many statements give evidence of a continued preoccupation with social aspects. Myrtle Imhoff writes, "Social skills are of key importance in the program." [1] Even more emphatically, Hazel Lambert states that in the modern school most of the child's first year should be devoted to "socializing him, help-

---

[1] Myrtle M. Imhoff, *Early Elementary Education* (New York: Appleton-Century-Crofts, 1959), p. 190.

ing him learn to cooperate in a group." [2] What evidence is there that this is an all-absorbing task for either the child or the teacher?

Kindergarten *is* a transitional period in which the child is introduced to democratic group living. The first school experience may have a long-lasting effect on the child's attitude toward authority figures, his feeling of mastery in a new situation, his ability to work with his peers. The literature concerning the self-concept indicates that the school situation needs to be viewed largely in terms of the individual. It is no longer in keeping with our knowledge of development to insist that each child adjust by conforming to specified social habits; more is involved in adjustment than gaining adult approval by meeting adult standards of behavior. Nor is it adequate to view adjustment only in terms of the child's ability to cooperate with the group. In the eyes of some educators today, "group adjustment" and "togetherness" have become fetishes that tend to sacrifice individual potential. Kneller charges the school with fostering a superficial sense of cooperation at the expense of individualism.[3] Some programs for young children have, no doubt, gone so far in stressing community life that they have done violence to individual integrity. The relationship between the teacher and the child demands greater intimacy and communion than presently exists in many classrooms. One suspects that as early childhood specialists become cognizant of the hitherto unrecognized realities emerging on the educational scene, there will be fewer adherents to strict socialization. In its place will be a broadened conception of function.

There is a formidable alliance of pressures to increase the function of the kindergarten in developing the child's intellectual powers. General pressures for excellence, derived essentially from our troubled world situation ,are manifest at all educational levels. This force reaches down into early childhood with the urgency to begin the acquisition of knowledge and skills at an earlier age. As Ilse Forest writes, "The demand of many parents and some administrators is for greater formality, more restrictions of play activities, a serious attempt to prepare children directly for later school work, in

[2] Hazel Lambert, *Teaching the Kindergarten Child* (New York: Harcourt, Brace, 1958), p. 165.

[3] George F. Kneller, "Education, Knowledge, and the Problem of Existence," *Harvard Educational Review,* XXXI (Fall, 1961), 432.

fact, more efforts to put small noses to the grindstone." [4] The explosion of knowledge has caused a new excitement and a fear that children might not be ready for the demands of space-age activities.

Accusations that the kindergarten is wasting children's time—especially gifted children—raise the question of whether five-year-olds entering kindergarten today are not in some aspects quite different from those of twenty-five years ago. Proponents of this view, which is merely speculative, look to sociological and technological changes as bringing about broadened backgrounds even in early childhood, particularly for children at upper socioeconomic levels.

The greatest preoccupation in promoting cognitive growth, however, is related to children who are labeled culturally deprived. Distress has mounted as educators have become increasingly aware of the insuperable handicaps of the educationally disadvantaged child in coping with the demands of the school. Since this position has already been discussed, it is mentioned here only to indicate that it is related to the problem of purpose.

A third position regarding the function of the kindergarten, that of individual self-actualization—or in existential terms, of the positive affirmation of the authentic self—may well subsume some aspects of the intellectual function, but it would repudiate the primary emphasis on socialization as it was previously understood. The direction would be *toward* helping the individual become an autonomous "being" and *away* from adjusting him to preconceived norms gained at the cost of the individual self. No premium would be placed on the techniques of social adaptation or social engineering. The affective side of man—his capacity to love, to appreciate, to become deeply involved in the world around him—would be cultivated. Specific knowledge would be included only as it contributed to the search for meaning in life. Donald Snygg effectively relates this to the surge for early skill development:

The purpose of teaching three-year-olds to read, if this is tried, should not be to hasten their graduation from school. The purpose is

[4] Ilse Forest, "The Responsibility of the Kindergarten in the School's Readiness Program," *Education in Transition,* Forty-seventh Annual Schoolmen's Week Proceedings (Philadelphia: University of Pennsylvania Press, 1960), p. 126.

to help them perceive themselves as individuals who can learn and to discover that their thoughts have significance before their homes and their community have taught them otherwise. It is obvious that applying present day first grade methods to three-year-olds will not automatically achieve these ends. In fact such methods may make matters worse by teaching the children at the age of three instead of at the age of six that they are incompetent and that school activities are meaningless.[5]

In a powerful statement, James Macdonald expresses this third position: "The basic function of the schools should become not the development of cultural intellect, or the production of specialists, or the creation of problem solvers or the developers of personality integration, but something in essence much simpler and a great deal more difficult. The schools should function to *protect the person* from dehumanization." [6] The trend toward dehumanized, impersonal living, accentuated by mass media, urbanization, and automation, can be counteracted if the schools buttress the person against the dehumanization of the broader society. This implies a person-oriented curriculum with all the related issues of how this is to be achieved. Can the child-centered curriculum grow into a person-centered one, fostering deep involvement for each person in the classroom?

Large-scale issues emanate from the varying emphases that are given to the function of the curriculum. Each function implies a value commitment that is essential for organizing the elements of the educational program into a meaningful curriculum design. Though not mutually exclusive orientations, they are, today, propelling diverse curricula.

A CURRICULUM RATIONALE

Three indispensable components are part of all learning situations: learners, something to be learned, and a process whereby learn-

---

[5] Donald Snygg, "A Cognitive Field Theory of Learning," in Walter B. Waetjen (ed.), *Learning and Mental Health in the School* (Washington, D.C.: Association for Supervision and Curriculum Development, 1966), p. 94.

[6] James B. Macdonald, "The Person in the Curriculum," in Helen F. Robison (ed.), *Precedents and Promise in the Curriculum Field* (New York: Teachers College Press, 1966), pp. 51-52.

ing takes place.[7] At the risk of over-simplifying the complicated task of weaving together the numerous factors requiring consideration in building kindergarten programs, let us look at these three components for they will help to pinpoint important curricular problems. Vastly different curricula emerge as these components are envisioned in a variety of relationships, but for a school program to have depth, breadth, and movement, all three dimensions must be recognized. Synthesizing these components into a curriculum that equips the child with the knowledge and skills needed in life, without interfering with his freedom for unique selfhood or robbing him of autonomy in learning, remains a frontier task in education. It demands a new arrangement of basic components.

Curriculum designs have tended to place great value on either the child or the subject matter. Our analysis of earlier kindergarten curricula reveals that attention was concentrated on the nature of the child and to a lesser degree on the process of early learning while less emphasis was placed on the content of learning experiences. Curiously, at the next level of education, the primary school, priority was given to skills and information and based on a different concept of the learning process. The resulting rationales used in curriculum decision-making are at such odds with each other that considerable discontinuity exists between the two levels despite efforts exerted ever since the early decades of this century to build continuity. While each educational level has tried to change the other, the disparity between the two rationales requires concerted assault in the sphere of theory as well as practice. This is another essential, future task of early childhood educators.

Key Concepts and Methods

A viable synthesis among curriculum components is contingent upon increasing rigor in learning more and more about each separate dimension. We have already explored briefly the new insights about the learner and the learning process. Curriculum planners are turning also to a new conception of the nature of knowledge. Whereas for-

[7] John I. Goodlad, "Three Dimensions in Organizing the Curriculum for Learning and Teaching," in Vincent J. Glennon (ed.), *Frontiers of Elementary Education, III* (Syracuse, N.Y.: Syracuse University Press, 1956), 13.

merly "factual and descriptive content" was emphasized in schools, now the stress is on "basic concepts and methods" designated by scholars.[8] Jerome Bruner, the Harvard professor who is largely responsible for introducing the concept of the structure of academic disciplines into educational discourse, argues that by such an approach both meaning and connectedness are added to the educational enterprise.[9] The idea of disciplinary structure is not new, of course; what is new is the insistence that structure be identified and given primacy in the teaching of disciplinary subjects. Early childhood educators are exploring the relevance of the structure of knowledge for the kindergarten curriculum. This conception of knowledge holds promise for adding substantive ideas to the program for young children while working within their own perceptual framework and natural thinking propensities.

The use of key ideas from a body of knowledge is proposed as a rational means for selecting content as opposed to the intuitive, accidental method formerly used.[10] No one intends the result to be rote learning of important generalizations, these ideas themselves would supply the content goals consistently lacking in kindergarten programs. Experiences would be selected to help children discover and build the meanings and relationships defined. To develop such programming the assistance of scholars in various disciplines—mathematics, geography, economics, or linguistics—is essential to identify major concepts and basic relationships within their area of knowledge; but the selection and organization of learning experiences that would help children fashion the basic generalizations rests in the hands of teachers. Active exploration, playful manipulation, imaginative re-creation, and individual choice might all be involved in the process of learning.

Experimentors have found that programs so designed offer rich intellectual potential for young children and purposeful direction in

[8] Arno Bellack, "The Structure of Knowledge and the Structure of the Curriculum," in Dwayne Huebner (ed.), *A Reassessment of the Curriculum* (New York: Teachers College Press, 1964), p. 26.

[9] Jerome Bruner, *On Knowing* (Cambridge, Mass.: Harvard University Press, 1962), p. 120.

[10] Helen F. Robison and Bernard Spodek, *New Directions in the Kindergarten* (New York: Teachers College Press, 1965), p. 13.

programming for teachers. Economic concepts identified by the National Task Force on Economics Education were utilized by Helen Robison in a kindergarten project introducing children to the concepts of work, money, prices, profit, and division of labor through such experiences as store play, a cookie sale, and a visit to the super-market.[11] The growth of concepts in geography and history has been explored in a similar manner by Bernard Spodek.[12] Robert Karplus is involved in working out a guided study of natural phenomena with children from kindergarten through grade six.[13] Karplus hypothesizes that if science material is presented so that it fits the child's way of thinking, the child can be helped to move steadily from mere observation to an understanding of higher order concepts.

Issues revolving around these recommendations relate both to *should* and *how* questions. Those welcoming this direction in the kindergarten program may question the feasibility of delineating an authoritative inventory of key ideas in content areas with their unique ways of knowing. Others may ask how the promised benefits of the program may be obtained while utilizing what we know about children and their ways of learning.

But some early chidhood educators may question this means of selecting learning experiences as being too far from the self of the learner. They would allow for greater freedom and choice on the part of the child in the interaction between persons, materials, ideas, and objects of the contrived school environment. If this latter alternative for curriculum building is chosen, teachers need to be given more extensive help in order to operate effectively with learners.

Reading in the Kindergarten

Not all learnings in the kindergarten can be derived through key concepts for many learnings are in the realm of skill development. The issue of teaching reading at the kindergarten level has been re-opened. There is a fast-growing trend across the nation to introduce

---

[11] *Ibid.*, pp. 39-67.

[12] *Ibid.*, pp. 19-38.

[13] Robert Karplus, *One Physicist Looks at Science Education,* Paper presented at the Eighth ASCD Curriculum Research Institute, Washington, D.C., April 27, 1963. Mimeographed.

reading instruction even earlier, for which parental and lay pressures are partly responsible.[14] Eye-catching periodical articles have aroused the anxiety of some parents about an early start in reading while leading others to regard precocity in reading as a status symbol. There is ample evidence that five-year-olds can learn to decode the symbol system of reading, the fundamental issue is whether or not this should be part of the kindergarten day. Many specialists in early childhood education oppose systematic teaching of reading skills to all young children. They argue that most young children are not sufficiently mature to withstand formal teaching without harmful results.[15] Furthermore, they ask whether this is the best use of time in the short kindergarten day: what experiences will need to be eliminated to make time for reading instruction? [16] Others point to new psychological theory and research studies that support beginning reading for all children in the kindergarten.[17]

Reading, like walking, is a developmental task. Many educators would like to see it included in a total program of language growth that includes perceptual skills, verbal adequacy, vocabulary expansion, meaningful listening, and other language abilities. Aware that language patterns are firmly implanted by the age of six, communities are turning to the preschool years for help with the language problems common to the economically disadvantaged. According to Kenneth Wann, recent advances in structural linguistics can be utilized to chart the language needs of the child so that earlier stages of language development can precede beginning reading.[18] For many specialists, learning to read then becomes simply an extension of

[14] Warren G. Cutts, "New Approaches to Reading for Young Children," in J. Allen Figurel (ed.), *Reading as an Intellectual Activity*, International Reading Association Conference Proceedings, 1963 (New York: Scholastic Magazines, 1963), p. 39.

[15] Nila Banton Smith, *Shall We Teach Formal Reading in the Kindergarten?* (Washington, D.C.: Association for Childhood Education International, 1965), p. 1.

[16] Edgar Dale, "Early Reading," *The News Letter* [Columbus, Ohio: Ohio State University, Bureau of Educational Research and Service] (February 1964), 3.

[17] Joseph E. Brzeinski, M. Lucile Harrison, Paul McKee, "Should Johnny Read in Kindergarten?" *NEA Journal*, 56 (March, 1967), 25.

[18] Kenneth Wann, "A Comment on the Denver Experiment," *NEA Journal*, 56 (March, 1967), 26.

other language experiences at the time the child is ready. Millie Almy suggests that a knowledge of Piaget's theory enables a teacher to become much more skillful in pacing instruction, including reading, to the individual child's apparent maturity and rate of learning.[19]

Resolution is complicated by the rigid age-grade organization of the public schools; from this has stemmed a tradition that no child should learn to read in the kindergarten, but that all children must learn to read in first grade. This is a denial of what we know about individual differences in learning. Some children move from first-hand experiences to symbolic learning much more readily than others. Children interested in the symbolism inherent in reading should be supported in this learning. For other children, we need to know much more about the kinds of experiences that will bridge the gap they experience between encounters with people and things and encounters with symbols. Multiple age groupings hold the promise of permitting children to learn to read at a time when they are willing to involve themselves deeply in the process. This type of school organization may help to break down rigid age-grade expectations. In this and in many other regards, probably the best thing would be for the kindergarten to cease to exist as a separate entity and to merge into a program of continuous education for children between the ages of three and eight. Certainly for some children, schooling cannot be postponed until the age of five.

Organizing for Learning

Some kindergarten programs are designated as structured, while others are called unstructured. This is a spurious distinction; all classroom environments are contrived and are therefore structured in various ways and in differing degrees of rigidity. In a broad curriculum sense, structure means a synthesis of curriculum components so that a succession of creative acts of teaching and learning are released. It means an educational environment that "takes care of students, keeps them alive, and makes them grow." [20]

[19] Millie Almy, *Young Children's Thinking* (New York: Teachers College Press, 1966), p. 140.

[20] Dwayne Huebner, "Curriculum As a Field of Study," in Helen F. Robison (ed.), *Precedents and Promise in the Curriculum Field* (New York: Teachers College Press, 1966), p. 109.

On an instructional level, structure is related to a series of alternatives: the degree to which the child's autonomous search takes precedence over the teacher's authority in learning; the amount of active, self-directed, manipulative activity permitted the child as opposed to drill and direct telling of facts by the teacher; the number of imposed tasks to which the child must comply contrasted with his opportunities to select experiences according to his interests; and the amount of total group activity compared to the freedom for small functional groups or individual experience. These determine the rigidity or flexibility of structure in the classroom.

Repeatedly in our discussion of the kindergarten we have pointed out that the issues revolve around the way in which sequential concept formation may be fostered while not inhibiting creative search. Barbara Biber proposes that traditional educational procedures have "imposed a structure of didactic instruction, right-wrong criteria, dominance of the logical-objective over the intuitive-subjective on the learning child" so early that creative potential has been stifled except for unusual individuals.[21] A frontier task for kindergarten specialists is to provide for continuous learning in a way that does not mitigate the flexibility that is traditionally part of the classroom. For the kindergarten curriculum has tended to be on the more flexible end of the continuum of structure. Though constant total group activities and workbook exercises have been a part of some classrooms, in others much freedom has been extended. In the latter situations, however, learning has been structured by the unchanging kindergarten materials. If the structured environment is to be opened to include more of the wide, wonderful world so appealing to young children, new materials need to be added. Some innovators would include technological teaching aids from television to automated responsive environments. The kind of educational value these aids can have in schools is a question that needs continued consideration.

From the point of view of Piaget, the early childhood period is one of transition in cognitive functioning, a time when the child is developing his own systematic way of thinking. Millie Almy suggests that the nature of this transition "raises many questions about

21 Barbara Biber, "Premature Structuring As a Deterrent to Creativity," *The American Journal of Orthopsychiatry*, XXIX (April, 1959), 281.

both the time and the way in which the child responds to the order and the structure that come from the adult." [22] Problems of determining the varieties of structure that may be effective within a program or for children of different backgrounds have yet to be resolved.

Evaluation

Evaluation is a process of judging growth in terms of objectives. The key word in evaluation is *value,* which implies that evaluation can be most effectively carried out when goals are clearly expressed. This relationship has presented continuous problems in the kindergarten; probably the clearest relationship existed when the trait rating scales were used as a means to determine character development. The techniques of measurement were indeed crude, but they were basically in keeping with the intent of the program. This has not always been true. Sometimes a program designed to achieve certain results has been evaluated by measures related to different goals. Programs clearly emphasizing social and emotional adjustment, for example, have been judged by how well children could perform on a reading readiness test. Two factors have contributed to the kindergarten teacher's dilemmas in evaluation. First, goals have persistently been related to personality development, but never stated in a behavioral form amenable to measurement. Second, measurement instruments are less developed in this area than in others. As Bloom points out, personality characteristics are difficult to measure and there is a general lack of testing instruments clearly regarded as valid.[23] Only when the gathering of data is carried on in relation to the educational purpose can evaluation have meaning for a specific kindergarten program. When the goals are self-actualization or the enhancment of personal growth, standards and evaluation can be determined only in individual terms.

CONCLUSION

When kindergarten teachers moved from the Froebelian program to the reconstructed curriculum developed under the leadership of Patty Smith Hill and Alice Temple, the transitional period

---

[22] Almy, *Young Children's Thinking,* p. 137.

[23] Benjamin S. Bloom, *Stability and Change in Human Characteristics* (New York: John Wiley, 1964), p. 133.

was long and painful. The new program arose from a process of trial and error. Trials were not based, however, on an *ad hoc* utilization of ideas, but were consistently guided by newly revealed theoretical insights. Leaders took ideas emerging from research and theory and worked out their implications at the practical level of kindergarten education. The same process needs to be repeated today. Kindergarten specialists need to push freshly recognized truths for their meaning for a revised kindergarten program, even though these meanings may be only dimly evident at this time. The transitional period may again be painful. Some mistakes may be made, but the efforts may well lead to a renaissance of early childhood education in which the kindergarten program assumes an importance far greater than ever before.

The beliefs that intellectual growth needs to be sacrificed so that affective and social nurturance can be maximized or that the emotions can be disregarded in the pursuit of academic skill present a false set of alternatives. Human growth moves along all of a piece; self-actualization includes all aspects of functioning. Intellectual and emotional abilities are inseparably interwoven. Indeed the success of innovative practice will rest on the *total* impact it makes on learners. The problem is one of fitting pieces together into the long-range goals of education, which must look ultimately beyond what the child can learn to the kind of person he should be. Programs designed to bring quick results may sacrifice long-range human objectives. The concept of self that is built through early school experience is vital to learning. The accepting, supporting, encouraging environment provided in many kindergarten classrooms needs careful preservation.

Narrow, single-dimensional curriculum reform holds the danger of freezing other segments of the school program desperately in need of reexamination. Not only programs at the kindergarten level, but those in succeeding years as well need readjustment. Head Start is lowering the barriers between nursery school and kindergarten education. New means for facilitating continuity in education for children from three to eight years old may be found in recent views of the nature of cognition and of the nature of knowledge. Central to problems of continuity is the crucial match between the child's expanding abilities and the experiences he encounters. Educators are still endeavoring to resolve the inner and outer aspects of learning so

~iportant to Froebel one hundred and twenty-five years ago. The promise seems greater today. As the underpinnings of logical thought become clearer and continuity in learning increasingly possible, better balanced programs at all age levels should result.

The fundamental kindergarten problem, as in all curriculum design, is one of balance—a synthesis of all the pieces into a coherent pattern of relationship. Within the school setting the child needs a chance to be known and understood as a person as well as the opportunity to learn and to develop a love of learning. Establishing kinship with other children in the context of learning and responsible functioning needs to be balanced with the fostering of uniqueness. Affective, cognitive, and psychomotor development all need consideration in depth and proportion. Symbolic experiences need the illumination of direct experience. Creative expression, so important in the growth of the person, must be nurtured by an evocative environment. The need for balance argues against piecemeal curriculum reform.

Elements pushing for a revised kindergarten curriculum are on the educational scene today: theory discrediting formerly accepted beliefs and propelling new directions, widespread public interest that recognizes the need for financial support, and program experimentation that indicates a readiness to move forward. The tasks ahead are Herculean, but the resolution of issues and the solution of perplexing problems promise more rational directives for the teacher of young children as well as more effective programs for early childhood.

BIBLIOGRAPHY

CHAPTER I

Books

Original Writings

Barop, Johannes Arnold, "Critical Moments in the Froebel Community," *Autobiography of Friedrich Froebel*. Translated by Emilie Michaelis and H. Keatley Moore. Syracuse: C. W. Bardeen, 1889.

Froebel, Friedrich, *Autobiography of Friedrich Froebel*. Translated by Emilie Michaelis and H. Keatley Moore. Syracuse: C. W. Bardeen, 1889.

————, *Education by Development*. Translated by Josephine Jarvis. New York: D. Appleton and Co., 1899.

————, *The Education of Man*. Translated by William Hailmann. New York: D. Appleton and Co., 1889.

————, *Mutter-und Kose Lieder*. Leipzig: A. Pichler's Witwe und Sohn, 1911.

————, *Pedagogics of the Kindergarten*. Translated by Josephine Jarvis. New York: D. Appleton and Co., 1895.

Heinemann, Arnold H., (Ed.), *Froebel's Letters*. Boston: Lee and Shepard, 1893.

Interpretive Writings

Bowen, Courthope, *Froebel and Education Through Self-Activity*. New York: Charles Scribner's Sons, 1903.

Brubacher, John S., *A History of the Problems of Education.* New York: McGraw Hill, 1947.

Eby, Frederick, and C. F. Arrowood, *The Development of Modern Education.* New York: Prentice-Hall, 1952.

Snider, Denton J., *The Life of Frederich Froebel.* Chicago: Sigma Publishing Co., 1900.

Ulich, Robert, *History of Educational Thought.* New York: American Book Co., 1945.

von Marenholtz-Bülow, Bertha, *Reminiscences of Friedrich Froebel.* Translated by Mary Mann. Boston: Lee and Shepard, 1882.

von Marenholtz-Bülow, Bertha, "The Mother Play and Nursery Songs." in *Kindergarten and Child Culture Papers.* Henry Barnard (Ed.), New York: D. Appleton and Co., 1898.

CHAPTER II

Books

Original Writings

Barnard, Henry (Ed.), *Kindergarten and Child Culture Papers.* Hartford: Office of Barnard's American Journal of Education, 1890.

Blow, Susan E., *Educational Issues in the Kindergarten.* New York: D. Appleton, 1908.

———, *Symbolic Education.* New York: D. Appleton, 1894.

Kraus-Boelte, Maria, and John Kraus, *The Kindergarten Guide.* New York: E. Steiger, 1877.

Peabody, Elizabeth, and Mary Mann, *Guide to the Kindergarten and Moral Culture of Infancy.* New York: E. Steiger, 1877.

Peabody, Elizabeth, *Lectures in the Training Schools for Kindergartners.* Boston: D. C. Heath, 1886.

Pollack, Louise, *National Kindergarten Manual.* Boston: DeWolfe, Fiske, 1888.

Wiggin, Kate Douglas, *Children's Rights.* Boston: Houghton Mifflin, 1892.

———, *The Story of Patsy.* Boston: Houghton Mifflin, 1889.

Interpretive Writings

Aborn, Caroline D., and Sarah A. Marble (Eds.), *History of the Kindergarten Movement in the Mid-western States and in New York.* Washington, D.C.: Association for Childhood Education, 1938.

Butts, R. Freeman, *A Cultural History of Western Education.* New York: McGraw-Hill, 1955.

Curti, Merle, *The Social Ideas of American Educators.* Paterson, New Jersey: Littlefield, Adams, 1959.

Greenwood, Barbara (Ed.), *History of the Kindergarten Movement in the Western States, Hawaii and Alaska.* Washington, D.C.: Association for Childhood Education, 1940.

Kiefer, Monica, *American Children Through Their Books.* Philadelphia: University of Pennsylvania Press, 1948.

Tharp, Louise Hall, *The Peabody Sisters of Salem.* Boston: Little, Brown, 1951.

Thursfield, Richard Emmons, *Henry Barnard's American Journal of Education.* Baltimore: Johns Hopkins Press, 1945.

Vandewalker, Nina C., *The Kindergarten in American Education.* New York: Macmillan, 1908.

Watkins, Catherine (Ed.), *History of the Kindergarten Movement in the Southeastern States.* Washington, D.C.: Association for Childhood Education, 1939.

Wheelock, Lucy, and Caroline D. Aborn (Eds.), *The Kindergarten in New England.* Printing by Charles Edward Newell, Massachusetts School of Art, 1935.

Articles and Addresses

Adler, Felix, "Free Kindergarten and Workingman's School," in Henry Barnard (Ed.), *Kindergarten and Child Culture Papers.* Hartford: Office of Barnard's American Journal of Education, 1890, pp. 687-691.

Blow, Susan E., "The Mother Play and Nursery Songs," and "Some Aspects of the Kindergarten," Henry Barnard (Ed.), *Kindergarten and Child Culture Papers.* Hartford: Office of Barnard's American Journal of Education, 1890, pp. 575-594, 595-616.

————, "The Service of Dr. William T. Harris to the Kindergarten," *Proceedings of the Seventeenth Annual Meeting of the International Kindergarten Union,* 1910, pp. 123-143.

Cooper, Sarah B., "Kindergarten for Neglected Children," Henry Barnard (Ed.), *Kindergarten and Child Culture Papers.* Hartford: Office of Barnard's American Journal of Education, 1890, pp. 731-736.

Dickinson, J. W., "What Froebel's System of Kindergarten Education Is, and How It Can Be Introduced Into Our Public Schools," *Journal of Addresses and Proceedings of the National Education Association,* 1873, pp. 230-241.

Hailmann, Eudora, "Some Essentials of Kindergarten Education," *Journal of Addresses and Proceedings of the National Education Association,* 1885, pp. 364-368.

Hailmann, William N., "The Adaptation of Froebel's System of Education to American Institutions," *Journal of Addresses and Proceedings of the National Education Association,* 1872, pp. 141-149.

———, "Schoolishness in the Kindergarten," *Journal of Addresses and Proceedings of the National Education Association,* 1890, pp. 565-573.

Harris, William T., "How Imitation Grows into Originality and Freedom," *Kindergarten Magazine,* XI (May, 1899), 600-601.

———, "Psychological Inquiry," *Journal of Addresses and Proceedings of the National Education Association,* 1885, pp. 91-101.

———, "Kindergarten Methods Contrasted with the Methods of the Primary School," *Journal of Addresses and Proceedings of the National Education Association,* 1889, pp. 448-453.

Jenkins, Elizabeth, "How the Kindergarten Found Its Way To America," *The Wisconsin Magazine of History,* XIV (September, 1930), 48-62.

Kraus, John, "The Kindergarten (Its Use and Abuse) in America," *Journal of Addresses and Proceedings of the National Education Association,* 1877, pp. 186-207.

Kraus-Boelte, Maria, "Characteristics of Froebel's Method, Kindergarten Training," *Journal of Addresses and Proceedings of the National Education Association,* 1876, pp. 211-230.

Pollock, Luise, "Kindergarten," *Journal of Addresses and Proceedings of the National Education Association,* 1881, pp. 129-131.

Schaeffer, Nathan C., "The Educational Value of the Beautiful," *Journal of Addresses and Proceedings of the National Education Association,* 1888, pp. 332-339.

CHAPTER III

Books

Original Writings

Burk, Frederic, and Caroline F. Burk, *A Study of the Kindergarten Problem.* San Francisco: Whitaker and Roy, 1899.

Dewey, John, *School and Society.* Chicago: University of Chicago Press, 1899.

Hall, G. Stanley, *The Contents of Children's Minds.* Boston: Ginn and Co., 1907.

————, *Educational Problems.* Vol. I. New York: D. Appleton, 1911.

————, *Life and Confessions of a Psychologist.* New York: D. Appleton, 1924.

National Society for the Study of Education, *The Kindergarten and Its Relation to Elementary Education.* Sixth Yearbook, Bloomington, Illinois: Public School Publishing Society, 1907.

Interpretive Writings

Committee of Nineteen, *Pioneers of the Kindergarten in America.* New York: Century Co., 1924.

Cremin, Lawrence, *The Transformation of the School.* New York: Knopf, 1961.

Forest, Ilse, *Preschool Education.* New York: Macmillan, 1927.

Good, Harry G., *A History of American Education.* New York: Macmillan, 1956.

Mayhew, Katherine C., and Anna Camp Edwards, *The Dewey School.* New York: D. Appleton Century, 1936.

Miller, Perry (Ed.), *American Thought Civil War to World War I.* New York: Rinehart and Co., 1954.

Articles and Addresses

Bryan, Anna E., "The Letter Killeth," *Journal of Proceedings and Addresses of the National Education Association,* 1890, pp. 573-581.

Clippinger, Geneva M., "A Visit to the Subprimary Class of Dr. Dewey's School," *Kindergarten Review,* XI (March, 1901), 424-426.

Cross, Ermine, "The Work of the Chicago Free Kindergarten Association," *Kindergarten Magazine,* X (April, 1898), 509-515.

Dewey, John, "My Pedagogic Creed," *The School Journal,* LIV (January 16, 1897), 77-80.

————, "Froebel's Educational Principles," *The Elementary School Record,* I (June, 1900), 143-151.

————, "The Situation As Regards the Course of Study," *Journal of Proceedings and Addresses of the National Education Association,* 1901, pp. 332-348.

Hailmann, William N., "The Kindergarten Occupations," *Proceedings of the Thirteenth Annual Meeting of the International Kindergarten Union,* 1906, pp. 88-89.

Hall, G. Stanley, "Editorial," *Pedagogical Seminary,* IV (April, 1897), 267-268.

————, "The Ideal School as Based on Child Study," *Journal of Proceedings and Addresses of the National Education Association,* 1901, pp. 474-488.

Thorndike, Edward L., "Notes on Psychology for Kindergartners," *Teachers College Record,* IV (Nov. 1903), 47-68.

Scates, Georgia P., "The Sub-Primary (Kindergarten) Department," *The Elementary School Record,* I (June, 1900), 129-142.

Temple, Alice, "The Kindergarten in America—Modern Period," *Childhood Education,* XIII (April, 1937), 358-363.

Wiltse, Sara E., "A Preliminary Sketch of the History of Child Study for the Year Ending September, 1896," *Pedagogical Seminary,* IV (October, 1896), 111-125.

CHAPTER IV

Books

Original Writings

Committee of Nineteen, *The Kindergarten.* Boston: Houghton Mifflin, 1913.

Fisher, Dorothy Canfield, *A Montessori Mother.* New York: Henry Holt, 1912.

Kilpatrick, William H., *Froebel's Kindergarten Principles Critically Examined.* New York: Macmillan, 1916.

————, *The Montessori System Examined.* New York: Houghton Mifflin, 1914.

Montessori, Maria, *The Montessori Method.* New York: Frederick A. Stokes, 1912.

Articles and Addresses

Amidon, Beaulah, "Forty Years in Kindergarten," *The Survey*, LVIII (September, 1927), 506-509.

Barnes, Earl, "Comparison of Froebelian and Montessori Methods and Principles," *Kindergarten Review*, XXIII (April, 1913), 487-490.

Beck, Robert W., "Kilpatrick's Critique of Montessori's Method and Theory," *Studies in Philosophy and Education*, I (November, 1961), 153-162.

Glidden, Minnie E. (Chairman), "Conference of Gifts and Occupations," *Proceedings of the Seventh Annual Convention of the International Kindergarten Union*, 1900, pp. 36-93.

Harrison, Elizabeth, "The Montessori Method and the Kindergarten," *U. S. Bureau of Education Bulletin, No. 28.* Washington, D.C.: Government Printing Office, 1914.

Haven, Caroline T., "International Kindergarten Union: Its Origin," *Proceedings of the Fifteenth Annual Meeting of the International Kindergarten Union*, 1908, pp. 115-119.

Kilpatrick, William H., "Montessori and Froebel," *Kindergarten Review*, XXIII (April, 1913), 491-496.

Logan, Anna E., "Montessori and Froebel," *Kindergarten Review*, XXIII (April, 1913), 553-561.

Montessori, Maria, "Education in Relation to the Imagination of the Little Child," *Journal of Addresses and Proceedings of the National Education Association*, 1915, pp. 663-666.

O'Grady, Geraldine (Chairman), "Round Table Conference on Programs," *Proceedings of the Eighth Annual Convention of the International Kindergarten Union*, 1901, pp. 48-73.

Palmer, Luella A., "Montessori and Froebelian Materials and Methods," *Kindergarten Review*, XXIV (November, 1913), 129-140.

Putnam, Alice H. (Chairman), "Conference on Training," *Proceedings of the Seventh Annual Convention of the International Kindergarten Union*, 1900, pp. 96-137.

Shaw, Elizabeth R., "The Effects of the Scientific Spirit in Education upon the Kindergarten: Its Relation to the Distinctive Characteristics of the Montessori Method," *Journal of Addresses and Proceedings of the National Education Association,* 1913, pp. 439-445.

Stannard, Margaret J. (Chairman), "Round Table on Home Discipline," *Proceedings of the Ninth Annual Convention of the International Kindergarten Union,* 1902, pp. 40-50.

Steward, Sarah, "Aims," *First Report of the International Kindergarten Union,* 1892, n.p.

Ward, Florence E., "The Montessori Method," *Kindergarten Review,* XXIII (November, 1912), 139-143.

Wheelock, Lucy, "Report of the Committee of Nineteen," *Proceedings of the Fourteenth Annual Meeting of the International Kindergarten Union,* 1907, pp. 43-49.

Witmer, Lightmer, "The Montessori Method," *Proceedings of the Twentieth Annual Meeting of the International Kindergarten Union,* 1913, pp. 122-127.

CHAPTER V

Articles and Addresses

Aborn, Caroline D., "The Game," *Proceedings of the Fifteenth Annual Meeting of the International Kindergarten Union,* 1908, pp. 145-147.

Alder, Louise, "General Principles Underlying the Course of Study," *Proceedings of the Twenty-third Annual Meeting of the International Kindergarten Union,* 1916, pp. 135-137.

Bailey, Liberty H., "What Is Nature Study?" *Kindergarten Review,* VIII (October, 1897), 85-86.

Bailey, Marion E., "Nursery Arts and Crafts," *Kindergarten Review,* XX (September, 1909), 39-44.

Baker, Edna Dean, "The Balanced Program," *Proceedings of the Thirtieth Annual Meeting of the International Kindergarten Union,* 1923, pp. 131-137.

Burke, Caroline F., "Free Play in the Kindergarten," *Proceedings of the Seventh Annual Convention of the International Kindergarten Union,* 1900, pp. 138-143.

Bryan, Anna (Chairman), "Report of the Child Study Committee," *Report of the Second Annual Meeting of the International Kindergarten Union,* 1897, pp. 36-42.

Comstalk, Anna Botsford, "Nature Study in the Kindergarten," *Kindergarten Review,* XIV (September, 1914), 28-35.

Cronise, Caroline C., "The Art Work of the Kindergarten," *Elementary School Teacher,* X (January, 1910), 240-247.

Hall, G. Stanley, "The Pedagogy of the Kindergarten," *Educational Problems,* Vol. I, New York: D. Appleton, 1911, 11-41.

————, "From Fundamental to Accessory in Education," *The Kindergarten Magazine,* XI (May, 1899), 599-600.

Hill, Patty Smith, "Shall the Supervisor Plan the General Program?" *Proceedings of the Eighth Annual Convention of the International Kindergarten Union,* 1901, pp. 44-45.

————, "Some Conservative and Progressive Phases of Kindergarten Education," *The Kindergarten and Its Relation to Elementary Education,* Sixth Yearbook of the National Society for the Study of Education, Part II. Bloomington, Illinois: Public School Publishing Co., 1907, 61-86.

————, "Some Hopes and Fears for the Kindergarten of the Future," *Proceedings of the Twentieth Annual Meeting of the International Kindergarten Union,* 1913, pp. 89-101.

————, "The Value of Constructive Work in the Kindergarten," *Proceedings of the Ninth Annual Convention of the International Kindergarten Union,* 1902, pp. 51-55.

Hofer-Hegner, Bertha, "A Story of a Settlement Garden," *Kindergarten Magazine,* XIII (May, 1901), 483-488.

————, "The Kindergarten Program in Relation to Home Environment and Activity," *Proceedings of the Twenty-second Annual Meeting of the International Kindergarten Union,* 1915, pp. 155-156.

Laidlow, Margaret, "Gardens of Kindergarten Children," *Kindergarten Review,* XIV (May, 1904), 577-581.

Lindgren, Ethel Roe, "Rhythm in the Kindergarten," *Kindergarten Review,* XII (September, 1901), 7-13.

Martindell, Charlotte Sherwood, "New Developments in Kindergarten Work," *Kindergarten Review,* IX (February, 1899), 358-361.

Newell, Bertha Payne, "The Kindergarten Program," *Kindergarten Review,* XXIII (January, 1913), 292-297.

Openheimer, Carol P., "Suggestions Concerning Rhythm Plays," *Kindergarten Review,* XXV (March, 1915), 480-484.

Page, Mary Boomer, "Plays and Games in the Kindergarten," *Elementary School Teacher,* IX (March, 1909), 341-357.

Palmer, Luella A., "Problems vs. Subject Matter as a Basis for Kindergarten Curricula," *Kindergarten Review,* XXV (November, 1914), 129-138.

Putnam, Alice, "Shall Reading and Writing be Taught in the Kindergarten?" *Journal of Proceedings and Addresses of the National Education Association,* 1894, pp. 327-328.

Sargent, Walter, "The Beginnings of Art in the Kindergarten," *Proceedings of the Seventeenth Annual Meeting of the International Kindergarten Union,* 1910, pp. 218-219.

Speed, Susan P., "How Far Should Imaginative Terminology Be Used in Nature Study?" *Kindergarten Review,* XVII (October, 1906), 90-91.

Subcommittee on Curriculum of the Bureau of Education Committee of the International Kindergarten Union, "The Kindergarten Curriculum," *U. S. Bureau of Education Bulletin, No. 16.* Washington, D.C.: Government Printing Office, 1919.

Tanner, Amy E., "The Child as the Center of Correlation in the Kindergarten," *Kindergarten Review,* XXV (November, 1914), 75-80.

Temple, Alice, "The Factor of Environment in the Making of a Kindergarten Program," *Kindergarten Review,* XIX (October, 1908), 77-81.

————, "Subject Matter in the Curriculum," *Journal of Proceedings and Addresses of the National Education Association,* 1919, pp. 175-178.

Thorne-Thomsen, Gudrun, "The Place of Literature in Child Life," *Kindergarten Review,* XIII (June, 1903), 587-594.

Vandewalker, Nina C., "The History of Kindergarten Influence in Elementary Education," *The Kindergarten and Its Relation to Elementary Education,* Sixth Yearbook of the National Society for the Study of Education, Part II. Bloomington, Illinois: Public School Publishing Co., 1907, 115-138.

————, "The Kindergarten Curriculum as Modified by Modern Educational Thought," *Journal of Proceedings and Addresses of the National Education Association,* 1919, pp. 171-175.

CHAPTER VI

Books

Original Writings

Bobbitt, Franklin, *How To Make A Curriculum*. Boston: Houghton Mifflin, 1924.

Charters, Werrett W., *Curriculum Construction*. New York: Macmillan, 1923.

Judd, Charles H., *Introduction to the Scientific Study of Education*. Boston: Ginn and Co., 1918.

Thorndike, Edward L., *The Principles of Teaching*. New York: A. G. Seiler, 1906.

———, *The Psychology of Learning*. New York: Columbia University Press, 1913.

Watson, John B., *Behavior*. New York: Henry Holt, 1914.

Interpretive Writings

Butts, R. Freeman, and Lawrence A. Cremin, *A History of Education in American Culture*. New York: Henry Holt, 1953.

Meyer, Adolph E., *An Educational History of the American People*. New York: McGraw-Hill, 1957.

———, *The Development of Education in the Twentieth Century*. New York: Prentice-Hall, 1949.

Woelfel, Norman, *Molders of the American Mind*. New York: Columbia University Press, 1933.

Articles and Addresses

Baker, Edna Dean, "The Balanced Program," *Proceedings of the Thirtieth Annual Meeting of the International Kindergarten Union*, 1923, pp. 131-137.

Binzel, Alma L., "General Character and Work of Measurement in the Grades and the Need for These in the Kindergarten Field," *Proceedings of the Twenty-fifth Annual Meeting of the International Kindergarten Union*, 1918, pp. 141-149.

Bobbitt, Franklin, "Education as Growth Through Experience," *Childhood Education*, I (October, 1924), 51-60.

Committee on Economy of Time in Education, Department of Super-intendents, "Report," *Journal of Proceedings and Addresses of the National Education Association,* 1911, pp. 222-226.

Hill, Patty Smith, "The Project, An Adaptation of a Life Method of Thought and Action," *Proceedings of the Twenty-eighth Annual Meeting of the International Kindergarten Union,* 1921, pp. 153-155.

Hutchinson, Ethel, "Some Practical Projects," *Proceedings of the Thirtieth Annual Meeting of the International Kindergarten Union,* 1923, pp. 138-139.

Kilpatrick, William H., "The Project Method," *Teachers College Record,* XIX (September, 1918), 319-335.

————, "Statement of Position," *The Foundations of Curriculum Making,* Twenty-Sixth Yearbook of the National Society for the Study of Education, Part II. Bloomington, Illinois: Public School Publishing Co., 1930, 119-146.

Moore, Annie E. (Chairman), "Report of the Committee on Minimum Essentials in Kindergarten and Primary Grades," *Proceedings of the Twenty-fourth Annual Meeting of the International Kinder-garten Union,* 1917, pp. 110-126.

Raymond, Mae, "Kalamazoo on the Project Method," *Proceedings of the Twenty-eighth Annual Meeting of the International Kinder-garten Union,* 1921, pp. 207-210.

Rogers, Agnes L., "The Relation of An Inventory of Habits to Charac-ter Development," *Proceedings of the Twenty-ninth Annual Meet-ing of the International Kindergarten Union,* 1922, pp. 136-146.

Symposium, "An Investigation of Record Making in the Kindergarten and First Grade," *Proceedings of the Thirtieth Annual Meeting of the International Kindergarten Union,* 1923, pp. 72-75.

Thorndike, Edward L., "The Nature, Purposes and General Methods of Measurement of Educational Products,' *The Measurement of Educational Products,* Seventeenth Yearbook of the National So-ciety for the Study of Education, Part II. Bloomington, Illinois: Public School Publishing Co., 1918, 16-24.

Vandewalker, Nina C. (Chairman), "Report of the Bureau of Educa-tion Committee," *Proceedings of the Twenty-fifth Annual Meet-ing of the International Kindergarten Union,* 1918, pp. 74-77.

Watson, John B., "The Pre-Kindergarten Age—A Laboratory Stage," *Proceedings of the Twenty-sixth Annual Meeting of the International Kindergarten Union*, 1919, pp. 184-206.

CHAPTER VII

Books

Original Writings

National Society for the Study of Education, *The Coordination of the Kindergarten and the Elementary School*, Seventh Yearbook, Part II. Bloomington, Illinois: Public School Publishing Society, 1908.

Parker, Francis W., *Talks on Teaching*. New York: E. L. Kellogg, 1896.

Interpretive Writings

Cremin, Lawrence A., David A. Shannon, and Mary Evelyn Townsend, *A History of Teachers College, Columbia University*. New York: Columbia University Press, 1954.

Forest, Ilse, *The School for the Child from Two to Eight*. Boston: Ginn and Co., 1935.

Russell, James Earl, *Founding Teachers College*. New York: Bureau of Publications, Teachers College, Columbia University, 1937.

Articles and Addresses

Abbott, Julia Wade, "Kindergarten Education 1918-1920," *U. S. Bureau of Education Bulletin, 1921, No. 19,* Washington, D.C.: Government Printing Office, 1921, 1-12.

————, "Kindergartens—Past and Present," *U. S. Bureau of Education Kindergarten Circular, No. 11*. Washington, D.C.: Government Printing Office, 1923.

Balliet, Thomas L., "Practical Meeans of Unifying the Work of the Kindergarten-Primary Grades," *Journal of Addresses and Proceedings of the National Education Association*, 1916, pp. 435-436.

Brown, Kate L., "Application of Froebel's Principles to the Primary School," *Journal of Proceedings and Addresses of the National Education Association*, 1887, pp. 338-350.

Browning, Lucy E., "A Discussion of the Training of Kindergartners Under Differing Conditions," *Proceedings of the Thirteenth Annual Meeting of the International Kindergarten Union,* 1906, pp. 45-48.

Davis, Mary Dabney, "Nursery-Kindergarten-Primary Education in 1924-1926," *U. S. Bureau of Education Bulletin, 1927, No. 28.* Washington, D.C.: Government Printing Office, 1927, 1-12.

Directory of Kindergarten Training in Colleges, Normal Schools and in Kindergarten Training Schools, *Proceedings of the Twenty-seventh Annual Meeting of the International Kindergarten Union,* 1920, pp. 151-155.

Fine, Benjamin, "Patty Smith Hill, A Great Educator," *American Childhood,* XXI (May, 1936), 17-18.

Frazier, Benjamin W., "History of the Professional Education of Teachers in the United States," *U. S. Office of Education Bulletin, No. 10.* Washington, D.C.: Government Printing Office, 1933, 42-86.

Gage, Lucy, "Kindergarten Progress During the Past Twenty-Five Years," *Journal of Proceedings and Addresses of the National Education Association,* 1925, pp. 480-484.

Meriam, J. L., "Practical Means of Unifying the Work of the Kindergarten and Primary Grades," *Journal of Proceedings and Addresses of the National Education Association,* 1916, pp. 430-431.

Putnam, Alice (Chairman), "Report of the Committee on Training," *Third Report of the International Kindergarten Union,* 1898, pp. 30-31.

Temple, Alice, "The Advantages and Disadvantages of the Kindergarten Training Course in the Independent Training School," *Proceedings of the Thirteenth Annual Meeting of the International Kindergarten Union,* 1906, pp. 49-51.

Vandewalker, Nina C., "An Evaluation of Kindergarten-Primary Courses of Study in Teacher Training Institutions," *U. S. Bureau of Education Bulletin, No. 3.* Washington, D.C.: Government Printing Office, 1924, 1-44.

———, "Conference on Training of Teachers," *Proceedings of the Eighth Annual Convention of the International Kindergarten Union,* 1901, pp. 95-105.

————, "The Curriculum and Methods of the Kindergarten Training School," *Proceedings of the Tenth Annual Convention of the International Kindergarten Union,* 1903, pp. 53-64.

Waite, Mary G., "How the Kindergarten Prepares Children for Primary Work," *U. S. Bureau of Education Kindergarten Circular, No. 15.* Washington, D.C.: Government Printing Office, 1924.

Wheelock, Lucy, "Ideal Relation of Kindergarten to Primary School," *Journal of Addresses and Proceedings of the National Education Association,* 1894, pp. 702-703.

CHAPTER VIII

Books

Original Writings

Burke, Agnes, *et al., A Conduct Curriculum for the Kindergarten and First Grade.* New York: Scribners, 1923.

Canty, Margaret, *et al., Kindergarten Activities.* Milwaukee: Board of School Directors, 1925.

DeLima, Agnes, *Our Enemy the Child.* New York: New Republic, 1926.

Dewey, John, and Evelyn Dewey, *Schools of Tomorrow.* New York: E. P. Dutton, 1915.

Garrison, Charlotte G., *Permanent Play Materials for Children.* New York: Scribners, 1926.

National Society for the Study of Education, *Preschool and Parental Education,* Twenty-eighth yearbook, Part I. Bloomington, Illinois: Public School Publishing Co., 1929.

Parker, Samuel Chester, and Alice Temple, *Unified Kindergarten and First Grade Teaching.* Boston: Ginn and Co., 1925.

Rogers, Agnes L., *A Tentative Inventory of Habits.* New York: Bureau of Publications, Teachers College, Columbia University, 1922.

Pickett, Lalla, and Duralde Boren, *Early Childhood Education.* Yonkers-on-Hudson, New York: World Book Co., 1925.

Staff of the Training School of the Southern Branch of the University of Los Angeles, *An Activity Curriculum for Kindergarten and the Primary Grades.* San Francisco: Harr Wagner Publishing Co., 1924.

Thorn, Alice G., *Music for Young Children*. New York: Scribners, 1929.

Articles and Addresses

Davis, Mary Dabney, *General Practice in Kindergarten Education*. Washington, D.C.: National Education Association, 1925.

Hill, Patty Smith, "Changes in Curricula and Method in Kindergarten Education," *Childhood Education*, II (November, 1925), 99-106.

————, "The Speyer School Experimental Play Room," *Kindergarten Review*, XVII (November, 1906), 136-140.

Kilpatrick, William H., "How Shall Early Education Conceive Its Objectives?" *Childhood Education*, II (September, 1925), 1-12.

Temple, Alice, "Extending the Child's Social Understandings," *Childhood Education*, V (April, 1929), 419-423.

————, "The Kindergarten-Primary Unit," *Elementary School Journal*, XX (March, 1920), 498-509.

Thorndike, Edward L., "Measurement in Education," *Teachers College Record*, XXII (November, 1921), 371-379.

Tracy, Catherine J., "Outline for a Study of Habits," *Kindergarten Review*, XXII (December, 1911), 238-241.

Vandewalker, Nina C., "The Kindergarten Curriculum as Modified by Modern Educational Thought," *Proceedings and Addresses of the National Education Association*, 1919, pp. 171-175.

CHAPTER IX

Books

Original Writings

Coleman, Satis N., *Creative Music for Children*. New York: G. P. Putnam, 1922.

Forest, Ilse, *Preschool Education*. New York: Macmillan, 1927.

Foster, Josephine C., and Marion L. Mattson, *Nursery School Procedure*. New York: D. Appleton, 1929.

Johnson, Harriet M., *Children in the Nursery School*. New York: John Day, 1928.

McMillan, Margaret, *The Nursery School*. New York: E. P. Dutton, 1919.

Mathias, Margaret E., *The Beginnings of Art in the Public Schools.* New York: Scribners, 1924.

Mearns, Hughes, *Creative Youth.* Garden City, New York: Doubleday, Doran, 1925.

Naumberg, Margaret, *The Child and the World.* New York: Harcourt, Brace, 1928.

Owen, Grace (Ed.), *Nursery School Education.* New York: E. P. Dutton, 1923.

Pratt, Caroline, *I Learn From Children.* New York: Simon and Schuster, 1948.

Pratt, Caroline, and Jessie Stanton, *Before Books.* New York: Adelphi, 1926.

Pratt, Caroline, and Lula E. Wright, *Experimental Practice in the City and Country School.* New York: E. P. Dutton, 1924.

Rugg, Harold, and Ann Shumaker, *The Child-Centered School.* Yonkers-on-Hudson, New York: World Book, 1928.

Articles and Addresses

Alschuler, Rose M., "The Franklin Street Nursery of the Chicago Public Schools," *Preschool and Parental Education,* Twenty-eighth Yearbook of the National Society for the Study of Education, Part I. Bloomington, Illinois: Public School Publishing Co., 1929, 157-164.

Baldwin, Bird T., "Preschool Laboratories at the Iowa Child Welfare Station," *Preschool and Parental Education,* Twenty-eight Yearbook of the National Society for the Study of Education, Part I. Bloomington, Illinois: Public School Publishing Co., 1929, 211-217.

Beck, Robert H., "Progressive Education and American Progressivism: Caroline Pratt," *Teachers College Record,* LX (December, 1958), 129-137.

————, "Progressive Education and American Progressivism: Margaret Naumberg," *Teachers College Record,* LX (January, 1959), 198-208.

Coleman, Satis M., "The Creative Music Experiment in the Lincoln School of Teachers College," *The New Era,* VIII (January, 1927), 7-10.

Davis, Mary Dabney, "Nursery Schools: Their Development and Current Practices in the United States" *U. S. Office of Education Bulletin, No. 9*, Washington, D.C.: Government Printing Office, 1932.

Dewey, John, "How Much Freedom in New Schools?" *The New Republic*, LXIII (July 9, 1930), 204-206.

Gesell, Arnold, "The Downward Extension of the Kindergarten," *Childhood Education*, II (October, 1926), 53-59.

————, "The Changing Status of the Pre-School Child," *Progressive Education*, II (January-March, 1925), 8-10.

————, "Significance of the Nursery School," *Childhood Education*, I (September, 1925), 11-20.

McMillan, Margaret, "The Nursery School in the Old Country," *Progressive Education*, II (January-March, 1925), 22-25.

Mearns, Hughes, "The Curriculum and the Creative Spirit," *The New Era*, X (April, 1929), 113-118.

Naumberg, Margaret, "The Crux of Progressive Education," *The New Republic*, LXIII (July 25, 1930), 145-146.

Pearson, Elizabeth W., "The Ruggles Street Nursery School," *Progressive Education, II* (January-March, 1925), 19-21.

Raymond, E. Mae, "The Nursery School as an Integral Part of Education," *Teachers College Record*, XXVII (May, 1926), 782-791.

Rugg, Harold, "The Reconstruction of the American School System," *The New Era*, X (April, 1929), 81-84.

Woolley, Helen T., "Preschool and Parental Education at the Merrill-Palmer School," *Progressive Education*, II (January-March, 1925), 35-37.

CHAPTER X

Books

Original Writings

Baruch, Dorothy W., *New Ways in Discipline*. New York: McGraw-Hill, 1949.

Cole, Natalie, *The Arts in the Classroom*. New York: John Day, 1940.
Curriculum Records of the Children's School. Evanston, Illinois: Bureau of Publication, National College of Education, 1932.

Foster, Josephine C., and Neith E. Headley, *Education in the Kinder-garten.* New York: American Book Co., 1936.

Garrison, Charlotte G., Emma D. Sheehy, and Alice Dalgliesh, *The Horace Mann Kindergarten.* New York. Bureau of Publications, Teachers College, Columbia University, 1937.

Gesell, Arnold, and Frances L. Ilg, *Infant and Child in the Culture of Today.* New York: Harper, 1943.

————, *The Child From Five to Ten.* New York: Harper, 1946.

Hartley, Ruth E., Lawrence K. Frank, and Robert M. Goldenson, *Understanding Children's Play.* New York: Columbia University Press, 1952.

Hymes, James L. Jr., *A Child Development Point of View.* Englewood Cliffs, New Jersey: Prentice-Hall, 1955.

Jersild, Arthur T., *Child Development and the Curriculum.* New York: Bureau of Publications, Teachers College, Columbia University, 1946.

Lambert, Hazel M., *Teaching the Kindergarten Child.* New York: Harcourt, Brace, 1958.

Lowenfeld, Viktor, *Creative and Mental Growth.* New York: Macmillan, 1947.

Murchison, Carl (Ed.), *A Handbook of Child Psychology.* Worcester, Massachusetts: Clark University Press, 1931.

National Society for the Study of Education, *Child Development and the Curriculum.* Thirty-eighth Yearbook, Part I. Bloomington, Illinois: Public School Publishing Co., 1939.

Sheehy, Emma D., *Children Discover Music and Dance.* New York: Henry Holt, 1959.

Wills, Clarice D., and William H. Stegeman. *Living in the Kinder-garten.* Chicago: Follett, 1950.

Articles and Addresses

Adlerblum, Evelyn D., "Mental Hygiene in the Kindergarten," *Journal of the National Education Association,* XLIV (February, 1955), 80-81.

Alshuler, Rose H., "Children's Paintings and Their Personalities," *The New Era,* XXXV (April, 1954), 61-66.

Anderson, John E., "Changing Emphasis in Early Childhood Education," *School and Society,* XLIX (January 7, 1939), 1-9.

————, "Child Development: An Historical Perspective," *Child Development,* XXVII (June, 1956), 181-196.

Arbuthnot, May Hill, "Content in the Kindergarten Curriculum,"
Journal of the National Education Association, XXIII (February,
1933), 41-43.

————, "The Unit of Work and Subject Matter Growth," *Childhood
Education,* IX (January, 1933), 182-188.

————, "Transitions in Discipline," *Childhood Education,* XV (November, 1938), 101-107.

Brogan, Peggy D., "Scientists in the Kindergarten," *Nation's Schools,*
XXXIV (December, 1944), 20-22.

Campbell, Elizabeth, "Kindergarten Shape Up," *Progressive Education,*
XXIII (May, 1946), 264-265.

Davis, Mary Dabney, "How NANE Grew," *Young Children,* XX
(November, 1964), 106-109.

Ginsberg, Sadie D., "Changing Attitudes About Children," *Partners in
Education.* Forty-fifth Annual Schoolman's Week Proceedings.
Philadelphia: University of Pennsylvania Press, 1958, pp. 328-
341.

Hooper, Laura, "Trends in the Modern Kindergarten," *American
Childhood,* XXIV (November, 1938), 51-52.

Hymes, James L. Jr., "A Newcomer: Early Childhood Education,"
Peabody Journal of Education, XXVII (March, 1950), 266-269.

Roth, Betty Ann, "Promising Practices in Kindergarten Education,"
Midlands Schools, LXXIV (March, 1960), 18-19.

Southhall, Maycie, "Meeting the Needs of Children," *Childhood
Education,* XIV (April, 1938), 339-340.

Stewart, Florence V., "The Modern Kindergarten," *California Journal
of Elementary Education,* XIV (February, 1946), 185-191.

Thompson, Ethel, "Effective Practices in the Kindergarten," *Education:
Intellectual, Moral, Physical,* Forty-eighth Annual Schoolmen's
Week Proceedings, Philadelphia: University of Pennsylvania
Press, 1961, pp. 175-182.

CHAPTER XI

Books

Original Writings

Bain, Winifred, *Parents Look At Modern Education*. New York: D. Appleton-Century, 1935.

Carr, William D. (Director), *Better Reading Instruction: A Survey of Research and Successful Practice, Research Bulletin XIII, No. 5*. Washington, D.C.: Research Division of the National Education Association, 1935.

Davis, Hazel (Project Director), *Kindergarten Practices, 1961*. M2. Washington, D.C.: Research Division of the National Education Association, 1962.

Gans, Roma, Celia B. Stendler, and Millie Almy, *Teaching Young Children*. Yonkers-on-Hudson, New York: World Book Co., 1952.

Gates, Arthur I., *Psychology for Students of Education*. New York: Macmillan, 1923.

Hardy, Marjorie (Ed.), *Reading Emphasis in School Activities*. Washington, D.C.: Association for Childhood Education, 1933.

Harrison, M. Lucile, *Reading Readiness*. Boston: Houghton Mifflin, 1936.

Headley, Neith, *Foundation Learnings in the Kindergarten*. Washington, D.C.: Department of Kindergarten-Primary Education, National Education Association, 1958.

Hildreth, Gertrude, *Learning the Three Rs*. Minneapolis: Educational Publishers, Inc., 1936.

Thorndike, Edward L., and Arthur I. Gates, *Elementary Principles of Education*. New York: Macmillan, 1929.

Storm, Grace E., and Nila Banton Smith. *Reading Activities in the Primary Grades*. Boston: Ginn and Co., 1930.

Articles and Addresses

Almy, Millie, "Programs for Young Children," *Educational Leadership*, VIII (February, 1951), 270-275.

Baker, Edna Dean, "Report of the Conferring Committee on Reorganization, International Kindergarten Union," *Childhood Education*, VI (June, 1930), 459-460.

————, "Interpreting the Kindergarten," *Journal of the National Educaiton Association,* XXII (April, 1933), 121-122.

Bowen, Harry, "A More Meaningful Kindergarten," *Ohio Schools,* XXXIII (April, 1955), 28-31.

Cowen, Shirley, "Reading Readiness Through Kindergarten Experiences," *Elementary School Journal,* LII (October, 1951), 96-99.

Culkin, Mabel Louise, "The Contemporary Kindergarten," *Educational Record,* XXIV (October, 1943), 345-357.

Deans, Edwina, "Is There a Reading Readiness Program?" *Viewpoints on Educational Issues and Problems,* Thirty-ninth Annual Schoolmen's Week Proceedings. Philadelphia: University of Pennsylvania Press, 1952, pp. 95-103.

Engelhardt, Fred, "How to Save the Kindergarten," *Journal of the National Education Association,* XXIII (April, 1934), 114-115.

Forest, Ilse, "The Responsibility of the Kindergarten in the School's Readiness Program," *Education in Transition,* Forty-seventh Annual Schoolmen's Week Proceedings. Philadelphia: University of Pennsylvania Press, 1960, pp. 124-135.

Gesell, Arnold, "Maturation and the Patterning of Behavior," in Carl Murchison (Ed.), *A Handbook of Child Psychology.* Worcester, Massachusetts: Clark University Press, 1933, pp. 209-235.

Gray, William S., "Training and Experiences That Prepare for Reading," *Childhood Education,* III (January, 1927), 210-214.

Hammond, Sarah Lou, "What Happens to the Five-Year-Olds?" *Educational Leadership,* XII (October, 1954), 9-14.

Headley, Neith E., "Kindergarten—1944 Model," *School Executive,* 63 (June, 1944), 34-36.

Hoppock, Anne, "Danger to Kindergartens," *Journal of the American Association of University Women,* LII (May, 1959), 227-228.

Lee, Dorris May, "What Should We Expect of Our Kindergarten?" *Education,* 77 (February, 1954), 362-368.

Lewis, Kathryn W., "Kindergarten Whys," *Kentucky School Journal,* XX (January, 1944), 28-29.

Robinson, Margaret E., "The Kindergarten Pre-Reading Program," *The School,* XXXIII (February, 1945), 492-499.

Strickland, Ruth G., "The Contribution of the Kindergarten," *Journal of the National Education Association,* XX (March, 1931), 77-78.

Stendler, Celia B., "Let Them Be Five," *Illinois Education,* XXXVII (April, 1949), 285-286.

Wann, Kenneth D., "Children Want to Know," *Childhood Education,* XXXVII (September, 1960), 8-12.

Willy, Dorothy E., "The Challenge To the Kindergarten," *Childhood Education,* XV (September, 1938), 4.

CHAPTER XII

Books

Almy, Millie, *et al., Young Children's Thinking.* New York: Teachers College Press, 1966.

Bloom, Benjamin, *Stability and Change in Human Characteristics.* New York: John Wiley, 1964.

Hunt, J. McVicker, *Intelligence and Experience.* New York: Ronald Press, 1961.

Kneller, George F., *Existentialism and Education.* New York: John Wiley, 1958.

May, Rollo (Ed.), *Existential Psychology.* New York: Random House, 1961.

Murphy, Lois B., *The Widening World of Childhood: Paths Toward Mastery.* New York: Basic Books, 1962.

Vygotsky, L. S., *Thought and Language.* Cambridge: Massachusetts Institute of Technology Press, 1962.

Articles and Addresses

Almy, Millie, "Child Development and the Curriculum," Dwayne Huebner (Ed.), *A Reassessment of the Curriculum.* New York: Bureau of Publications, Teachers College, Columbia University, 1964, pp. 41-52.

Biber, Barbara, "Preschool Education," Robert Ulich (Ed.), *Education and the Idea of Mankind.* New York: Harcourt, Brace, and World, 1964, pp. 71-96.

Borrowman, Merle, "Traditional Values and the Shaping of American Education," *Social Forces Influencing Education,* Nelson B. Henry (Ed.), Sixtieth Yearbook of the National Society for the Study of Education. Chicago: University of Chicago Press, 1961, pp. 144-170.

Bronfenbrenner, Urie, "Developmental Theory in Transition," *Child Psychology,* Harold Stevenson (Ed.), Sixty-second Yearbook of the National Society for the Study of Education. Chicago: University of Chicago Press, 1963, pp. 517-542.

Combs, Arthur W., "Personality Theory and Its Implications for Curriculum Development," Alexander Frazier (Ed.), *Learning More About Learning.* Washington, D.C.: Association for Supervison and Curriculum Development, 1959, pp. 5-20.

Deutsch, Martin, "Nursery Education: The Influence of Social Programming On Early Development," *Journal of Nursery Education,* XVIII (April, 1963), 191-197.

Gordon, Ira J., "New Conceptions of Children's Learning and Development," Walter Waetjen (Ed.), *Learning and Mental Health in the School.* Washington, D.C.: Association for Supervision and Curriculum Development, 1966, pp. 49-73.

Hechinger, Fred M., "Passport to Equality," Fred M. Hechinger (Ed.), *Pre-School Education Today.* New York: Doubleday, 1966, pp. 1-12.

Hughes, Marie, "Learning and Becoming—New Meanings to Teachers," Walter Waetjen (Ed.), *Learning and Mental Health in the School.* Washington, D.C.: Association for Supervision and Curriculum Development, 1966, pp. 127-144.

Kessen, William, "The Strategy of Instruction," Jerome Bruner (Ed.), *Learning About Learning.* Washington, D.C.: U. S. Government Printing Office, 1966, pp. 98-104.

Martin, William E., "Rediscovering the Mind of the Child," *Merrill-Palmer Quarterly,* VI (January, 1960), pp. 67-76.

Murphy, Lois Barclay, "Self-Management Capacities in Children," Alexander Frazier (Ed.), *New Insights and the Curriculum.* Washington, D.C.: Association for Supervision and Curriculum Development, 1963, pp. 107-120.

Piaget, Jean, "Foreward," Millie Almy, *et al., Young Children's Thinking.* New York: Teachers College Press, 1966, pp. iii-vii.

Roeper, Annamarie, and Irving Sigel, "Finding the Clue to Children's Thought Processes," *Young Children,* XXI (September, 1966), 335-349.

Snygg, Donald, "A Cognitive Field Theory of Learning," Walter Waet-jen (Ed.), *Learning and Mental Health in the School*. Washington, D.C.: Association for Supervision and Curriculum Development, 1966, pp. 77-96.

Torrance, E. Paul, "Factors Affecting Creative Thinking in Children," *Merrill-Palmer Quarterly*, VII (July, 1961), 171-180.

CHAPTER XIII

Books

Bruner, Jerome, *On Knowing*. Cambridge, Massachusetts: Harvard University Press, 1962.

Robison, Helen F., and Bernard Spodek, *New Directions in the Kindergarten*. New York: Teachers College Press, 1965.

Articles and Addresses

Almy, Millie, "New Views on Intellectual Development in Early Childhood Education," A. Harry Passow (Ed.), *Intellectual Development: Another Look*. Washington, D.C.: Association for Supervision and Curriculum Development, 1964, pp. 12-26.

Bellack, Arno, "The Structure of Knowledge and the Structure of the Curriculum," Dwayne Huebner (Ed.), *A Reassessment of the Curriculum*. New York: Bureau of Publications, Teachers College, Columbia University, 1964, pp. 25-40.

Biber, Barbara, "Premature Structuring As a Deterrent to Creativity," *The American Journal of Orthopsychiatry*, XXIX (April, 1959), 280-290.

Cutts, Warren G., "New Approaches to Reading for Young Children," J. Allen Figurel (Ed.), *Reading as an Intellectual Activity*, International Reading Association Conference Proceedings. New York: Scholastic Magazines, 1963, pp. 39-43.

Dale, Edgar, "Early Reading," *The News Letter*. Columbus, Ohio: Ohio State University, Bureau of Educational Research and Service, February, 1964, p. 3.

Goodlad, John I., "Three Dimensions in Organizing the Curriculum for Learning and Teaching," Vincent J. Glennon (Ed.), *Frontiers of Elementary Education III*. Syracuse, New York: Syracuse University Press, 1956, pp. 11-22.

Huebner, Dwayne, "Curriculum As A Field of Study," Helen F. Robison (Ed.), *Precedents and Promise in the Curriculum Field.* New York: Teachers College Press, 1966, pp. 94-112.

Karplus, Robert, *One Physicist Looks At Science Education,* paper presented at the Eighth ASCD Curriculum Research Institute, Washington, D.C., April 27, 1963. Mimeographed.

Macdonald, James B., "The Person in the Curriculum," Helen F. Robison (Ed.), *Precedents and Promise in the Curriculum Field.* New York: Teachers College Press, 1966, pp. 38-52.

Smith, Nila Banton, *Shall We Teach Formal Reading in the Kindergarten?* Washington, D.C.: Association for Childhood Education International, 1965, pp. 1-8.

BIBLIOGRAPHICAL NOTE

All books cited as published by the Bureau of Publications, Teachers College, Columbia University, are now copyrighted as published by Teachers College Press.

The kindergarten has drawn wide interest from educators and lay persons from its earliest introduction into the United States. Consequently, the literature about the kindergarten has been voluminous. For its development and expansion in the United States into the 1890's Henry Barnard's *Kindergaren and Child Culture Papers* and the *Journal of Proceedings and Addresses of the National Education Association* are particularly helpful. From 1892 to the early 1920's the *Proceedings of the Annual Meetings of the International Kindergarten Union* present the curriculum controversy in great detail. After 1920 there is no one particularly valuable source but an ever increasing wealth of writing in a variety of publications.

The listings in each bibliography contain some of the most influential writing for each time period, and literature that is illustrative of the discussions of the day. Though some pieces of literature are useful for more than one period, they are listed only once.

For the *Journal of Addresses and Proceedings of the National Education Association* only the appropriate year is indicated. This is true also for the *Proceedings of the Annual Meetings of the International Kindergarten Union,* which were consistently published by the Union. These exist now only in libraries where they have been preserved.

INDEX

269